THE BIRTH OF TRAGEDY
and
THE CASE OF WAGNER

THE BIRTH
OF TRAGEDY
and
THE CASE
OF WAGNER

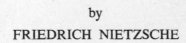

by

FRIEDRICH NIETZSCHE

Translated, with Commentary,

by

WALTER KAUFMANN

VINTAGE BOOKS

A Division of Random House

NEW YORK

FIRST VINTAGE EDITION,
February, 1967

© Copyright, 1967, by Random House, Inc.

All rights reserved under International and Pan-American Copyright
Conventions. Published simultaneously in Canada by Random House
of Canada Limited, Toronto.

Library of Congress Catalog Card Number: 67–11589

Manufactured in the United States of America

VINTAGE BOOKS
are published by

Alfred A. Knopf, Inc. / and / *Random House, Inc.*

For
My Apollinian Grandfather
ARNOLD SELIGSOHN (1854–1939)
and
My Dionysian Grandmother
JULIE KAUFMANN (1857–1940)

A Note on This Edition

The two books in this volume belong together in theme. *The Birth of Tragedy,* Nietzsche's first book, ends with a lengthy panegyric on the rebirth of tragedy in Wagner's operas. In his "Attempt at a Self-Criticism," added as a preface to the "new edition" of 1886, Nietzsche regretted that he had "spoiled the grandiose Greek problem . . . by introducing the most modern problems," and he explained that he had meanwhile come to see Wagner in a very different light. Two years later, in 1888, Nietzsche brought out the last book whose publication he himself experienced: *The Case of Wagner. The Birth of Tragedy* is probably Nietzsche's least humorous book; *The Case of Wagner,* his wittiest. Those reading the former without the latter are sure to get a very misleading view of Nietzsche.

My English versions of these two books, with commentary, have not appeared before. But I owe a debt to Clifton Fadiman, whose early translation of *The Birth of Tragedy,* done when he was a graduate student, I have used as a basis for parts of my new version. Even where I did not start from scratch, I have compared every sentence with the original, and my revisions are so extensive that the new version is probably more different from his than most Nietzsche translations—including Fadiman's—are from those that preceded them. And in large parts I did work from scratch.

The commentary is presented in the form of introductions, footnotes, and translations of pertinent letters. All footnotes are mine, except three in *The Case of Wagner* which are clearly identified: these are the only footnotes Nietzsche himself included in any of his books.

WALTER KAUFMANN

Princeton
July 1966

Acknowledgments

But for Jason Epstein, I should never have translated another Nietzsche book after 1954. He persevered; he left the choice of books and all particulars entirely up to me; and eventually he got me to undertake a second series of translations. There were times when I wished he hadn't; but now that the work is completed, I want to thank him as well as Berenice Hoffman, whose editorial queries have made this volume less imperfect than it would have been without her.

Most of the work on the two indices was done by Stephen Watson, but Sonia Volochova made valuable additions.

WALTER KAUFMANN

CONTENTS

THE
BIRTH OF TRAGEDY

Translator's Introduction

This was Nietzsche's first book. It is far from being his best book, but the "Attempt at a Self-Criticism" that Nietzsche placed at the beginning of the "new edition" of 1886 is among the finest things he ever wrote. Perhaps no other great writer has written a comparable preface to one of his own works. Certainly this self-criticism is far superior to most of the criticisms others have directed against *The Birth of Tragedy*.

Before considering briefly the most famous critique of the book, it may be well to suggest something of its importance. Apart from the fact that this essay has been widely admired and is generally taken for one of Nietzsche's major works, its significance may be said to be threefold.

First of all, *The Birth of Tragedy* is, for all its faults, one of the most suggestive and influential studies of tragedy ever written. Perhaps only Aristotle's *Poetics* excels it. What other study of tragedy could one place beside it? Only Hegel's scattered remarks on the subject—many of them to be found only in posthumously published, and very badly edited, lectures. It is arguable that all three philosophers were wrong about the fourteen extant plays of Aeschylus and Sophocles and the nineteen of Euripides. But there is no denying that Aristotle, Hegel, and Nietzsche have vastly enriched the discussion of tragedy—probably more so than anyone else.

Secondly, *The Birth of Tragedy* does not deal only with tragedy—nor only with tragedy and with Wagner: it also deals with the relation of art to science, with the whole phenomenon of Greek civilization, and with the modern age. On all these subjects Nietzsche has much to say that is interesting, and a good deal that is exceptionally brilliant and penetrating.

Finally, some of the distressing faults of the essay are inseparable from its third claim to importance. Nietzsche was probably Germany's greatest prose stylist as well as one of the most profound and influential modern philosophers. But much of *The Birth of Tragedy* is badly overwritten and murky, as Nietzsche himself pointed out in section 3 of his "Attempt at a Self-Criticism"; and occasionally a more extreme contrast to his later style—both literary and philosophical—would be difficult to imagine. To appreciate fully his later accomplishment, one should know his beginnings. Indeed, it is one of Nietzsche's central points in the book that we cannot do justice to the achievement of the Greeks and the triumph of those powers of restraint that he calls Apollinian unless we first behold the unrestrained Dionysian energies that the Greeks managed to harness. Similarly, his own later style, so remarkable for its lucidity and aphoristic brevity, seems doubly impressive when we compare it with the prose he himself found so embarrassing by 1886—prose that at times, particularly in the last ten sections, reads like a parody of Wagner.

It is partly, though not only, on account of this third point that the book should not be read by itself, without knowledge of Nietzsche's later writings. And no other essay forms as perfect a pair with it as the exceedingly brief and malicious *Case of Wagner,* here offered in the same volume.

One corollary of what has just been said must be noted expressly. Confronted with the occasionally hyperromantic and turgid prose of *The Birth of Tragedy,* it is tempting for the translator to tone down what offends his own taste and to make the style leaner and drier. But I have made a point of resisting this temptation. To the extent to which one gives in to it, one makes nonsense of parts of Nietzsche's brilliant "Attempt at a Self-Criticism," and one deprives those interested in Nietzsche's development of the opportunity to see for themselves to what extent Nietzsche changed. A faithful translator should strive to let Rilke sound like Rilke, Heidegger like Heidegger, *The Case of Wagner* like *Der Fall Wagner* —and *The Birth of Tragedy* like *Die Geburt der Tragödie.*

2

The first edition of *The Birth of Tragedy* was published in 1872, when Nietzsche was twenty-seven. It was immediately attacked by a young philologist, Ulrich Wilamowitz-Moellendorff, in an unbridled polemical pamphlet entitled *Zukunftsphilologie!* [1] Wagner's music was then called "music of the future," and Wilam-

---

[1] Berlin, Gebrüder Bornträger, 1872.

owitz tried to expose Nietzsche's "philology of the future"—a philology devoid of Greek quotations and footnotes.

Actually, there was much more to the attack than this. Nietzsche had been called to a chair at the University of Basel in Switzerland in 1869, and promoted to a full professorship of classical philology the following year—at the age of twenty-five. His doctoral degree had been conferred by the University of Leipzig without his having written a dissertation, on the basis of the call to Basel. That call, in turn, had been based on a superlative recommendation by Professor Ritschl, who had published articles by Nietzsche in the philological journal he edited and who had informed Basel that Nietzsche "is the first from whom I have ever accepted any contribution at all while he was still a student." The tenor of Ritschl's estimate of Nietzsche is perhaps best summed up in his sentence: "He will simply be able to do anything he wants to do." [2] Nietzsche's appointment to a chair at twenty-four was a sensation in professional circles, and it was to be expected that in his first book he would try to show the world of classical philology that his meteoric rise had been justified. Instead—he published *The Birth of Tragedy,* the kind of volume that could not be expected to appeal to the guild at any time, least of all to German professors in the new Empire, founded the year before.

Wilamowitz (1848–1931) was four years Nietzsche's junior, had just received his doctorate but not yet the title of professor—and the attack on Nietzsche was *his* first "book." He *did* try to establish the range and solidity of his scholarship by cataloguing Nietzsche's faults—and he saw nothing good at all in *The Birth.* His attack culminated in a charge of "ignorance and lack of love of truth" (p. 32).

Nietzsche's friend Erwin Rohde replied, still in 1872, in a pamphlet he called *Afterphilologie*[3] to signify a perversion of philology. Luther had liked the prefix *After,* which refers literally to the human posterior; Kant, too, had used it in his book on religion (1793); and Schopenhauer had spoken of *Afterphilosophie* when he attacked the philosophy of the universities. Rohde tried to show

---

[2] For Ritschl's letter, see *The Portable Nietzsche* (ed. and tr. by Walter Kaufmann), pp. 7–8.

[3] Leipzig, E. W. Fritzsch, 1872.

how many of the mistakes Wilamowitz claimed to have found in *The Birth* involved errors on *his* part. But Rohde also called Wilamowitz repeatedly "our Dr. phil." (our Ph.D.)—Rohde himself had just received the title of professor, though he was not yet a full professor—and "the pasquinader"; [4] and the level of his polemic was no higher than that of the attack he sought to meet. Two quotations may show this:

"I have emphasized this example because it may serve you as a sample at the outset of the manner in which throughout this pasquinade ignorance, the art of eager slander, and speculative reliance on the blind prejudices of the general reader are woven together into an attractive whole" (p. 10).

". . . really no more similar than an ape is to Heracles—indeed, even less; about as similar as our Dr. phil. von Wilamowitz is to the type of the 'Socratic man' whom our friend [Nietzsche] designates as the 'noblest opponent' of an artistic culture, although our Dr. phil. rather amusingly supposes that the designation fits him and the likes of him" (p. 12).

This last passage is important because it also illustrates Nietzsche's high esteem of the "Socratic man." *Afterphilologie,* to be sure, was written by Rohde, not Nietzsche; but the two men were very close friends at that time, and the point of Rohde's pamphlet was to expose misinterpretations of *The Birth of Tragedy.*

In 1873 Wilamowitz replied once more with a sequel to his *Zukunftsphilologie.*[5] The tenor of his reply may be gleaned from a remark near the end: "I should waste my time and energy on the inanities and wretchednesses of a couple of rotted brains?" (p. 23). Later, both Wilamowitz and Rohde made great reputations as classical philologists and never reprinted these early essays—presumably because they felt embarrassed by them.

Rohde, incidentally, had published a review of *The Birth of Tragedy* in the *Norddeutsche allgemeine Zeitung,* Sunday, May 26, 1872, before Wilamowitz's pamphlet appeared. And in 1882 he published a very critical and hostile review of Wilamowitz's *Antigonos von Karystos* (1881) in the *Litterarische Centralblatt.*

---

[4] Libeler.

[5] *Zukunftsphilologie: Zweites Stück* (Berlin, Gebrüder Bornträger, 1873).

Both of these reviews were reprinted in his *Kleine Schriften* (2 vols., 1901).

Nietzsche never referred to Wilamowitz in any of his works and went his own way without letting resentment eat into his soul. There are a few references to Wilamowitz in Nietzsche's letters of 1872 and 1873; but the most revealing passage is found in a letter to Rohde, March 19, 1874:

"To refute Dräseke's[6] contribution to the question of Wagner, of belly-shaking memory, Herr Bruno Meier[7] has written a lengthy and weighty treatise in which I am solemnly denounced as an 'enemy of our culture,' besides being represented as a wily deceiver among those who are deceived. He sent me his treatise personally, even furnishing his home address; I will send him the two essays of Wilamops. That's surely Christian beneficence toward one's enemies. For the delight of this dear Meier over Wilamops will surpass all words."

To explain Nietzsche's nickname for Wilamowitz: *Mops* is the German word for a pug, but the term was actually used to refer to a person with a disgruntled facial expression before it was transferred to the dog; it designates the quintessence of the comic, stupid, coarse, unfriendly, and inelegant. *Mopsig* means "boring"; *sich mopsen*, "to be bored." *Mops* seems to be related etymologically to the English "mope."

Nietzsche took Wilamowitz's attack very lightly; yet it has been claimed that Wilamowitz finished Nietzsche as a philologist, and even that Nietzsche retired in 1879, after only ten years as a professor, because the students stayed away as a result of Wilamowitz's polemics. In fact, the size of enrollments had nothing to do with Nietzsche's decision.

It may be of some interest to indicate what he taught and to note how few students he had all along. During his first year he gave the following courses (the number of students is indicated in

---

6 Johannes Dräseke, "Beiträge zur Wagner-Frage" (contributions to the problem of Wagner), in *Musikalisches Wochenblatt*, IV (1873).

7 Bruno Meyer (Nietzsche wrote "Meier"), "Beiträge zur Wagner-Frage: In eigener Sache" (in my cause), in *Deutsche Warte*, V, 641–73. Dräseke replied in *Musikalisches Wochenblatt*, V (1874), 403–05, 418–20, and 438–442, condemning Meyer's attack on Nietzsche.

each case in parentheses): Aeschylus' *Choephori* (6), Greek Lyric
Poets (7), Latin Grammar (8). The next year: Sophocles' *Oedi-
pus Rex* (11), Metrics (5), Hesiod's *Erga* (11). The third year:
Introduction to the Study of Philology (9), Introduction to the
Study of Plato's Dialogues (6), Introduction to Latin Epigraphy
(9). In the summer of 1872, after the publication of *The Birth,*
Nietzsche lectured on Pre-Platonic Philosophers (10) and Aeschylus *Choephori* (7); but that winter he had only two students in his
Greek and Roman Rhetoric, and neither was a philologist. This
drop in the number of students was surely due to Wilamowitz's first
polemic. By the next summer, however, his lectures on the Pre-
Platonic Philosophers drew eleven students; in 1876 the same
course drew ten, and his lectures On Plato's Life and Doctrines
nineteen. In 1878, finally, just before his retirement, he had more
students than ever, though certainly not many: Hesiod's *Works and
Days* (13), Plato's *Apology of Socrates* (6), Greek Lyrical Poets
(13), Introduction to the Study of Plato (8). These data may give
some idea of Nietzsche's career as a professor of classical philology, which was not exhausted by *The Birth of Tragedy.*

About the book opinions still differ, as they do about all of
Nietzsche's works. F. M. Cornford, one of the leading British clas-
sicists of the first half of the twentieth century, known to generations of students for his translations of many Platonic dialogues
and his remarkable commentaries, said in *From Religion to Philosophy* (1912) that *The Birth* was "a work of profound imaginative
insight, which left the scholarship of a generation toiling in the
rear."

For all that, Wilamowitz had a point, though he was completely blind to Nietzsche's merits. Some of the "philology" of the
future aped the manifest defects of Nietzsche's book without par-
taking of his genius—and, by a remarkable irony of fate, Nietzsche
himself was to suffer a great deal, posthumously, from pseudo-
scholars who substituted effusive prose for precision and correct-
ness.

On the whole, however, the general estimate of posterity has
been much closer to Cornford's view, and he himself and Jane Har-
rison have done a good deal to sustain Nietzsche's central intu-
itions.

In 1965 Professor Gerald F. Else followed up his monumental analysis of *Aristotle's Poetics* (1957) with a short study of *The Origin and Early Form of Greek Tragedy*[8] in which he argues that Aristotle, Nietzsche, Gilbert Murray, and the Cambridge school have all been importantly wrong about the origin of tragedy. He shows his usual mastery of the whole literature, and in his notes at the end of the volume he gives abundant references to recent literature on the subject. Those wondering about the current status of some of the problems raised by Nietzsche may be referred to Else's work. But it is noteworthy that, in spite of his radical disagreement with Nietzsche, Else should say, *"The Birth of Tragedy* is a great book, by whatever standard one cares to measure it" (p. 10). And he adds: *"The Birth of Tragedy* has cast a spell on almost everybody who has dealt with the subject since 1871."

3

What is of lasting importance is not the contrast of the Apollinian[9] and Dionysian as such: that smacks of Schopenhauer's contrast of the world as representation and the world as will; and playing off two concepts against each other like that is rarely very fruitful, though it has been a popular pastime among German scholars.

When *The Birth* appeared, the prevalent conception of the Greeks was still that pioneered by Johann Joachim Winckelmann (1717–1768) and adopted by Goethe (1749–1832): *edle Einfalt, stille Grösse,* "noble simplicity, calm grandeur." Matthew Arnold (1822–1888), utterly unable as a critic to maintain the level of his poem "Dover Beach," had only recently led this view to the absurd with his famous formulation: "sweetness and light."[10] Nietzsche used Apollo as a symbol for this aspect of Greek culture which found superb expression in classical Greek temples and sculptures: the genius of restraint, measure, and harmony. Far from depreciating what he called "the Apollinian," he argued that one could not

---

[8] Cambridge, Mass., Harvard University Press, 1965.

[9] *Apollinisch* has often been rendered by "Apollonian"; but I follow Brinton, Morgan, and the translator of Spengler's *Decline of the West* in preferring "Apollinian": after all, Nietzsche did not say *Apollonisch.*

[10] This is the title of the first chapter of Arnold's *Culture and Anarchy* (1869). The text itself was originally presented as Arnold's last Oxford lecture, June 15, 1867, under the title "Culture and Its Enemies."

appreciate it sufficiently until one became aware of another side of Greek culture that was barbarous by comparison and found expression in the Dionysian festivals. Surely, *The Bacchae* of Euripides shows us passions that are worlds removed from the Greece of Winckelmann, Goethe, and Arnold; and Nietzsche claimed that the same boundless and cruel longing to exceed all norms is also occasionally encountered in the *Iliad* [11] and in subsequent Greek poetry —and "the birth of tragedy" cannot be understood apart from it.

A careful reading of *The Birth* shows that Nietzsche, far from glorifying "the Dionysian," argues that the achievements of the Greeks generally, and their tragedies in particular, cannot be understood adequately so long as we do not realize what potentially destructive forces had to be harnessed to make them possible. On this central point Nietzsche was surely right. If one wants a single well-written book which abounds in quotations and references that document this "dark" side of ancient Greece, there is probably none better than E. R. Dodds's superb study of *The Greeks and the Irrational*,[12] which also abounds in references to other recent literature on this subject.

The Birth of Tragedy reaches its first great climax in section 7, which is of interest also in connection with French existentialism. Then the book moves on to suggestions about the death of tragedy. For over forty years the ridiculous claims of Richard Oehler, in *Friedrich Nietzsche und die Vorsokratiker* (1904),[13] were repeated by one interpreter after another—even after Oehler had thoroughly discredited himself with one of the most unscrupulous books ever to have come from a writer with some scholarly pretensions, *Friedrich Nietzsche und die Deutsche Zukunft* (1935),[14] an attempt to identify Nietzsche with the aspirations of the Nazis, who had come to power in 1933. In the interim, Oehler had compiled two huge indices for the two most complete editions of Nietzsche's works, the latter index (for the so-called Musarion edition) comprising two and a half volumes. This did not prevent

---

[11] Compare also Nietzsche's early fragment "Homer's Contest" (pp. 32–39 in *Portable Nietzsche*).

[12] Berkeley, University of California Press, 1951; Boston, Beacon Press paperback, 1951.

[13] Leipzig, Dürr, 1904.

[14] Leipzig, Armanen, 1935.

him—on the contrary, it enabled him to stud his book of 1935 with utterly misleading quotations that seem to say the opposite of what Nietzsche actually says on the pages from which they are taken. At best the carlier volume shows that Oehler's stunning lack of intellectual integrity was fused with a limited intelligence and an appalling inability to understand Nietzsche. But this man was one of the pillars of the Nietzsche Archive, established by the philosopher's sister, and one of the editors of the works.[15]

Neither Oehler nor his early book would deserve mention here if that book had not been used and echoed uncritically by A. H. J. Knight in the only English full-length study of Nietzsche's relation to the Greeks,[16] and if Knight had not been relied on uncritically by Ernest Newman, Crane Brinton, and Erich Podach.[17] To catalogue Oehler's mistakes here would be pointless; but two of them have been repeated so often that it seems necessary to repudiate them specifically.

First, the young Oehler claimed that the early Nietzsche "was completely under the influence of Schopenhauer," and a pessimist (p. 28). In fact, however, Nietzsche's very first book, *The Birth,* constitutes a declaration of independence from Schopenhauer: while Nietzsche admires him for honestly facing up to the terrors of existence, Nietzsche himself celebrates Greek tragedy as a superior alternative to Schopenhauer's "Buddhistic negation of the will." From tragedy Nietzsche learns that one can affirm life as sublime, beautiful, and joyous in spite of all suffering and cruelty.

Second, Oehler understood *The Birth* as a manifesto against Socrates and Socratism. In fact, Nietzsche is no more against (or for) Socrates than he is against (or for) Apollo or Dionysus. His

---

[15] Cf. *Beyond Good and Evil,* Kaufmann translation, section 251, note 27; also Kaufmann's *Nietzsche,* check the references to Richard Oehler in the Index.

[16] Knight's *Some Aspects of the Life and Work of Nietzsche and particularly of His Connection with Greek Literature and Thought* (Cambridge, England: Cambridge University Press, 1933) is generally unreliable, and some of the many errors in the book are pointed out in Kaufmann's *Nietzsche.* In other words, the two monographs devoted to Nietzsche and the Greeks (Oehler's and Knight's) are both quite unhelpful.

[17] Erich Podach, *Nietzsches Werke des Zusammenbruchs* (Heidelberg, Wolfgang Rothe Verlag, 1961), p. 407. Cf. Kaufmann, "Nietzsche in the Light of His Suppressed Manuscripts," *Journal of the History of Philosophy* (1964), p. 216, note 13.

whole way of thinking is far removed from such crudities. And Nietzsche was as right as most of his interpreters, following Oehler, have been wrong when he said in 1888, in *Ecce Homo,* in the first section of his own analysis of *The Birth:* "It smells offensively Hegelian, and the cadaverous perfume of Schopenhauer sticks only to a few formulas."

Socrates is introduced in *The Birth* with the reverence befitting a god, the equal of Apollo and Dionysus. Of course, Nietzsche's critical powers do not spare even gods, and he finds Socrates deeply problematic. He always approached Socrates in this manner, stressing now his admiration, now his objections, and sometimes, as here, both at once.[18] Indeed, the two sections (14 and 15) in which the discussion of the death of tragedy reaches its climax—the second great highpoint of the book—suggest that but for Socrates Greek culture might have perished altogether; also that "the influence of Socrates necessitates ever again the regeneration of art"; and finally even that we need an "artistic Socrates."

Apollo and Dionysus reached a synthesis in tragedy; this synthesis was negated by Socrates; and now another synthesis is wanted, an artistic Socrates. Could Plato be meant? On the contrary. Those who feel that Nietzsche is unfair to Socrates and that Socratism is *not* opposed to tragedy should reconsider Plato's resolve, in the *Republic,* to tolerate no tragic poets in his ideal city, as well as the older Plato's remarks on tragedy in *The Laws.* The "artistic Socrates" is Nietzsche himself. He looks forward to a philosophy that admits the tragic aspect of life, as the Greek poets did, but does not sacrifice the critical intellect; a philosophy that denies Socrates' optimistic faith that knowledge and virtue and happiness are, as it were, Siamese triplets; a philosophy as sharply critical as Socrates' but able and willing to avail itself of the visions and resources of art.

For all that, one need not accept Nietzsche's view of the death of tragedy, though it has been served up to us again and again in the twentieth century. This is not the place to offer sustained criticisms of his theses; but to stimulate reflection I suggest that Nietzsche is blatantly unfair not to Socrates but to Euripides—and that

---

[18] All the relevant passages are considered in Chapter 13 of Kaufmann's *Nietzsche.*

the death of tragedy was far better explained by Goethe, when he said to Eckermann, May 1, 1825:

"Man is simple. And however rich, manifold, and unfathomable he may be, yet the circle of his states is soon run through. If the circumstances had been like those among us poor Germans where Lessing wrote two or three, I myself three or four, and Schiller five or six passable plays, there would have been room for a fourth, fifth, and sixth tragic poet. But among the Greeks with their abundant production, where each of the three great ones had written over one hundred, or close to one hundred, plays, and the tragic subjects of Homer and the heroic tradition had in some cases been treated three or four times—in view of such an abundance, I say, one may suppose that subject matter and contents had gradually been exhausted and poets writing after the three great ones did not really know what next. And when you stop to think about it, why should they? Wasn't it really enough for a while? . . . After all, these few grandiose views that have come down to us are of such dimension and significance that we poor Europeans have been occupying ourselves with them for centuries and will yet have food and work enough for a few more centuries."

Unfortunately, *The Birth of Tragedy* does not end with Section 15, as an early draft did and as the book clearly ought to. Another ten sections follow that weaken the whole book immeasurably.

Sections 1 through 6 are introductory and inferior stylistically. The heart of the book is found in Sections 7 through 15, which deal with the birth and death of tragedy. This is by far the best part of the book and can probably be understood fairly well by itself. Sections 16–25 are less worthy of Nietzsche than anything else of comparable length he ever published—and he himself soon felt this. The book as a whole, though it has a touch of genius, is marred by the faults Nietzsche enumerates in his "Attempt at a Self-Criticism." This "Attempt," however, shows us not only a brilliant writer who has grown far beyond the level of his first performance, but a great human being.

W. K.

The
BIRTH OF TRAGEDY
Or:
Hellenism And Pessimism

———◆———

by
FRIEDRICH NIETZSCHE

———◆———

New Edition

With an Attempt at a Self-Criticism[1]

---

[1] In the first edition of 1872 the title was *The Birth of Tragedy out of the Spirit of Music.* A second edition with very slight textual changes was printed in 1874 and appeared in 1878. In 1886, the same year that saw the publication of *Beyond Good and Evil,* the remaining copies of *both* editions were reissued with the new title page, above. The original title page was also retained but it now followed the "Attempt at a Self-Criticism."

Attempt at a Self-Criticism

Whatever may be at the bottom of this questionable book, it must have been an exceptionally significant and fascinating question, and deeply personal at that: the time in which it was written, in *spite* of which it was written, bears witness to that—the exciting time of the Franco-Prussian War of 1870/71. As the thunder of the battle of Wörth was rolling over Europe, the muser and riddle-friend who was to be the father of this book sat somewhere in an Alpine nook, very bemused and beriddled, hence very concerned and yet unconcerned, and wrote down his thoughts about the *Greeks*—the core of the strange and almost inaccessible book to which this belated preface (or postscript) shall now be added. A few weeks later—and he himself was to be found under the walls of Metz, still wedded to the question marks that he had placed after the alleged "cheerfulness" of the Greeks and of Greek art. Eventually, in that month of profoundest suspense when the peace treaty was being debated at Versailles, he, too, attained peace with himself and, slowly convalescing from an illness contracted at the front, completed the final draft of *The Birth of Tragedy out of the Spirit of Music*.— Out of music? Music and tragedy? Greeks and the music of tragedy? Greeks and the art form of pessimism? The best turned out, most beautiful, most envied type of humanity to date, those most apt to seduce us to life, the Greeks—how now? They of all people should have *needed* tragedy? Even more—art? For what—Greek art?

You will guess where the big question mark concerning the value of existence had thus been raised. Is pessimism *necessarily* a sign of decline, decay, degeneration, weary and weak instincts—as it once was in India and now is, to all appearances, among us, "modern" men and Europeans? Is there a pessimism of *strength?* An intellectual predilection for the hard, gruesome, evil, problematic aspect of existence, prompted by well-being, by overflowing health, by the *fullness* of existence? Is it perhaps possible to suffer precisely from overfullness? The sharp-eyed courage that tempts and attempts, that *craves* the frightful as the enemy, the worthy enemy, against whom one can test one's strength? From whom one can learn what it means "to be frightened"? What is the significance of the *tragic* myth among the Greeks of the best, the strongest, the most courageous period? And the tremendous phenomenon of the Dionysian—and, born from it, tragedy—what might they signify?— And again: that of which tragedy died, the Socratism of morality, the dialectics, frugality, and cheerfulness of the theoretical man—how now? might not this very Socratism be a sign of decline, of weariness, of infection, of the anarchical dissolution of the instincts? And the "Greek cheerfulness" of the later Greeks— merely the afterglow of the sunset? The Epicureans' resolve *against* pessimism—a mere precaution of the afflicted? And science itself, our science—indeed, what is the significance of all science, viewed as a symptom of life? For what—worse yet, *whence*—all science? How now? Is the resolve to be so scientific about everything perhaps a kind of fear of, an escape from, pessimism? A subtle last resort against—*truth?* And, morally speaking, a sort of cowardice and falseness? Amorally speaking, a ruse? O Socrates, Socrates, was that perhaps *your* secret? O enigmatic ironist, was that perhaps your—irony?

2

What I then got hold of, something frightful and dangerous, a problem with horns but not necessarily a bull, in any case a *new* problem—today I should say that it was *the problem of science itself,* science considered for the first time as problematic, as questionable. But the book in which my youthful courage and suspicion found an outlet—what an *impossible* book had to result from a task so uncongenial to youth! Constructed from a lot of immature, overgreen personal experiences, all of them close to the limits of communication, presented in the context of *art*—for the problem of science cannot be recognized in the context of science—a book perhaps for artists who also have an analytic and retrospective penchant (in other words, an exceptional type of artist for whom one might have to look far and wide and really would not care to look); a book full of psychological innovations and artists' secrets, with an artists' metaphysics in the background; a youthful work full of the intrepid mood of youth, the moodiness of youth, independent, defiantly self-reliant even where it seems to bow before an authority and personal reverence; in sum, a first book, also in every bad sense of that label. In spite of the problem which seems congenial to old age, the book is marked by every defect of youth, with its "length in excess" and its "storm and stress." On the other hand, considering its success (especially with the great artist to whom it addressed itself as in a dialogue, Richard Wagner), it is a *proven* book, I mean one that in any case satisfied "the best minds of the time." [1] In view of that, it really ought to be treated with some consideration and taciturnity. Still, I do not want to suppress entirely how disagreeable it now seems to me, how strange it appears now, after sixteen years—before a much older, a hundred times more demanding, but by no means colder eye which has not become a stranger to the task which this audacious book dared to tackle for the first time: *to look at science in the perspective of the artist, but at art in that of life.*

3

To say it once more: today I find it an impossible book: I consider it badly written, ponderous, embarrassing, image-mad and image-confused, sentimental, in places saccharine to the point of effeminacy, uneven in tempo, without the will to logical cleanliness, very convinced and therefore disdainful of proof, mistrustful even of the *propriety* of proof, a book for initiates, "music" for those dedicated to music, those who are closely related to begin with on the basis of common and rare aesthetic experiences, "music" meant as a sign of recognition for close relatives *in artibus*[2]—an arrogant and rhapsodic book that sought to exclude right from the beginning the *profanum vulgus*[3] of "the educated" even more than "the mass" or "folk." Still, the effect of the book proved and proves that it had a knack for seeking out fellow-rhapsodizers and for luring them on to new secret paths and dancing places. What found expression here was anyway—this was admitted with as much cu-

---

[1] An allusion to Schiller's lines in *Wallensteins Lager:* "He that has satisfied the best minds of the time has lived for all times."

[2] In the arts.

[3] The profane crowd.

riosity as antipathy—a *strange* voice, the disciple of a still "unknown God," one who concealed himself for the time being under
the scholar's hood, under the gravity and dialectical ill humor of
the German, even under the bad manners of the Wagnerian. Here
was a spirit with strange, still nameless needs, a memory bursting
with questions, experiences, concealed things after which the name
of Dionysus was added as one more question mark. What spoke
here—as was admitted, not without suspicion—was something like
a mystical, almost maenadic soul that stammered with difficulty, a
feat of the will, as in a strange tongue, almost undecided whether it
should communicate or conceal itself. It should have *sung,* this
"new soul"—and not spoken! [4] What I had to say then—too bad
that I did not dare say it as a poet: perhaps I had the ability. Or at
least as a philologist: after all, even today practically everything in
this field remains to be discovered and dug up by philologists!
Above all, the problem that there *is* a problem here—and that the
Greeks, as long as we lack an answer to the question "what is Dionysian?" remain as totally uncomprehended and unimaginable as
ever.[5]

4

Indeed, what is Dionysian?— This book contains an answer:
one "who knows" is talking, the initiate and disciple of his god.
Now I should perhaps speak more cautiously and less eloquently
about such a difficult psychological question as that concerning the

---

[4] When Nietzsche died in 1900, Stefan George, the most remarkable German
poet of his generation, after Rilke, wrote a poem on "Nietzsche" that ends:
"it should have sung, not spoken, this new soul." For George's whole poem,
see *Twenty German Poets: A Bilingual Collection* (New York, The Modern
Library, 1963).

[5] The conception of the Dionysian in *The Birth* differs from Nietzsche's later
conception of the Dionysian. He originally introduced the term to symbolize
the tendencies that found expression in the festivals of Dionysus, and contrasted the Dionysian with the Apollinian; but in his later thought the
Dionysian stands for the creative employment of the passions and the affirmation of life in spite of suffering—as it were, for the synthesis of the
Dionysian, as originally conceived, with the Apollinian—and it is contrasted
with the Christian negation of life and extirpation of the passions. In the
Twilight of the Idols, written in 1888, the outlook of the old Goethe can
thus be called Dionysian (section 49).

origin of tragedy among the Greeks. The question of the Greek's relation to pain, his degree of sensitivity, is basic: did this relation remain constant? Or did it change radically? The question is whether his ever stronger *craving for beauty,* for festivals, pleasures, new cults was rooted in some deficiency, privation, melancholy, pain? Supposing that this were true—and Pericles (or Thucydides) suggests as much in the great funeral oration—how should we then have to explain the origin of the opposite craving, which developed earlier in time, the *craving for the ugly;* the good, severe will of the older Greeks to pessimism, to the tragic myth, to the image of everything underlying existence that is frightful, evil, a riddle, destructive, fatal? What, then, would be the origin of tragedy? Perhaps *joy,* strength, overflowing health, overgreat fullness? And what, then, is the significance, physiologically speaking, of that madness out of which tragic and comic art developed—the Dionysian madness? How now? Is madness perhaps not necessarily the symptom of degeneration, decline, and the final stage of culture? Are there perhaps—a question for psychiatrists—neuroses of *health?* of the youth and youthfulness of a people? Where does that synthesis of god and billy goat in the satyr point? What experience of himself, what urge compelled the Greek to conceive the Dionysian enthusiast and primeval man as a satyr? And regarding the origin of the tragic chorus: did those centuries when the Greek body flourished and the Greek soul foamed over with health perhaps know endemic ecstasies? Visions and hallucinations shared by entire communities or assemblies at a cult? How now? Should the Greeks, precisely in the abundance of their youth, have had the will to the tragic and have been pessimists? Should it have been madness, to use one of Plato's phrases, that brought the greatest blessings upon Greece? On the other hand, conversely, could it be that the Greeks became more and more optimistic, superficial, and histrionic precisely in the period of dissolution and weakness—more and more ardent for logic and logicizing the world and thus more "cheerful" and "scientific"? How now? Could it be possible that, in spite of all "modern ideas" and the prejudices of a democratic taste, the triumph of *optimism,* the gradual prevalence of *rationality,* practical and theoretical *utilitarianism,* no less than democracy itself which developed at the same time, might all have been symptoms of a decline of strength, of impending old age, and of physio-

logical weariness? These, and not pessimism? Was Epicure an optimist—precisely because he was *afflicted?*

It is apparent that it was a whole cluster of grave .questions
with which this book burdened itself. Let us add the gravest question of all. What, seen in the perspective of *life,* is the significance
of morality?

5

Already in the preface addressed to Richard Wagner, art,
and *not* morality, is presented as the truly *metaphysical* activity of
man. In the book itself the suggestive sentence is repeated several
times, that the existence of the world is *justified* only as an aesthetic phenomenon. Indeed, the whole book knows only an artistic
meaning and crypto-meaning behind all events—a "god," if you
please, but certainly only an entirely reckless and amoral artist-god
who wants to experience, whether he is building or destroying, in
the good and in the bad, his own joy and glory—one who, creating
worlds, frees himself from the *distress* of fullness and *overfullness*
and from the *affliction* of the contradictions compressed in his
soul.[6] The world—at every moment the *attained* salvation of God,
as the eternally changing, eternally new vision of the most deeply
afflicted, discordant, and contradictory being who can find salvation
only in *appearance:* you can call this whole artists' metaphysics
arbitrary, idle, fantastic; what matters is that it betrays a spirit who
will one day fight at any risk whatever the *moral* interpretation and
significance of existence. Here, perhaps for the first time, a pessimism "beyond good and evil" [7] is suggested. Here that "perversity
of mind" gains speech and formulation against which Schopenhauer never wearied of hurling in advance his most irate curses and
thunderbolts: a philosophy that dares to move, to demote, morality
into the realm of appearance—and not merely among "appearances" or phenomena (in the sense assigned to these words by

---

[6] Cf. the words which Heine, in his *Schöpfungslieder,* attributes to God:
"Disease was the most basic ground/of my creative urge and stress;/creating,
I could convalesce,/creating, I again grew sound."

[7] The book with that title was published in 1886, the same year that the new
edition of *The Birth of Tragedy* appeared, with this preface.

Idealistic philosophers), but among "deceptions," as semblance, delusion, error, interpretation, contrivance, art.

Perhaps the depth of this *antimoral* propensity is best inferred from the careful and hostile silence with which Christianity is treated throughout the whole book—Christianity as the most prodigal elaboration of the moral theme to which humanity has ever been subjected. In truth, nothing could be more opposed to the purely aesthetic interpretation and justification of the world which are taught in this book than the Christian teaching, which is, and wants to be, *only* moral and which relegates art, *every* art, to the realm of *lies;* with its absolute standards, beginning with the truthfulness of God, it negates, judges, and damns art. Behind this mode of thought and valuation, which must be hostile to art if it is at all genuine, I never failed to sense a *hostility to life*—a furious, vengeful antipathy to life itself: for all of life is based on semblance, art, deception, points of view, and the necessity of perspectives and error. Christianity was from the beginning, essentially and fundamentally, life's nausea and disgust with life, merely concealed behind, masked by, dressed up as, faith in "another" or "better" life. Hatred of "the world," condemnations of the passions, fear of beauty and sensuality, a beyond invented the better to slander this life, at bottom a craving for the nothing, for the end, for respite, for "the sabbath of sabbaths"—all this always struck me, no less than the unconditional will of Christianity to recognize *only* moral values, as the most dangerous and uncanny form of all possible forms of a "will to decline" [8]—at the very least a sign of abysmal sickness, weariness, discouragement, exhaustion, and the impoverishment of life. For, confronted with morality (especially Christian, or unconditional, morality), life *must* continually and inevitably be in the wrong, because life *is* something essentially amoral—and eventually, crushed by the weight of contempt and the eternal No, life *must* then be felt to be unworthy of desire and altogether worthless. Morality itself—how now? might not morality be "a will to negate life," a secret instinct of annihilation, a principle of decay, diminution, and slander—the beginning of the end? Hence, the danger of dangers?

---

[8] *Untergang,* as in the title of Spengler's *Decline of the West,* which was influenced decisively by this discussion. Spengler himself says in his preface that he owes "everything" to Goethe and to Nietzsche.

It was *against* morality that my instinct turned with this questionable book, long ago; it was an instinct that aligned itself with life and that discovered for itself a fundamentally opposite doctrine and valuation of life—purely artistic and *anti-Christian*. What to call it? As a philologist and man of words I baptized it, not without taking some liberty—for who could claim to know the rightful name of the Antichrist?—in the name of a Greek god: I called it Dionysian.

6

It is clear what task I first dared to touch with this book? How I regret now that in those days I still lacked the courage (or immodesty?) to permit myself in every way an individual language of my own for such individual views and hazards—and that instead I tried laboriously to express by means of Schopenhauerian and Kantian formulas strange and new valuations which were basically at odds with Kant's and Schopenhauer's spirit and taste! What, after all, did Schopenhauer think of tragedy?

"That which bestows on everything tragic its peculiar elevating force"—he says in *The World as Will and Representation,*[9] volume II, p. 495—"is the discovery that the world, that life, can never give real satisfaction and hence is *not worthy* of our affection: this constitutes the tragic spirit—it leads to *resignation.*"

How differently Dionysus spoke to me! How far removed I was from all this resignationism!—[10] But there is something far worse in this book, something I now regret still more than that I obscured and spoiled Dionysian premonitions with Schopenhauerian formulations: namely, that I *spoiled* the grandiose *Greek problem,* as it had arisen before my eyes, by introducing the most modern problems! That I appended hopes where there was no ground for hope, where everything pointed all too plainly to an end! That on the basis of the latest German music I began to rave about "the German spirit" as if that were in the process even then of discover-

---

[9] *Welt als Wille und Vorstellung,* ed. Julius Frauenstädt (Leipzig, F. A. Brockhaus, 1873). Translated by R. B. Haldane and J. Kemp as *World as Will and Idea* (London, Kegan Paul, 1907).

[10] Nietzsche's coinage.

ing and finding itself again—at a time when the German spirit, which not long before had still had the will to dominate Europe and the strength to lead Europe,[11] was just making its testament and *abdicating* forever, making its transition, under the pompous pretense of founding a *Reich,* to a leveling mediocrity, democracy, and "modern ideas"!

Indeed, meanwhile I have learned to consider this "German spirit" with a sufficient lack of hope or mercy; also, contemporary *German music,* which is romanticism through and through and most un-Greek of all possible art forms—moreover, a first-rate poison for the nerves, doubly dangerous among a people who love drink and who honor lack of clarity as a virtue, for it has the double quality of a narcotic that both intoxicates and spreads a *fog.*

To be sure, apart from all the hasty hopes and faulty applications to the present with which I spoiled my first book, there still remains the great Dionysian question mark I raised—regarding music as well: what would a music have to be like that would no longer be of romantic origin, like German music—but *Dionysian?*

7

But, my dear sir, what in the world is romantic if *your* book isn't? Can deep hatred against "the Now," against "reality" and "modern ideas" be pushed further than you pushed it in your artists' metaphysics? believing sooner in the Nothing, sooner in the devil than in "the Now"? Is it not a deep bass of wrath and the lust for destruction that we hear humming underneath all of your contrapuntal vocal art and seduction of the ear, a furious resolve against everything that is "now," a will that is not too far removed from practical nihilism and seems to say: "sooner let nothing be true than that *you* should be right, than that *your* truth should be proved right!"

Listen yourself, my dear pessimist and art-deifier, but with open ears, to a single passage chosen from your book—to the not ineloquent dragon-slayer passage which may have an insidious pied-

---

[11] The allusion is to the time of Goethe when Germany, at her cultural zenith, was at her political nadir. The whole passage illustrates Nietzsche's conception of the "will to dominate" and the "will to power."

piper sound for young ears and hearts. How now? Isn't this the typical creed of the romantic of 1830, masked by the pessimism of 1850? Even the usual romantic finale is sounded—break, breakdown, return and collapse before an old faith, before *the* old God. How now? Is your pessimists' book not itself a piece of anti-Hellenism and romanticism? Is it not itself something "equally intoxicating and befogging," in any case a narcotic, even a piece of music, *German* music? But listen:

"Let us imagine a coming generation with such intrepidity of vision, with such a heroic penchant for the tremendous; let us imagine the bold stride of these dragon-slayers, the proud audacity with which they turn their back on all the weakling's doctrines of optimism in order to 'live resolutely' in wholeness and fullness: *would it not be necessary* for the tragic man of such a culture, in view of his self-education for seriousness and terror, to desire a new art, the *art of metaphysical comfort,* to desire tragedy as his own proper Helen, and to exclaim with Faust:

> *Should not my longing overleap the distance*
> *And draw the fairest form into existence?"* [12]

"Would it not be *necessary?"*—No, thrice no! O you young romantics: it would *not* be necessary! But it is highly probable that it will *end* that way, that *you* end that way—namely, "comforted," as it is written, in spite of all self-education for seriousness and terror, "comforted metaphysically"—in sum, as romantics end, as *Christians.*

No! You ought to learn the art of *this-worldly* comfort first; you ought to learn to laugh, my young friends, if you are hell-bent on remaining pessimists. Then perhaps, as laughers, you may some day dispatch all metaphysical comforts to the devil—metaphysics in front. Or, to say it in the language of that Dionysian monster who bears the name of Zarathustra:

"Raise up your hearts, my brothers, high, higher! And don't forget your legs! Raise up your legs, too, good dancers; and still better: stand on your heads!

"This crown of the laugher, the rose-wreath crown: I crown

---

[12] Section 18 below.

myself with this crown; I myself pronounced holy my laughter. I did not find anyone else today strong enough for that.

"Zarathustra, the dancer; Zarathustra, the light one who beckons with his wings, preparing for a flight, beckoning to all birds, ready and heady, blissfully lightheaded;

"Zarathustra, the soothsayer; Zarathustra, the sooth-laugher; not impatient; not unconditional; one who loves leaps and side-leaps: I crown myself with this crown.

"This crown of the laugher, the rose-wreath crown: to you, my brothers, I throw this crown. Laughter I have pronounced holy: you higher men, *learn*—to laugh!"

Thus Spoke Zarathustra, Part IV.[13]

Sils-Maria, Oberengadin,
August 1886—

---

[13] "On the Higher Man," sections 17–20, quoted by Nietzsche with omissions.

THE
BIRTH OF TRAGEDY

Out of the Spirit of Music

Preface to Richard Wagner

To keep at a distance all the possible scruples, excitements, and misunderstandings that the thoughts united in this essay will occasion, in view of the peculiar character of our aesthetic public, and to be able to write these introductory remarks, too, with the same contemplative delight whose reflection—the distillation of good and elevating hours—is evident on every page, I picture the moment when you, my highly respected friend, will receive this essay. Perhaps after an evening walk in the winter snow, you will behold Prometheus unbound on the title page, read my name, and be convinced at once that, whatever this essay should contain, the author certainly has something serious and urgent to say; also that, as he hatched these ideas, he was communicating with you as if you were present, and hence could write down only what was in keeping with that presence. You will recall that it was during the same period when your splendid *Festschrift* on Beethoven came into being, amid the terrors and sublimities of the war that had just broken out, that I collected myself for these reflections. Yet anyone would be mistaken if he associated my reflections with the contrast between patriotic excitement and aesthetic enthusiasm, of courageous seriousness and a cheerful game: if he really read this essay, it would dawn on him, to his surprise, what a seriously German problem is faced here and placed right in the center of German hopes, as a vortex and turning point.[1] But perhaps such readers will find it offensive that an aesthetic problem should be taken so seriously— assuming they are unable to consider art more than a pleasant sideline, a readily dispensable tinkling of bells that accompanies the "seriousness of life," just as if nobody knew what was involved in such a contrast with the "seriousness of life." Let such "serious" readers learn something from the fact that I am convinced that art represents the highest task and the truly metaphysical activity of

---

[1] This image occurs also in section 15 below.

this life, in the sense of that man to whom, as my sublime predecessor on this path, I wish to dedicate this essay.

Basel, end of the year 1871

1

We shall have gained much for the science of aesthetics, once we perceive not merely by logical inference, but with the immediate certainty of vision, that the continuous development of art is bound up with the *Apollinian* and *Dionysian* duality—just as procreation depends on the duality of the sexes, involving perpetual strife with only periodically intervening reconciliations. The terms Dionysian and Apollinian we borrow from the Greeks, who disclose to the discerning mind the profound mysteries of their view of art, not, to be sure, in concepts, but in the intensely clear figures of their gods. Through Apollo and Dionysus, the two art deities of the Greeks, we come to recognize that in the Greek world there existed a tremendous opposition, in origin and aims,[1] between the Apollinian art of sculpture, and the nonimagistic, Dionysian art of music. These two different tendencies run parallel to each other, for the most part openly at variance; and they continually incite each other to new and more powerful births, which perpetuate an antagonism, only superficially reconciled by the common term "art"; till eventually,[2] by a metaphysical miracle of the Hellenic "will," they appear coupled with each other, and through this coupling ultimately generate an equally Dionysian and Apollinian form of art—Attic tragedy.

In order to grasp these two tendencies, let us first conceive of them as the separate art worlds of *dreams* and *intoxication*. These physiological phenomena present a contrast analogous to that existing between the Apollinian and the Dionysian. It was in dreams, says Lucretius, that the glorious divine figures first appeared to the souls of men; in dreams the great shaper beheld the splendid bodies of superhuman beings; and the Hellenic poet, if questioned about the mysteries of poetic inspiration, would likewise have suggested

---

[1] In the first edition: ". . . an opposition of style: two different tendencies run parallel in it, for the most part in conflict; and they . . ." Most of the changes in the revision of 1874 are as slight as this (compare the next footnote) and therefore not indicated in the following pages. This translation, like the standard German editions, follows Nietzsche's revision.

[2] First edition: "till eventually, at the moment of the flowering of the Hellenic 'will,' they appear fused to generate together the art form of Attic tragedy."

dreams and he might have given an explanation like that of Hans
Sachs in the *Meistersinger:*

> *The poet's task is this, my friend,*
> *to read his dreams and comprehend.*
> *The truest human fancy seems*
> *to be revealed to us in dreams:*
> *all poems and versification*
> *are but true dreams' interpretation.*[3]

The beautiful illusion[4] of the dream worlds, in the creation of
which every man is truly an artist, is the prerequisite of all plastic
art, and, as we shall see, of an important part of poetry also. In our
dreams we delight in the immediate understanding of figures; all
forms speak to us; there is nothing unimportant or superfluous. But
even when this dream reality is most intense, we still have, glim-
mering through it, the sensation that it is *mere appearance:* at least
this is my experience, and for its frequency—indeed, normality—I
could adduce many proofs, including the sayings of the poets.

Philosophical men even have a presentiment that the reality in
which we live and have our being is also mere appearance, and that
another, quite different reality lies beneath it. Schopenhauer actually indicates as the criterion of philosophical ability the occasional
ability to view men and things as mere phantoms or dream images.
Thus the aesthetically sensitive man stands in the same relation to
the reality of dreams as the philosopher does to the reality of existence; he is a close and willing observer, for these images afford him
an interpretation of life, and by reflecting on these processes he
trains himself for life.

It is not only the agreeable and friendly images that he experiences as something universally intelligible: the serious, the trou-

---

[3] Wagner's original text reads:
> *Mein Freund, das grad' ist Dichters Werk,*
> *dass er sein Träumen deut' und merk'.*
> *Glaubt mir, des Menschen wahrster Wahn*
> *wird ihm im Traume aufgethan:*
> *all' Dichtkunst und Poëterei*
> *ist nichts als Wahrtraum-Deuterei.*

[4] *Schein* has been rendered in these pages sometimes as "illusion" and sometimes as "mere appearance."

bled, the sad, the gloomy, the sudden restraints, the tricks of accident, anxious expectations, in short, the whole divine comedy of
life, including the inferno, also pass before him, not like mere shadows on a wall—for he lives and suffers with these scenes—and yet
not without that fleeting sensation of illusion. And perhaps many
will, like myself, recall how amid the dangers and terrors of dreams
they have occasionally said to themselves in self-encouragement,
and not without success: "It is a dream! I will dream on!" I have
likewise heard of people who were able to continue one and the
same dream for three and even more successive nights—facts
which indicate clearly how our innermost being, our common
ground, experiences dreams with profound delight and a joyous necessity.

This joyous necessity of the dream experience has been embodied by the Greeks in their Apollo: Apollo, the god of all plastic
energies, is at the same time the soothsaying god. He, who (as the
etymology of the name indicates) is the "shining one," [5] the deity
of light, is also ruler over the beautiful illusion of the inner world of
fantasy. The higher truth, the perfection of these states in contrast
to the incompletely intelligible everyday world, this deep consciousness of nature, healing and helping in sleep and dreams, is at
the same time the symbolical analogue of the soothsaying faculty
and of the arts generally, which make life possible and worth living.
But we must also include in our image of Apollo that delicate
boundary which the dream image must not overstep lest it have a
pathological effect (in which case mere appearance would deceive
us as if it were crude reality). We must keep in mind that measured
restraint, that freedom from the wilder emotions, that calm of the
sculptor god. His eye must be "sunlike," as befits his origin; even
when it is angry and distempered it is still hallowed by beautiful
illusion. And so, in one sense, we might apply to Apollo the words
of Schopenhauer when he speaks of the man wrapped in the veil of
māyā [6] (*Welt als Wille und Vorstellung,* I, p. 416[7]): "Just as in a

---

[5] *Der "Scheinende."* The German words for illusion and appearance are
Schein and *Erscheinung.*

[6] A Sanskrit word usually translated as illusion. For detailed discussions see,
e.g., *A Source Book of Indian Philosophy,* ed. S. Radhakrishnan and Charles
Moore (Princeton, N.J., Princeton University Press, 1957); Heinrich Zim-
mer, *Philosophies of India,* ed. Joseph Campbell (New York, Meridian

stormy sea that, unbounded in all directions, raises and drops mountainous waves, howling, a sailor sits in a boat and trusts in his frail bark: so in the midst of a world of torments the individual human being sits quietly, supported by and trusting in the *principium individuationis*." [8] In fact, we might say of Apollo that in him the unshaken faith in this *principium* and the calm repose of the man wrapped up in it receive their most sublime expression; and we might call Apollo himself the glorious divine image of the *principium individuationis,* through whose gestures and eyes all the joy and wisdom of "illusion," together with its beauty, speak to us.

In the same work Schopenhauer has depicted for us the tremendous *terror* which seizes man when he is suddenly dumfounded by the cognitive form of phenomena because the principle of sufficient reason, in some one of its manifestations, seems to suffer an exception. If we add to this terror the blissful ecstasy that wells from the innermost depths of man, indeed of nature, at this collapse of the *principium individuationis,* we steal a glimpse into the nature of the *Dionysian,* which is brought home to us most intimately by the analogy of intoxication.

Either under the influence of the narcotic draught, of which the songs of all primitive men and peoples speak, or with the potent coming of spring that penetrates all nature with joy, these Dionysian emotions awake, and as they grow in intensity everything subjective vanishes into complete self-forgetfulness. In the German Middle Ages, too, singing and dancing crowds, ever increasing in number, whirled themselves from place to place under this same Dionysian impulse. In these dancers of St. John and St. Vitus, we rediscover the Bacchic choruses of the Greeks, with their prehistory in Asia Minor, as far back as Babylon and the orgiastic Sacaea.[9] There are some who, from obtuseness or lack of experience,

---

Books, 1956); and Helmuth von Glasenapp, *Die Philosophie der Inder* (Stuttgart, Kröner, 1949), consulting the indices.

[7] This reference, like subsequent references to the same work, is Nietzsche's own and refers to the edition of 1873 edited by Julius Frauenstädt—still one of the standard editions of Schopenhauer's works.

[8] Principle of individuation.

[9] A Babylonian festival that lasted five days and was marked by general license. During this time slaves are said to have ruled their masters, and a

turn away from such phenomena as from "folk-diseases," with contempt or pity born of the consciousness of their own "healthy-mindedness." But of course such poor wretches have no idea how corpselike and ghostly their so-called "healthy-mindedness" looks when the glowing life of the Dionysian revelers roars past them.

Under the charm of the Dionysian not only is the union between man and man reaffirmed, but nature which has become alienated, hostile, or subjugated, celebrates once more her reconciliation with her lost son,[10] man. Freely, earth proffers her gifts, and peacefully the beasts of prey of the rocks and desert approach. The chariot of Dionysus is covered with flowers and garlands; panthers and tigers walk under its yoke. Transform Beethoven's "Hymn to Joy" into a painting; let your imagination conceive the multitudes bowing to the dust, awestruck—then you will approach the Dionysian. Now the slave is a free man; now all the rigid, hostile barriers that necessity, caprice, or "impudent convention" [11] have fixed between man and man are broken. Now, with the gospel of universal harmony, each one feels himself not only united, reconciled, and fused with his neighbor, but as one with him, as if the veil of *māyā* had been torn aside and were now merely fluttering in tatters before the mysterious primordial unity.

In song and in dance man expresses himself as a member of a higher community; he has forgotten how to walk and speak and is on the way toward flying into the air, dancing. His very gestures express enchantment. Just as the animals now talk, and the earth yields milk and honey, supernatural sounds emanate from him, too: he feels himself a god, he himself now walks about enchanted, in ecstasy, like the gods he saw walking in his dreams. He is no longer an artist, he has become a work of art: in these paroxysms of intoxication the artistic power of all nature reveals itself to the highest gratification of the primordial unity. The noblest clay, the most costly marble, man, is here kneaded and cut, and to the sound of the chisel strokes of the Dionysian world-artist rings out the cry

---

criminal was given all royal rights before he was put to death at the end of the festival. For references, see, e.g., *The Oxford Classical Dictionary*.

[10] In German, "the prodigal son" is *der verlorene Sohn* (the lost son).

[11] An allusion to Friedrich Schiller's hymn *An die Freude* (to joy), used by Beethoven in the final movement of his Ninth Symphony.

of the Eleusinian mysteries: "Do you prostrate yourselves, millions? Do you sense your Maker, world?" [12]

2

Thus far we have considered the Apollinian and its opposite, the Dionysian, as artistic energies which burst forth from nature herself, *without the mediation of the human artist*—energies in which nature's art impulses are satisfied in the most immediate and direct way—first in the image world of dreams, whose completeness is not dependent upon the intellectual attitude or the artistic culture of any single being; and then as intoxicated reality, which likewise does not heed the single unit, but even seeks to destroy the individual and redeem him by a mystic feeling of oneness. With reference to these immediate art-states of nature, every artist is an "imitator," that is to say, either an Apollinian artist in dreams, or a Dionysian artist in ecstasies, or finally—as for example in Greek tragedy—at once artist in both dreams and ecstasies; so we may perhaps picture him sinking down in his Dionysian intoxication and mystical self-abnegation, alone and apart from the singing revelers, and we may imagine how, through Apollinian dream-inspiration, his own state, i.e., his oneness with the inmost ground of the world, is revealed to him in a *symbolical dream image*.

So much for these general premises and contrasts. Let us now approach the *Greeks* in order to learn how highly these *art impulses of nature* were developed in them. Thus we shall be in a position to understand and appreciate more deeply that relation of the Greek artist to his archetypes which is, according to the Aristotelian expression, "the imitation of nature." In spite of all the dream literature and the numerous dream anecdotes of the Greeks, we can speak of their *dreams* only conjecturally, though with reasonable assurance. If we consider the incredibly precise and unerring plastic power of their eyes, together with their vivid, frank delight in colors, we can hardly refrain from assuming even for their dreams (to the shame of all those born later) a certain logic of line and contour, colors and groups, a certain pictorial sequence reminding us of their finest bas-reliefs whose perfection would cer-

---

[12] Quotation from Schiller's hymn.

tainly justify us, if a comparison were possible, in designating the dreaming Greeks as Homers and Homer as a dreaming Greek—in a deeper sense than that in which modern man, speaking of his dreams, ventures to compare himself with Shakespeare.

On the other hand, we need not conjecture regarding the immense gap which separates the *Dionysian Greek* from the Dionysian barbarian. From all quarters of the ancient world—to say nothing here of the modern—from Rome to Babylon, we can point to the existence of Dionysian festivals, types which bear, at best, the same relation to the Greek festivals which the bearded satyr, who borrowed his name and attributes from the goat, bears to Dionysus himself. In nearly every case these festivals centered in extravagant sexual licentiousness, whose waves overwhelmed all family life and its venerable traditions; the most savage natural instincts were unleashed, including even that horrible mixture of sensuality and cruelty which has always seemed to me to be the real "witches' brew." For some time, however, the Greeks were apparently perfectly insulated and guarded against the feverish excitements of these festivals, though knowledge of them must have come to Greece on all the routes of land and sea; for the figure of Apollo, rising full of pride, held out the Gorgon's head to this grotesquely uncouth Dionysian power—and really could not have countered any more dangerous force. It is in Doric art that this majestically rejecting attitude of Apollo is immortalized.

The opposition between Apollo and Dionysus became more hazardous and even impossible, when similar impulses finally burst forth from the deepest roots of the Hellenic nature and made a path for themselves: the Delphic god, by a seasonably effected reconciliation, now contented himself with taking the destructive weapons from the hands of his powerful antagonist. This reconciliation is the most important moment in the history of the Greek cult: wherever we turn we note the revolutions resulting from this event. The two antagonists were reconciled; the boundary lines to be observed henceforth by each were sharply defined, and there was to be a periodical exchange of gifts of esteem. At bottom, however, the chasm was not bridged over. But if we observe how, under the pressure of this treaty of peace, the Dionysian power revealed itself, we shall now recognize in the Dionysian orgies of the Greeks, as compared with the Babylonian Sacaea with their reversion of man to the tiger and the ape, the significance of festivals of world redemption and days of transfiguration. It is with them that nature for the first time attains her artistic jubilee; it is with them that the destruction of the *principium individuationis* for the first time becomes an artistic phenomenon.

The horrible "witches' brew" of sensuality and cruelty becomes ineffective; only the curious blending and duality in the emotions of the Dionysian revelers remind us—as medicines remind us of deadly poisons—of the phenomenon that pain begets joy, that ecstasy may wring sounds of agony from us. At the very climax of joy there sounds a cry of horror or a yearning lamentation for an irretrievable loss. In these Greek festivals, nature seems to reveal a sentimental [1] trait; it is as if she were heaving a sigh at her dismemberment into individuals. The song and pantomime of such dually-minded revelers was something new and unheard-of in the Homeric-Greek world; and the Dionysian *music* in particular excited awe and terror. If music, as it would seem, had been known previously as an Apollinian art, it was so, strictly speaking, only as the wave beat of rhythm, whose formative power was developed for the representation of Apollinian states. The music of Apollo was Doric architectonics in tones, but in tones that were merely suggestive, such as those of the cithara. The very element which forms the essence of Dionysian music (and hence of music in general) is carefully excluded as un-Apollinian—namely, the emotional power of the tone, the uniform flow of the melody, and the utterly incomparable world of harmony. In the Dionysian dithyramb man is incited to the greatest exaltation of all his symbolic faculties; something never before experienced struggles for utterance—the annihilation of the viel of *māyā*, oneness as the soul of the race and of nature itself. The essence of nature is now to be expressed symbolically; we need a new world of symbols; and the entire symbolism of the body is called into play, not the mere symbolism of the lips, face, and speech but the whole pantomime of dancing, forcing every member into rhythmic movement. Then the other symbolic powers suddenly press forward, particularly those of music, in rhythmics, dynamics, and harmony. To grasp this collective release

---

[1] *Sentimentalisch* (not *sentimental*): an allusion to Schiller's influential contrast of *naïve* (Goethean) poetry with his own *sentimentalische Dichtung*.

of all the symbolic powers, man must have already attained that
height of self-abnegation which seeks to express itself symbolically
through all these powers—and so the dithyrambic votary of Dionysus is understood only by his peers. With what astonishment must
the Apollinian Greek have beheld him! With an astonishment that
was all the greater the more it was mingled with the shuddering
suspicion that all this was actually not so very alien to him after all,
in fact, that it was only his Apollinian consciousness which, like a
veil, hid this Dionysian world from his vision.

3

To understand this, it becomes necessary to level the artistic
structure of the *Apollinian culture,* as it were, stone by stone, till the
foundations on which it rests become visible. First of all we see the
glorious *Olympian* figures of the gods, standing on the gables of
this structure. Their deeds, pictured in brilliant reliefs, adorn its
friezes. We must not be misled by the fact that Apollo stands side
by side with the others as an individual deity, without any claim to
priority of rank. For the same impulse that embodied itself in
Apollo gave birth to this entire Olympian world, and in this sense
Apollo is its father. What terrific need was it that could produce
such an illustrious company of Olympian beings?

Whoever approaches these Olympians with another religion
in his heart, searching among them for moral elevation, even for
sanctity, for disincarnate spirituality, for charity and benevolence,
will soon be forced to turn his back on them, discouraged and
disappointed. For there is nothing here that suggests asceticism,
spirituality, or duty. We hear nothing but the accents of an exuberant, triumphant life in which all things, whether good or evil,
are deified.[1] And so the spectator may stand quite bewildered
before this fantastic excess of life, asking himself by virtue of what
magic potion these high-spirited men could have found life so en-
joyable that, wherever they turned, their eyes beheld the smile of
Helen, the ideal picture of their own existence, "floating in sweet
sensuality." But to this spectator, who has already turned his back,

---

[1] This presage of the later coinage "beyond good and evil" is lost when *böse*
is mistranslated as "bad" instead of "evil."

we must say: "Do not go away, but stay and hear what Greek folk wisdom has to say of this very life, which with such inexplicable gaiety unfolds itself before your eyes.

"There is an ancient story that King Midas hunted in the forest a long time for the wise Silenus, the companion of Dionysus, without capturing him. When Silenus at last fell into his hands, the king asked what was the best and most desirable of all things for man. Fixed and immovable, the demigod said not a word, till at last, urged by the king, he gave a shrill laugh and broke out into these words: 'Oh, wretched ephemeral race, children of chance and misery, why do you compel me to tell you what it would be most expedient for you not to hear? What is best of all is utterly beyond your reach: not to be born, not to *be*, to be *nothing*. But the second best for you is—to die soon.' " [2]

How is the world of the Olympian gods related to this folk wisdom? Even as the rapturous vision of the tortured martyr to his suffering.

Now it is as if the Olympian magic mountain[3] had opened before us and revealed its roots to us. The Greek knew and felt the terror and horror of existence. That he might endure this terror at all, he had to interpose between himself and life the radiant dream-birth of the Olympians. That overwhelming dismay in the face of the titanic powers of nature, the Moira[4] enthroned inexorably over all knowledge, the vulture of the great lover of mankind, Prometheus, the terrible fate of the wise Oedipus, the family curse of the Atridae which drove Orestes to matricide: in short, that entire philosophy of the sylvan god, with its mythical exemplars, which caused the downfall of the melancholy Etruscans—all this was again and again overcome by the Greeks with the aid of the Olympian *middle world* of art; or at any rate it was veiled and withdrawn from sight. It was in order to be able to live that the Greeks had to create these gods from a most profound need. Perhaps we may picture the process to ourselves somewhat as follows: out of the original Titanic divine order of terror, the Olympian divine order of joy gradually evolved through the Apollinian impulse toward

---

[2] Cf. Sophocles, *Oedipus at Colonus*, lines 1224ff.
[3] *Zauberberg*, as in the title of Thomas Mann's novel.
[4] Fate.

beauty, just as roses burst from thorny bushes. How else could this people, so sensitive, so vehement in its desires, so singularly capable of *suffering,* have endured existence, if it had not been revealed to them in their gods, surrounded with a higher glory?

The same impulse which calls art into being, as the complement and consummation of existence, seducing one to a continuation of life, was also the cause of the Olympian world which the Hellenic "will" made use of as a transfiguring mirror. Thus do the gods justify the life of man: they themselves live it—the only satisfactory theodicy! Existence under the bright sunshine of such gods is regarded as desirable in itself, and the real pain of Homeric men is caused by parting from it, especially by early parting: so that now, reversing the wisdom of Silenus, we might say of the Greeks that "to die soon is worst of all for them, the next worst—to die at all." Once heard, it will ring out again; do not forget the lament of the short-lived Achilles, mourning the leaflike change and vicissitudes of the race of men and the decline of the heroic age. It is not unworthy of the greatest hero to long for a continuation of life, even though he live as a day laborer.[5] At the Apollinian stage of development, the "will" longs so vehemently for this existence, the Homeric man feels himself so completely at one with it, that lamentation itself becomes a song of praise.

Here we should note that this harmony which is contemplated with such longing by modern man, in fact, this oneness of man with nature (for which Schiller introduced the technical term "naïve"), is by no means a simple condition that comes into being naturally and as if inevitably. It is not a condition that, like a terrestrial paradise, *must* necessarily be found at the gate of every culture. Only a romantic age could believe this, an age which conceived of the artist in terms of Rousseau's *Emile* and imagined that in Homer it had found such an artist Emile, reared at the bosom of nature. Where we encounter the "naïve" in art, we should recognize the highest effect of Apollinian culture—which always must first overthrow an empire of Titans and slay monsters, and which must have triumphed over an abysmal and terrifying view of the world and the keenest susceptibility to suffering through recourse to the most forceful and pleasurable illusions. But how rarely is the naïve at-

---

[5] An allusion to Homer's *Odyssey,* XI, lines 489ff.

tained—that consummate immersion in the beauty of mere appearance! How unutterably sublime is *Homer* therefore, who, as an individual being, bears the same relation to this Apollinian folk culture as the individual dream artist does to the dream faculty of the people and of nature in general.

The Homeric "naïveté" can be understood only as the complete victory of Apollinian illusion: this is one of those illusions which nature so frequently employs to achieve her own ends. The true goal is veiled by a phantasm: and while we stretch out our hands for the latter, nature attains the former by means of our illusion. In the Greeks the "will" wished to contemplate itself in the transfiguration of genius and the world of art; in order to glorify themselves, its creatures had to feel themselves worthy of glory; they had to behold themselves again in a higher sphere, without this perfect world of contemplation acting as a command or a reproach. This is the sphere of beauty, in which they saw their mirror images, the Olympians. With this mirroring of beauty the Hellenic will combated its artistically correlative talent for suffering and for the wisdom of suffering—and, as a monument of its victory, we have Homer, the naïve artist.

4

Now the dream analogy may throw some light on the naïve artist. Let us imagine the dreamer: in the midst of the illusion of the dream world and without disturbing it, he calls out to himself: "It is a dream, I will dream on." What must we infer? That he experiences a deep inner joy in dream contemplation; on the other hand, to be at all able to dream with this inner joy in contemplation, he must have completely lost sight of the waking reality and its ominous obtrusiveness. Guided by the dream-reading Apollo, we may interpret all these phenomena in roughly this way.

Though it is certain that of the two halves of our existence, the waking and the dreaming states, the former appeals to us as infinitely preferable, more important, excellent, and worthy of being lived, indeed, as that which alone is lived—yet in relation to that mysterious ground of our being of which we are the phenomena, I should, paradoxical as it may seem, maintain the very opposite estimate of the value of dreams. For the more clearly I perceive in nature those omnipotent art impulses, and in them an ardent longing for illusion, for redemption through illusion, the more I feel myself impelled to the metaphysical assumption that the truly existent primal unity, eternally suffering and contradictory, also needs the rapturous vision, the pleasurable illusion, for its continuous redemption. And we, completely wrapped up in this illusion and composed of it, are compelled to consider this illusion as the truly nonexistent—i.e., as a perpetual becoming in time, space, and causality—in other words, as empirical reality. If, for the moment, we do not consider the question of our own "reality," if we conceive of our empirical existence, and of that of the world in general, as a continuously manifested representation of the primal unity, we shall then have to look upon the dream as a *mere appearance of mere appearance,* hence as a still higher appeasement of the primordial desire for mere appearance. And that is why the innermost heart of nature feels that ineffable joy in the naïve artist and the naïve work of art, which is likewise only "mere appearance of mere appearance."

In a symbolic painting, *Raphael,* himself one of these immortal "naïve" ones, has represented for us this demotion of appearance to the level of mere appearance, the primitive process of the naïve artist and of Apollinian culture. In his *Transfiguration,* the lower half of the picture, with the possessed boy, the despairing bearers, the bewildered, terrified disciples, shows us the reflection of suffering, primal and eternal, the sole ground of the world: the "mere appearance" here is the reflection of eternal contradiction, the father of things. From this mere appearance arises, like ambrosial vapor, a new visionary world of mere appearances, invisible to those wrapped in the first appearance—a radiant floating in purest bliss, a serene contemplation beaming from wide-open eyes. Here we have presented, in the most sublime artistic symbolism, that Apollinian world of beauty and its substratum, the terrible wisdom of Silenus; and intuitively we comprehend their necessary interdependence. Apollo, however, again appears to us as the apotheosis of the *principium individuationis,* in which alone is consummated the perpetually attained goal of the primal unity, its redemption through mere appearance. With his sublime gestures, he shows us how necessary is the entire world of suffering, that by means of it the individual may be impelled to realize the redeeming vision, and then, sunk in contemplation of it, sit quietly in his tossing bark, amid the waves.

If we conceive of it at all as imperative and mandatory, this apotheosis of individuation knows but one law—the individual, i.e., the delimiting of the boundaries of the individual, *measure* in the Hellenic sense. Apollo, as ethical deity, exacts measure of his disciples, and, to be able to maintain it, he requires self-knowledge. And so, side by side with the aesthetic necessity for beauty, there occur the demands "know thyself" and "nothing in excess"; consequently overweening pride and excess are regarded as the truly hostile demons of the non-Apollinian sphere, hence as characteristics of the pre-Apollinian age—that of the Titans; and of the extra-Apollinian world—that of the barbarians. Because of his titanic love for man, Prometheus must be torn to pieces by vultures; because of his excessive wisdom, which could solve the riddle of the Sphinx, Oedipus must be plunged into a bewildering vortex of crime. Thus did the Delphic god interpret the Greek past.

The effects wrought by the *Dionysian* also seemed "titanic" and "barbaric" to the Apollinian Greek; while at the same time he could not conceal from himself that he, too, was inwardly related to these overthrown Titans and heroes. Indeed, he had to recognize even more than this: despite all its beauty and moderation, his entire existence rested on a hidden substratum of suffering and of knowledge, revealed to him by the Dionysian. And behold: Apollo could not live without Dionysus! The "titanic" and the "barbaric" were in the last analysis as necessary as the Apollinian.

And now let us imagine how into this world, built on mere appearance and moderation and artificially dammed up, there penetrated, in tones ever more bewitching and alluring, the ecstatic sound of the Dionysian festival; how in these strains all of nature's *excess* in pleasure, grief, and knowledge became audible, even in piercing shrieks; and let us ask ourselves what the psalmodizing artist of Apollo, with his phantom harp-sound, could mean in the face of this demonic folk-song! The muses of the arts of "illusion" paled before an art that, in its intoxication, spoke the truth. The wisdom of Silenus cried "Woe! woe!" to the serene Olympians. The individual, with all his restraint and proportion, succumbed to the self-oblivion of the Dionysian states, forgetting the precepts of Apollo. *Excess* revealed itself as truth. Contradiction, the bliss born of pain, spoke out from the very heart of nature. And so, wherever the Dionysian prevailed, the Apollinian was checked and destroyed. But, on the other hand, it is equally certain that, wherever the first Dionysian onslaught was successfully withstood, the authority and majesty of the Delphic god exhibited itself as more rigid and menacing than ever. For to me the *Doric* state[1] and Doric art are explicable only as a permanent military encampment of the Apollinian. Only incessant resistance to the titanic-barbaric nature of the Dionysian could account for the long survival of an art so defiantly prim and so encompassed with bulwarks, a training so warlike and rigorous, and a political structure so cruel and relentless.

Up to this point we have simply enlarged upon the observation made at the beginning of this essay: that the Dionysian and the Apollinian, in new births ever following and mutually augmenting one another, controlled the Hellenic genius; that out of the age of "bronze," with its wars of the Titans and its rigorous folk philosophy, the Homeric world developed under the sway of the Apollinian impulse to beauty; that this "naïve" splendor was again overwhelmed by the influx of the Dionysian; and that against this new power the Apollinian rose to the austere majesty of Doric art and the Doric view of the world. If amid the strife of these two hostile principles, the older Hellenic history thus falls into four great periods of art, we are now impelled to inquire after the final goal of these developments and processes, lest perchance we should regard the last-attained period, the period of Doric art, as the climax and aim of these artistic impulses. And here the sublime and celebrated art of *Attic tragedy* and the dramatic dithyramb presents itself as the common goal of both these tendencies whose mysterious union, after many and long precursory struggles, found glorius consummation in this child—at once Antigone and Cassandra.[2]

---

[1] Sparta.

[2] In footnote 32 of his first polemic (1872) Wilamowitz said: "Whoever explains these last words, to which Mephistopheles' remark about the witch's arithmetic [Goethe's *Faust*, lines 2565–66] applies, receives a suitable reward from me." It would seem that Sophocles' Antigone is here seen as representative of the Apollinian, while Aeschylus' Cassandra (in *Agamemnon*) is associated with the Dionysian.

5

We now approach the real goal of our investigation, which is directed toward knowledge of the Dionysian-Apollinian genius and its art product, or at least toward some feeling for and understanding of this mystery of union. Here we shall begin by seeking the first evidence in Greece of that new germ which subsequently developed into tragedy and the dramatic dithyramb. The ancients themselves give us a symbolic answer, when they place the faces of *Homer* and *Archilochus*,[1] as the forefathers and torchbearers of Greek poetry, side by side on gems, sculptures, etc., with a sure feeling that consideration should be given only to these two, equally completely original, from whom a stream of fire flows over the whole of later Greek history. Homer, the aged self-absorbed dreamer, the type of the Apollinian naïve artist, now beholds with astonishment the passionate head of the warlike votary of the muses, Archilochus, who was hunted savagely through life. Modern aesthetics, by way of interpretation, could only add that here the first "objective" artist confronts the first "subjective" artist. But this interpretation helps us little, because we know the subjective artist only as the poor artist, and throughout the entire range of art we demand first of all the conquest of the subjective, redemption from the "ego," and the silencing of the individual will and desire; indeed, we find it impossible to believe in any truly artistic production, however insignificant, if it is without objectivity, without pure contemplation devoid of interest.[2] Hence our aesthetics must first solve the problem of how the "lyrist" is possible as an artist—he who, according to the experience of all ages, is continually saying "I" and running through the entire chromatic scale of his passions and desires. Compared with Homer, Archilochus appalls us by his cries of hatred and scorn, by his drunken outbursts of desire. Therefore is not he, who has been called the first subjective artist, essentially the non-artist? But in this case, how explain the rever-

---

[1] An early Greek poet whose dates are disputed. He mentions an eclipse that some believe to be the one of 711 B.C., others that of 648 B.C. *The Oxford Classical Dictionary* considers the earlier date more probable. His mother was a slave, and he was killed in battle.

[2] This conception of contemplation devoid of interest, as well as much else that is indebted to Schopenhauer, was later expressly criticized by Nietzsche.

ence which was shown to him—the poet—in very remarkable utterances by the Delphic oracle itself, the center of "objective" art?

Schiller has thrown some light on the poetic process by a psychological observation, inexplicable but unproblematic to his own
mind. He confessed that before the act of creation he did not have
before him or within him any series of images in a causal arrangement, but rather a *musical mood.* ("With me the perception has at
first no clear and definite object; this is formed later. A certain
musical mood comes first, and the poetical idea only follows
later.") Let us add to this the most important phenomenon of all
ancient lyric poetry: they took for granted *the union,* indeed the
identity, of the lyrist with the musician. Compared with this, our
modern lyric poetry seems like the statue of a god without a head.
With this in mind we may now, on the basis of our aesthetical
metaphysics set forth above, explain the lyrist to ourselves in this
manner.

In the first place, as a Dionysian artist he has identified himself with the primal unity, its pain and contradiction. Assuming that
music has been correctly termed a repetition and a recast of the
world, we may say that he produces the copy of this primal unity as
music. Now, however, under the Apollinian dream inspiration, this
music reveals itself to him again as a *symbolic dream image.* The
inchoate, intangible reflection of the primordial pain in music, with
its redemption in mere appearance, now produces a second mirroring as a specific symbol or example. The artist has already surren-
dered his subjectivity in the Dionysian process. The image that now
shows him his identity with the heart of the world is a dream scene
that embodies the primordial contradiction and primordial pain,
together with the primordial pleasure, of mere appearance. The "I"
of the lyrist therefore sounds from the depth of his being: its "subjectivity," in the sense of modern aestheticians is a fiction. When
Archilochus, the first Greek lyrist, proclaims to the daughters of
Lycambes both his mad love and his contempt, it is not his passion
alone that dances before us in orgiastic frenzy; but we see Dionysus
and the Maenads, we see the drunken reveler Archilochus sunk
down in slumber—as Euripides depicts it in the *Bacchae,*[3] the
sleep on the high mountain pasture, in the noonday sun. And now

[3] Lines 677ff.

Apollo approaches and touches him with the laurel. Then the Dionysian-musical enchantment of the sleeper seems to emit image sparks, lyrical poems, which in their highest development are called tragedies and dramatic dithyrambs.

The plastic artist, like the epic poet who is related to him, is absorbed in the pure contemplation of images. The Dionysian musician is, without any images, himself pure primordial pain and its primordial re-echoing. The lyric genius is conscious of a world of images and symbols—growing out of his state of mystical self-abnegation and oneness. This world has a coloring, a causality, and a velocity quite different from those of the world of the plastic artist and the epic poet. For the latter lives in these images, and only in them, with joyous satisfaction. He never grows tired of contemplating lovingly even their minutest traits. Even the image of the angry Achilles is only an image to him whose angry expression he enjoys with the dreamer's pleasure in illusion. Thus, by this mirror of illusion, he is protected against becoming one and fused with his figures. In direct contrast to this, the images of the *lyrist* are nothing but *his very* self and, as it were, only different projections of himself, so he, as the moving center of this world, may say "I": of course, this self is not the same as that of the waking, empirically real man, but the only truly existent and eternal self resting at the basis of things, through whose images the lyric genius sees this very basis.

Now let us suppose that among these images he also beholds *himself* as nongenius, i.e., his subject, the whole throng of subjective passions and agitations of the will directed to a definite object which appears real to him. It might seem as if the lyric genius and the allied non-genius were one, as if the former had of its own accord spoken that little word "I." But this mere appearance will no longer be able to lead us astray, as it certainly led astray those who designated the lyrist as the subjective poet. For, as a matter of fact, Archilochus, the passionately inflamed, loving, and hating man, is but a vision of the genius, who by this time is no longer merely Archilochus, but a world-genius expressing his primordial pain symbolically in the symbol of the man Archilochus—while the subjectively willing and desiring man, Archilochus, can never at any time be a poet. It is by no means necessary, however, that the lyrist should see nothing but the phenomenon of the man Archilochus before him as a reflection of eternal being; and tragedy shows how far the visionary world of the lyrist may be removed from this phenomenon which, to be sure, is closest at hand.[4]

Schopenhauer, who did not conceal from himself the difficulty the lyrist presents in the philosophical contemplation of art, thought he had found a way out on which, however, I cannot follow him. Actually, it was in his profound metaphysics of music that he alone held in his hands the means for a solution. I believe I have removed the difficulty here in his spirit and to his honor. Yet he describes the peculiar nature of song as follows (*Welt als Wille und Vorstellung,* I, p. 295):

"It is the subject of the will, *i.e.,* his own volition, which fills the consciousness of the singer, often as a released and satisfied desire (joy), but still oftener as an inhibited desire (grief), always as an affect, a passion, a moved state of mind. Besides this, however, and along with it, by the sight of surrounding nature, the singer becomes conscious of himself as the subject of pure will-less knowing, whose unbroken blissful peace now appears, in contrast to the stress of desire, which is always restricted and always needy. The feeling of this contrast, this alternation, is really what the song as a whole expresses and what principally constitutes the lyrical state. In it pure knowing comes to us as it were to deliver us from willing and its strain; we follow, but only for moments; willing, the remembrance of our own personal ends, tears us anew from peaceful contemplation; yet ever again the next beautiful environment in which pure will-less knowledge presents itself to us lures us away from willing. Therefore, in the song and the lyrical mood, willing (the personal interest of the ends) and pure perception of the environment are wonderfully mingled; connections between them are sought and imagined; the subjective mood, the affection of the will, imparts its own hue to the perceived environment, and vice versa. Genuine song is the expression of the whole of this mingled and divided state of mind."

Who could fail to recognize in this description that lyric poetry is here characterized as an incompletely attained art that arrives at its goal infrequently and only, as it were, by leaps? Indeed, it is de-

---

[4] The poet's ego is closest at hand, but the tragic poet can use Cassandra or Hamlet as a mask no less than his own empirical self.

scribed as a semi-art whose *essence* is said to consist in this, that willing and pure contemplation, i.e., the unaesthetic and the aesthetic condition, are wonderfully mingled with each other. We contend, on the contrary, that the whole opposition between the subjective and objective, which Schopenhauer still uses as a measure of value in classifying the arts, is altogether irrelevant in aesthetics, since the subject, the willing individual that furthers his own egoistic ends, can be conceived of only as the antagonist, not as the origin of art. Insofar as the subject is the artist, however, he has already been released from his individual will, and has become, as it were, the medium through which the one truly existent subject celebrates his release in appearance. For to our humiliation *and* exaltation, one thing above all must be clear to us. The entire comedy of art is neither performed for our betterment or education nor are we the true authors of this art world. On the contrary, we may assume that we are merely images and artistic projections for the true author, and that we have our highest dignity in our significance as works of art—for it is only as an *aesthetic phenomenon* that existence and the world are eternally *justified*[5]—while of course our consciousness of our own significance hardly differs from that which the soldiers painted on canvas have of the battle represented on it. Thus all our knowledge of art is basically quite illusory, because as knowing beings we are not one and identical with that being which, as the sole author and spectator of this comedy of art, prepares a perpetual entertainment for itself. Only insofar as the genius in the act of artistic creation coalesces with this primordial artist of the world, does he know anything of the eternal essence of art; for in this state he is, in a marvelous manner, like the weird image of the fairy tale which can turn its eyes at will and behold itself; he is at once subject and object, at once poet, actor, and spectator.

6

In connection with Archilochus, scholarly research has discovered that he introduced the *folk song* into literature and on account

---

[5] This parenthetical remark, repeated in section 24, is one of the most famous dicta in *The Birth of Tragedy*.

of this deserved, according to the general estimate of the Greeks, his unique position beside Homer. But what is the folk song in contrast to the wholly Apollinian epos? What else but the *perpetuum vestigium* of a union of the Apollinian and the Dionysian? Its enormous diffusion among all peoples, further re-enforced by ever-new births, is testimony to the power of this artistic dual impulse of nature, which leaves its vestiges in the folk song just as the orgiastic movements of a people immortalize themselves in its music. Indeed, it might also be historically demonstrable that every period rich in folk songs has been most violently stirred by Dionysian currents, which we must always consider the substratum and prerequisite of the folk song.

First of all, however, we must conceive the folk song as the musical mirror of the world, as the original melody, now seeking for itself a parallel dream phenomenon and expressing it in poetry. *Melody is therefore primary and universal,* and so may admit of several objectifications in several texts. Likewise, in the naïve estimation of the people, it is regarded as by far the more important and essential element. Melody generates the poem out of itself, ever again: that is what *the strophic form of the folk song* signifies; a phenomenon which I had always beheld with astonishment, until at last I found this explanation. Anyone who in accordance with this theory examines a collection of folk songs, such as *Des Knaben Wunderhorn,*[1] will find innumerable instances of the way the continuously generating melody scatters image sparks all around, which in their variegation, their abrupt change, their mad precipitation, manifest a power quite unknown to the epic and its steady flow. From the standpoint of the epos, this unequal and irregular image world of lyrical poetry is simply to be condemned: and it certainly has been thus condemned by the solemn epic rhapsodists of the Apollinian festivals in the age of Terpander.[2]

Accordingly, we observe that in the poetry of the folk song, language is strained to its utmost that it may *imitate music;* and with Archilochus begins a new world of poetry, basically op-

---

[1] An anthology of medieval German folk songs (1806–08), edited by Achim von Arnim (1781–1831) and his brother-in-law, Clemens Brentano (1778–1842). The title means "The Boy's Magic Horn."

[2] Middle of the seventh century B.C. Terpander, a poet, was born in Lesbos and lived in Sparta.

posed to the Homeric. And in saying this we have indicated the only possible relation between poetry and music, between word and tone: the word, the image, the concept here seeks an expression analogous to music and now feels in itself the power of music. In this sense we may discriminate between two main currents in the history of the language of the Greek people, according to whether their language imitated the world of image and phenomenon or the world of music. One need only reflect more deeply on the linguistic difference with regard to color, syntactical structure, and vocabulary in Homer and Pindar, in order to understand the significance of this contrast; indeed, it becomes palpably clear that in the period between Homer and Pindar the *orgiastic flute tones of Olympus* must have been sounded, which, even in Aristotle's time, when music was infinitely more developed, transported people to drunken ecstasy, and which, in their primitive state of development, undoubtedly incited to imitation all the poetic means of expression of contemporaneous man.

I here call attention to a familiar phenomenon of our own times, against which our aesthetic raises many objections. Again and again we have occasion to observe that a Beethoven symphony compels its individual auditors to use figurative speech in describing it, no matter how fantastically variegated and even contradictory may be the composition and make-up of the different worlds of images produced by a piece of music. To exercise its poor wit on such compositions, and to overlook a phenomenon which is certainly worth explaining, are quite in keeping with this aesthetic. Indeed, even when the tone-poet expresses his composition in images, when for instance he designates a certain symphony as the "pastoral" symphony, or a passage in it as the "scene by the brook," or another as the "merry gathering of rustics," these two are only symbolical representations born of music—and not the imitated objects of music—representations which can teach us nothing whatsoever concerning the *Dionysian* content of music, and which indeed have no distinctive value of their own beside other images. We have now to transfer this process of a discharge of music in images to some fresh, youthful, linguistically creative people, in order to get some notion of the way in which the strophic folk song originates, and the whole linguistic capacity is excited by this new principle of the imitation of music.

If, therefore, we may regard lyric poetry as the imitative ful-guration of music in images and concepts, we should now ask: "As what does music *appear* in the mirror of images and concepts?" It *appears as* will, taking the term in Schopenhauer's sense, i.e., as the opposite of the aesthetic, purely contemplative, and passive frame of mind. Here, however, we must make as sharp a distinction as possible between the concepts of essence and phenomenon; for music, according to its essence, cannot possibly be will. To be will it would have to be wholly banished from the realm of art—for the will is the unaesthetic-in-itself; but it *appears* as will. For in order to express its appearance in images, the lyrist needs all the agitations of passion, from the whisper of mere inclination to the roar of madness. Impelled to speak of music in Apollinian symbols, he conceives of all nature, and himself in it, as willing, as desiring, as eternal longing. But insofar as he interprets music by means of images, he himself rests in the calm sea of Apollinian contemplation, though everything around him that he beholds through the medium of music is in urgent and active motion. Indeed, when he beholds himself through this same medium, his own image appears to him as an unsatisfied feeling: his own willing, longing, moaning, rejoicing, are to him symbols by which he interprets music. This is the phenomenon of the lyrist: as Apollinian genius he interprets music through the image of the will, while he himself, completely released from the greed of the will, is the pure, undimmed eye of the sun.

Our whole discussion insists that lyric poetry is dependent on the spirit of music just as music itself in its absolute sovereignty does not *need* the image and the concept, but merely *endures* them as accompaniments. The poems of the lyrist can express nothing that did not already lie hidden in that vast universality and abso-luteness in the music that compelled him to figurative speech. Language can never adequately render the cosmic symbolism of music, because music stands in symbolic relation to the primordial contra-diction and primordial pain in the heart of the primal unity, and therefore symbolizes a sphere which is beyond and prior to all phe-nomena. Rather, all phenomena, compared with it, are merely symbols: hence *language,* as the organ and symbol of phenomena, can never by any means disclose the innermost heart of music; lan-guage, in its attempt to imitate it, can only be in superficial contact with music; while all the eloquence of lyric poetry cannot bring the deepest significance of the latter one step nearer to us.

7

We must now avail ourselves of all the principles of art considered so far, in order to find our way through the labyrinth, as we must call it, of *the origin of Greek tragedy.* I do not think I am unreasonable in saying that the problem of this origin has as yet not even been seriously posed, to say nothing of solved, however often the ragged tatters of ancient tradition have been sewn together in various combinations and torn apart again. This tradition tells us quite unequivocally *that tragedy arose from the tragic chorus,* and was originally only chorus and nothing but chorus. Hence we consider it our duty to look into the heart of this tragic chorus as the real proto-drama, without resting satisfied with such arty clichés as that the chorus is the "ideal spectator" or that it represents the people in contrast to the aristocratic region of the scene. This latter explanation has a sublime sound to many a politician—as if the immutable moral law had been embodied by the democratic Athenians in the popular chorus, which always won out over the passionate excesses and extravagances of kings. This theory may be ever so forcibly suggested by one of Aristotle's observations; still, it has no influence on the original formation of tragedy, inasmuch as the whole opposition of prince and people—indeed the whole politico-social sphere—was excluded from the purely religious origins of tragedy. But even regarding the classical form of the chorus in Aeschylus and Sophocles, which is known to us, we should deem it blasphemy to speak here of intimations of "constitutional popular representation." From this blasphemy, however, others have not shrunk. Ancient constitutions knew of no constitutional representation of the people in *praxi,* and it is to be hoped that they did not even "have intimations" of it in tragedy.

Much more famous than this political interpretation of the chorus is the idea of A. W. Schlegel,[1] who advises us to regard the

---

[1] One of the leading spirits of the early German romantic movement, especially renowned for his translations of about half of Shakespeare's plays; born 1767, died 1845.

chorus somehow as the essence and extract of the crowd of spectators—as the "ideal spectator." This view, when compared with the historical tradition that originally tragedy was only chorus, reveals itself for what it is—a crude, unscientific, yet brilliant claim that owes its brilliancy only to its concentrated form of expression, to the typically Germanic bias in favor of anything called "ideal," and to our momentary astonishment. For we are certainly astonished the moment we compare our familiar theatrical public with this chorus, and ask ourselves whether it could ever be possible to idealize from such a public something analogous to the Greek tragic chorus. We tacitly deny this, and now wonder as much at the boldness of Schlegel's claim as at the totally different nature of the Greek public. For we had always believed that the right spectator, whoever he might be, must always remain conscious that he was viewing a work of art and not an empirical reality. But the tragic chorus of the Greeks is forced to recognize real beings in the figures on the stage. The chorus of the Oceanides really believes that it sees before it the Titan Prometheus, and it considers itself as real as the god of the scene. But could the highest and purest type of spectator regard Prometheus as bodily present and real, as the Oceanides do? Is it characteristic of the ideal spectator to run onto the stage and free the god from his torments? We had always believed in an aesthetic public and considered the individual spectator the better qualified the more he was capable of viewing a work of art as art, that is, aesthetically. But now Schlegel tells us that the perfect, ideal spectator does not at all allow the world of the drama to act on him aesthetically, but corporally and empirically. Oh, these Greeks! we sigh; they upset all our aesthetics! But once accustomed to this, we repeated Schlegel's saying whenever the chorus came up for discussion.

Now the tradition, which is quite explicit, speaks against Schlegel. The chorus as such, without the stage—the primitive form of tragedy—and the chorus of ideal spectators do not go together. What kind of artistic genre could possibly be extracted from the concept of the spectator, and find its true form in the "spectator as such"? The spectator without the spectacle is an absurd notion. We fear that the birth of tragedy is to be explained neither by any high esteem for the moral intelligence of the masses nor by the concept of the spectator without a spectacle; and we consider the problem too deep to be even touched by such superficial considerations.

An infinitely more valuable insight into the significance of the chorus was displayed by Schiller in the celebrated Preface to his *Bride of Messina,* where he regards the chorus as a living wall that tragedy constructs around itself in order to close itself off from the world of reality and to preserve its ideal domain and its poetical freedom.

With this, his chief weapon, Schiller combats the ordinary conception of the natural, the illusion usually demanded in dramatic poetry. Although the stage day is merely artificial, the architecture only symbolical, and the metrical language ideal in character, nevertheless an erroneous view still prevails in the main, as he points out: it is not sufficient that one merely tolerates as poetic license what is actually the essence of all poetry. The introduction of the chorus, says Schiller, is the decisive step by which war is declared openly and honorably against all naturalism in art.

It would seem that to denigrate this view of the matter our would-be superior age has coined the disdainful catchword "pseudo-idealism." I fear, however, that we, on the other hand, with our present adoration of the natural and the real, have reached the opposite pole of all idealism, namely, the region of wax-work cabinets. There is an art in these, too, as there is in certain novels much in vogue at present; but we really should not be plagued with the claim that such art has overcome the "pseudo-idealism" of Goethe and Schiller.

It is indeed an "ideal" domain, as Schiller correctly perceived, in which the Greek satyr chorus, the chorus of primitive tragedy, was wont to dwell. It is a domain raised high above the actual paths of mortals. For this chorus the Greek built up the scaffolding of a fictitious *natural state* and on it placed fictitious *natural beings.* On this foundation tragedy developed and so, of course, it could dispense from the beginning with a painstaking portrayal of reality. Yet it is no arbitrary world placed by whim between heaven and earth; rather it is a world with the same reality and credibility that Olympus with its inhabitants possessed for the believing Hellene. The satyr, as the Dionysian chorist, lives in a religiously acknowledged reality under the sanction of myth and cult. That tragedy should begin with him, that he should be the voice of the Dionysian wisdom of tragedy, is just as strange a phenomenon for us as the general derivation of tragedy from the chorus.

Perhaps we shall have a point of departure for our inquiry if I put forward the proposition that the satyr, the fictitious natural being, bears the same relation to the man of culture that Dionysian music bears to civilization. Concerning the latter, Richard Wagner says that it is nullified [2] by music just as lamplight is nullified by the light of day. Similarly, I believe, the Greek man of culture felt himself nullified in the presence of the satyric chorus; and this is the most immediate effect of the Dionysian tragedy, that the state and society and, quite generally, the gulfs between man and man give way to an overwhelming feeling of unity leading back to the very heart of nature. The metaphysical comfort—with which, I am suggesting even now, every true tragedy leaves us—that life is at the bottom of things, despite all the changes of appearances, indestructibly powerful and pleasurable—this comfort appears in incarnate clarity in the chorus of satyrs, a chorus of natural beings who live ineradicably, as it were, behind all civilization and remain eternally the same, despite the changes of generations and of the history of nations.

With this chorus the profound Hellene, uniquely susceptible to the tenderest and deepest suffering, comforts himself, having looked boldly right into the terrible destructiveness of so-called world history as well as the cruelty of nature, and being in danger of longing for a Buddhistic negation of the will.[3] Art saves him, and through art—life.

For the rapture of the Dionysian state with its annihilation of the ordinary bounds and limits of existence contains, while it lasts, a *lethargic* element in which all personal experiences of the past become immersed. This chasm of oblivion separates the worlds of everyday reality and of Dionysian reality. But as soon as this everyday reality re-enters consciousness, it is experienced as such,

---

[2] *Aufgehoben:* one of Hegel's favorite words, which can also mean lifted up or preserved.

[3] Here Nietzsche's emancipation from Schopenhauer becomes evident, and their difference from each other concerns the central subject of the whole book: the significance of tragedy. Nietzsche writes about tragedy as the great life-affirming alternative to Schopenhauer's negation of the will. One can be as honest and free of optimistic illusions as Schopenhauer was, and still celebrate life as fundamentally powerful and pleasurable as the Greeks did.

with nausea: an ascetic, will-negating mood is the fruit of these states.

In this sense the Dionysian man resembles Hamlet: both have once looked truly into the essence of things, they have *gained knowledge,* and nausea inhibits action; for their action could not change anything in the eternal nature of things; they feel it to be ridiculous or humiliating that they should be asked to set right a world that is out of joint. Knowledge kills action; action requires the veils of illusion: that is the doctrine of Hamlet, not that cheap wisdom of Jack the Dreamer who reflects too much and, as it were, from an excess of possibilities does not get around to action. Not reflection, no—true knowledge, an insight into the horrible truth, outweighs any motive for action, both in Hamlet and in the Dionysian man.

Now no comfort avails any more; longing transcends a world after death, even the gods; existence is negated along with its glittering reflection in the gods or in an immortal beyond. Conscious of the truth he has once seen, man now sees everywhere only the horror or absurdity of existence; now he understands what is symbolic in Ophelia's fate; now he understands the wisdom of the sylvan god, Silenus: he is nauseated.

Here, when the danger to his will is greatest, *art* approaches as a saving sorceress, expert at healing. She alone knows how to turn these nauseous thoughts about the horror or absurdity of existence into notions with which one can live: these are the *sublime* as the artistic taming of the horrible, and the *comic* as the artistic discharge of the nausea of absurdity. The satyr chorus of the dithyramb is the saving deed of Greek art; faced with the intermediary world of these Dionysian companions, the feelings described here exhausted themselves.[4]

---

[4] Having finally broken loose from Schopenhauer, Nietzsche for the first time shows the brilliancy of his own genius. It is doubtful whether anyone before him had illuminated *Hamlet* so extensively in so few words: the passage invites comparison with Freud's great footnote on *Hamlet* in the first edition of *Die Traumdeutung* (interpretation of dreams), 1900. Even more obviously, the last three paragraphs invite comparison with existentialist literature, notably, but by no means only, Sartre's *La Nausée* (1938).

8

The satyr, like the idyllic shepherd of more recent times, is the offspring of a longing for the primitive and the natural; but how firmly and fearlessly the Greek embraced the man of the woods, and how timorously and mawkishly modern man dallied with the flattering image of a sentimental, flute-playing, tender shepherd! Nature, as yet unchanged by knowledge, with the bolts of culture still unbroken—that is what the Greek saw in his satyr who nevertheless was not a mere ape. On the contrary, the satyr was the archetype of man, the embodiment of his highest and most intense emotions, the ecstatic reveler enraptured by the proximity of his god, the sympathetic companion in whom the suffering of the god is repeated, one who proclaims wisdom from the very heart of nature, a symbol of the sexual omnipotence of nature which the Greeks used to contemplate with reverent wonder.

The satyr was something sublime and divine: thus he had to appear to the painfully broken vision of Dionysian man. The contrived shepherd in his dress-ups would have offended him: on the unconcealed and vigorously magnificent characters of nature, his eye rested with sublime satisfaction; here the true human being was disclosed, the bearded satyr jubilating to his god. Confronted with him, the man of culture shriveled into a mendacious caricature.

Schiller is right about these origins of tragic art, too: the chorus is a living wall against the assaults of reality because it—the satyr chorus—represents existence more truthfully, really, and completely than the man of culture does who ordinarily considers himself as the only reality. The sphere of poetry does not lie outside the world as a fantastic impossibility spawned by a poet's brain: it desires to be just the opposite, the unvarnished expression of the truth, and must precisely for that reason discard the mendacious finery of that alleged reality of the man of culture.

The contrast between this real truth of nature and the lie of culture that poses as if it were the only reality is similar to that between the eternal core of things, the thing-in-itself, and the whole world of appearances:[1] just as tragedy, with its metaphysical com-

---

[1] The word translated as "appearances" in this passage is *Erscheinungen*.

fort, points to the eternal life of this core of existence which abides
through the perpetual destruction of appearances, the symbolism of
the satyr chorus proclaims this primordial relationship between the
thing-in-itself and appearance.[2] The idyllic shepherd of modern
man is merely a counterfeit of the sum of cultural illusions that are
allegedly nature; the Dionysian Greek wants truth and nature in
their most forceful form—and sees himself changed, as by magic,
into a satyr.

The reveling throng, the votaries of Dionysus jubilate under
the spell of such moods and insights whose power transforms them
before their own eyes till they imagine that they are beholding
themselves as restored geniuses of nature, as satyrs. The later con-
stitution of the chorus in tragedy is the artistic imitation of this
natural phenomenon, though, to be sure, at this point the separation of Dionysian spectators and magically enchanted Dionysians
became necessary. Only we must always keep in mind that the public at an Attic tragedy found itself in the chorus of the *orchestra*,[3]
and there was at bottom no opposition between public and chorus:
everything is merely a great sublime chorus of dancing and singing
satyrs or of those who permit themselves to be represented by such
satyrs.

Now we are ready to understand Schlegel's formulation in a
deeper sense. The chorus is the "ideal spectator" [4] insofar as it is
the only beholder, the beholder of the visionary world of the
scene.[5] A public of spectators as we know it was unknown to the

---

[2] Here Nietzsche returns to Schopenhauer's perspective.

[3] "The Greek theatre appears to have been originally designed for the performance of dithyrambic choruses in honour of Dionysus. The centre of it
was the *orchēstrā* ('dancing-place'), a circular space, in the middle of which
stood the *thumelē* or altar of the god. Round more than half of the *orchestra*,
forming a kind of horse-shoe, was the *theātron* ('seeing-place') proper, circular tiers of seats, generally cut out of the side of a hill . . . Behind the
orchestra and facing the audience was the *skēnē* [called "scene" in the above
translation], originally a wooden structure, a façade with three doors, through
which, when the drama had developed from the dithyrambic chorus, the
actors made their entrances" (*The Oxford Companion to Classical Literature*,
ed. Sir Paul Harvey, revised edition, 1946, pp. 422f.).

[4] *Der "idealische Zuschauer."*

[5] *Der einzige* Schauer *ist, der Schauer der Visionswelt der Scene*. The word
Schauer could also mean shudder, the shudder of holy awe; and while this is
certainly not the primary meaning intended here, it somehow enters into the
coloring of the sentence.

Greeks: in their theaters the terraced structure of concentric arcs made it possible for everybody to actually *overlook*[6] the whole world of culture around him and to imagine, in absorbed contemplation, that he himself was a chorist.

In the light of this insight we may call the chorus in its primitive form, in proto-tragedy, the mirror image in which the Dionysian man contemplates himself. This phenomenon is best made clear by imagining an actor who, being truly talented, sees the role he is supposed to play quite palpably before his eyes. The satyr chorus is, first of all, a vision of the Dionysian mass of spectators, just as the world of the stage, in turn, is a vision of this satyr chorus: the force of this vision is strong enough to make the eye insensitive and blind to the impression of "reality," to the men of culture who occupy the rows of seats all around. The form of the Greek theater recalls a lonely valley in the mountains: the architecture of the scene appears like a luminous cloud formation that the Bacchants swarming over the mountains behold from a height— like the splendid frame in which the image of Dionysus is revealed to them.

In the face of our learned views about elementary artistic processes, this artistic proto-phenomenon which we bring up here to help explain the tragic chorus is almost offensive, although nothing could be more certain than the fact that a poet is a poet only insofar as he sees himself surrounded by figures who live and act before him and into whose inmost nature he can see. Owing to a peculiar modern weakness, we are inclined to imagine the aesthetic proto-phenomenon in a manner much too complicated and abstract.

For a genuine poet, metaphor is not a rhetorical figure but a vicarious image that he actually beholds in place of a concept. A character is for him not a whole he has composed out of particular traits, picked up here and there, but an obtrusively alive person before his very eyes, distinguished from the otherwise identical vision of a painter only by the fact that it continually goes on living and acting. How is it that Homer's descriptions are so much more vivid

---

[6] *Übersehen,* like overlook, can mean both survey and ignore. Francis Golffing, in his translation, opts for "quite literally survey," which makes nonsense of the passage. The context unequivocally requires oblivion of the whole world of culture: nothing is between the beholder and the chorus. Golffing's translation is altogether more vigorous than it is reliable.

than those of any other poet? Because he visualizes so much more vividly. We talk so abstractly about poetry because all of us are usually bad poets. At bottom, the aesthetic phenomenon is simple: let anyone have the ability to behold continually a vivid play and to live constantly surrounded by hosts of spirits, and he will be a poet; let anyone feel the urge to transform himself and to speak out of other bodies and souls, and he will be a dramatist.

The Dionysian excitement is capable of communicating this artistic gift to a multitude, so they can see themselves surrounded by such a host of spirits while knowing themselves to be essentially one with them. This process of the tragic chorus is the *dramatic* proto-phenomenon: to see oneself transformed before one's own eyes and to begin to act as if one had actually entered into another body, another character. This process stands at the beginning of the origin of drama. Here we have something different from the rhapsodist who does not become fused with his images but, like a painter, sees them outside himself as objects of contemplation. Here we have a surrender of individuality and a way of entering into another character. And this phenomenon is encountered epidemically: a whole throng experiences the magic of this transformation.

The dithyramb is thus essentially different from all other choral odes. The virgins who proceed solemnly to the temple of Apollo, laurel branches in their hands, singing a processional hymn, remain what they are and retain their civic names: the dithyrambic chorus is a chorus of transformed characters whose civic past and social status have been totally forgotten: they have become timeless servants of their god who live outside the spheres of society. All the other choral lyric poetry of the Hellenes is merely a tremendous intensification of the Apollinian solo singer, while in the dithyramb we confront a community of unconscious actors who consider themselves and one another transformed.

Such magic transformation is the presupposition of all dramatic art. In this magic transformation the Dionysian reveler sees himself as a satyr, *and as a satyr, in turn, he sees the god,* which means that in his metamorphosis he beholds another vision outside himself, as the Apollinian complement of his own state. With this new vision the drama is complete.

In the light of this insight we must understand Greek tragedy as the Dionysian chorus which ever anew discharges itself in an Apollinian world of images. Thus the choral parts with which tragedy is interlaced are, as it were, the womb that gave birth to the whole of the so-called dialogue, that is, the entire world of the stage, the real drama. In several successive discharges this primal ground of tragedy radiates this vision of the drama which is by all means a dream apparition and to that extent epic in nature; but on the other hand, being the objectification of a Dionysian state, it represents not Apollinian redemption through mere appearance but, on the contrary, the shattering of the individual and his fusion with primal being. Thus the drama is the Dionysian embodiment of Dionysian insights and effects and thereby separated, as by a tremendous chasm, from the epic. (A - one step, D - two.

The *chorus* of the Greek tragedy, the symbol of the whole excited Dionysian throng, is thus fully explained by our conception. Accustomed as we are to the function of our modern stage chorus, especially in operas, we could not comprehend why the tragic chorus of the Greeks should be older, more original and important than the "action" proper, as the voice of tradition claimed unmistakably. And with this traditional primacy and originality we could not reconcile the fact that the chorus consisted only of humble beings who served—indeed, initially only of goatlike satyrs. Finally, there remained the riddle of the orchestra in front of the scene. But now we realize that the scene, complete with the action, was basically and originally thought of merely as a *vision;* the chorus is the only "reality" and generates the vision, speaking of it with the entire symbolism of dance, tone, and words. In its vision this chorus beholds its lord and master Dionysus and is therefore eternally the *serving* chorus: it sees how the god suffers and glorifies himself and therefore does not itself *act*. But while its attitude toward the god is wholly one of service, it is nevertheless the highest, namely the Dionysian, expression of *nature* and therefore pronounces in its rapture, as nature does, oracles and wise sayings: *sharing his suffering* it also shares something of his *wisdom* and proclaims the truth from the heart of the world. That is the origin of the fantastic and seemingly so offensive figure of the wise and rapturous satyr who is at the same time "the simple man" as opposed to the god—the image of nature and its strongest urges, even their symbol, and at the same time the proclaimer of her wisdom *drama—acting out Dionysus?*

and art—musician, poet, dancer, and seer of spirits in one person.

Dionysus, the real stage hero and center of the vision, was, according both to this insight and to the tradition, not actually present at first, in the very oldest period of tragedy; he was merely imagined as present, which means that originally tragedy was only "chorus" and not yet "drama." Later the attempt was made to show the god as real and to represent the visionary figure together with its transfiguring frame as something visible for every eye—and thus "drama" in the narrower sense began. Now the dithyrambic chorus was assigned the task of exciting the mood of the listeners to such a Dionysian degree that, when the tragic hero appeared on the stage, they did not see the awkwardly masked human being but rather a visionary figure, born as it were from their own rapture.

Consider Admetus as he is brooding over the memory of his recently departed wife Alcestis, consuming himself in her spiritual contemplation, when suddenly a similarly formed, similarly walking woman's figure is led toward him, heavily veiled; let us imagine his sudden trembling unrest, his tempestuous comparisons, his instinctive conviction—and we have an analogy with what the spectator felt in his Dionysian excitement when he saw the approach on the stage of the god with whose sufferings he had already identified himself. Involuntarily, he transferred the whole magic image of the god that was trembling before his soul to that masked figure and, as it were, dissolved its reality into the unreality of spirits.

This is the Apollinian state of dreams in which the world of the day becomes veiled, and a new world, clearer, more understandable, more moving than the everyday world and yet more shadowy, presents itself to our eyes in continual rebirths. Accordingly, we recognize in tragedy a sweeping opposition of styles: the language, color, mobility, and dynamics of speech fall apart into the Dionysian lyrics of the chorus and, on the other hand, the Apollinian dream world, and become two utterly different spheres of expression. The Apollinian appearances in which Dionysus objectifies himself are no longer "an eternal sea, changeful strife, a glowing life," [7] like the music of the chorus, no longer those forces, merely felt and not condensed into images, in which the enraptured servant of Dionysus senses the nearness of the god: now the clarity

---

[7] Quoted from Goethe's *Faust,* lines 505–507.

and firmness of epic form addresses him from the scene; now Dionysus no longer speaks through forces but as an epic hero, almost in the language of Homer.

9

Everything that comes to the surface in the Apollinian part of Greek tragedy, in the dialogue, looks simple, transparent, and beautiful. In this sense, the dialogue is an image of the Hellene whose nature is revealed in the dance because in the dance the greatest strength remains only potential but betrays itself in the suppleness and wealth of movement. Thus the language of Sophocles' heroes amazes us by its Apollinian precision and lucidity, so we immediately have the feeling that we are looking into the innermost ground of their being, with some astonishment that the way to this ground should be so short. But suppose we disregard the character of the hero as it comes to the surface, visibly—after all, it is in the last analysis nothing but a bright image projected on a dark wall, which means appearance[1] through and through; suppose we penetrate into the myth that projects itself in these lucid reflections: then we suddenly experience a phenomenon that is just the opposite of a familiar optical phenomenon. When after a forceful attempt to gaze on the sun we turn away blinded, we see dark-colored spots before our eyes, as a cure, as it were. Conversely, the bright image projections of the Sophoclean hero—in short, the Apollinian aspect of the mask—are necessary effects of a glance into the inside and terrors of nature; as it were, luminous spots to cure eyes damaged by gruesome night. Only in this sense may we believe that we properly comprehend the serious and important concept of "Greek cheerfulness." The misunderstanding of this concept as cheerfulness in a state of unendangered comfort is, of course, encountered everywhere today.

Sophocles understood the most sorrowful figure of the Greek stage, the unfortunate Oedipus, as the noble human being who, in spite of his wisdom, is destined to error and misery but who eventually, through his tremendous suffering, spreads a magical power of blessing that remains effective even beyond his decease. The

[1] *Erscheinung*.

noble human being does not sin, the profound poet wants to tell us:
though every law, every natural order, even the moral world may
perish through his actions, his actions also produce a higher magical circle of effects which found a new world on the ruins of the old
one that has been overthrown. That is what the poet wants to say to
us insofar as he is at the same time a religious thinker. As a poet he
first shows us a marvelously tied knot of a trial, slowly unraveled
by the judge, bit by bit, for his own undoing. The genuinely Hellenic delight at this dialectical solution is so great that it introduces
a trait of superior cheerfulness into the whole work, everywhere
softening the sharp points of the gruesome presuppositions of this
process.

In *Oedipus at Colonus* we encounter the same cheerfulness,
but elevated into an infinite transfiguration. The old man, struck
by an excess of misery, abandoned solely to *suffer* whatever befalls
him, is confronted by the supraterrestrial cheerfulness that de-
scends from the divine sphere and suggests to us that the hero attains his highest activity, extending far beyond his life, through his
purely passive posture, while his conscious deeds and desires, earlier
in his life, merely led him into passivity. Thus the intricate legal
knot of the Oedipus fable that no mortal eye could unravel is
gradually disentangled—and the most profound human joy overcomes us at this divine counterpart of the dialectic.

If this explanation does justice to the poet one may yet ask
whether it exhausts the contents of the myth—and then it becomes
evident that the poet's whole conception is nothing but precisely
that bright image which healing nature projects before us after a
glance into the abyss. Oedipus, the murderer of his father, the hus-
band of his mother, the solver of the riddle of the Sphinx! What
does the mysterious triad of these fateful deeds tell us?

There is a tremendously old popular belief, especially in Per-
sia, that a wise magus can be born only from incest. With the riddle-
solving and mother-marrying Oedipus in mind, we must immediately interpret this to mean that where prophetic and magical
powers have broken the spell of present and future, the rigid
law of individuation, and the real magic of nature, some enor-
mously unnatural event—such as incest—must have occurred earlier, as a cause. How else could one compel nature to surrender her
secrets if not by triumphantly resisting her, that is, by means of

something unnatural? It is this insight that I find expressed in that horrible triad of Oedipus' destinies: the same man who solves the riddle of nature—that Sphinx of two species[2]—also must break the most sacred natural orders by murdering his father and marrying his mother. Indeed, the myth seems to wish to whisper to us that wisdom, and particularly Dionysian wisdom, is an unnatural abomination; that he who by means of his knowledge plunges nature into the abyss of destruction must also suffer the dissolution of nature in his own person. "The edge of wisdom turns against the wise: wisdom is a crime against nature": such horrible sentences are proclaimed to us by the myth; but the Hellenic poet touches the sublime and terrible Memnon's Column of myth like a sunbeam, so that it suddenly begins to sound—in Sophoclean melodies.[3]

Let me now contrast the glory of activity, which illuminates Aeschylus' *Prometheus,* with the glory of passivity. What the thinker Aeschylus had to say to us here, but what as a poet he only allows us to sense in his symbolic image, the youthful Goethe was able to reveal to us in the audacious words of his Prometheus:

> *Here I sit, forming men*
> *in my own image,*
> *a race to be like me,*
> *to suffer, to weep,*
> *to delight and to rejoice,*
> *and to defy you,*
> *as I do.*[4]

Man, rising to Titanic stature, gains culture by his own efforts and forces the gods to enter into an alliance with him because in his

---

[2] Lion and human. Actually, the Sphinx also has wings in ancient Greek representations.

Nietzsche's comments on incest are influenced by Wagner and should be compared with *The Case of Wagner,* section 4, third paragraph.

[3] Memnon's Column was an ancient name given to one of the two colossal statues of the pharaoh Amenophis III, near the Egyptian Thebes between the Nile and the valley of the kings, across the river from Karnak. When the first rays of the sun struck the weathered statue in the morning, it is said to have produced a musical sound—a phenomenon that stopped when an earthquake damaged the statue still further. The "statue of Memnon" also appears in Ibsen's *Peer Gynt* (1867), in Act IV.

[4] Goethe's poem—original text and verse translation on facing pages—is included in *Twenty German Poets,* trans. W. Kaufmann.

very own wisdom he holds their existence and their limitations in his hands. But what is most wonderful in this Prometheus poem, which in its basic idea is the veritable hymn of impiety, is the profoundly Aeschylean demand for *justice*. The immeasurable suffering of the bold "individual" on the one hand and the divine predicament and intimation of a twilight of the gods on the other, the way the power of these two worlds of suffering compels a reconciliation, a metaphysical union—all this recalls in the strongest possible manner the center and main axiom of the Aeschylean view of the world which envisages Moira enthroned above gods and men as eternal justice.

In view of the astonishing audacity with which Aeschylus places the Olympian world on the scales of his justice, we must call to mind that the profound Greek possessed an immovably firm foundation for metaphysical thought in his mysteries, and all his skeptical moods could be vented against the Olympians. The Greek artist in particular had an obscure feeling of mutual dependence when it came to the gods; and precisely in the *Prometheus* of Aeschylus this feeling is symbolized. In himself the Titanic artist found the defiant faith that he had the ability to create men and at least destroy Olympian gods, by means of his superior wisdom which, to be sure, he had to atone for with eternal suffering. The splendid "ability" of the great genius for which even eternal suffering is a slight price, the stern pride of the *artist*—that is the content and soul of Aeschylus' poem, while Sophocles in his *Oedipus* sounds as a prelude the *holy man's* song of triumph.

But Aeschylus' interpretation of the myth does not exhaust the astounding depth of its terror. Rather the artist's delight in what becomes, the cheerfulness of artistic creation that defies all misfortune, is merely a bright image of clouds and sky mirrored in a black lake of sadness. The Prometheus story is an original possession of the entire Aryan community of peoples and evidences their gift for the profoundly tragic. Indeed, it does not seem improbable that this myth has the same characteristic significance for the Aryan character which the myth of the fall has for the Semitic character, and that these two myths are related to each other like brother and sister.[5] The presupposition of the Prometheus myth is

---

[5] After his emancipation from Wagner, Nietzsche came to consider the

to be found in the extravagant value which a naïve humanity attached to *fire* as the true palladium of every ascending culture. But that man should freely dispose of fire without receiving it as a present from heaven, either as a lightning bolt or as the warming rays of the sun, struck these reflective primitive men as sacrilege, as a robbery of divine nature. Thus the very first philosophical problem immediately produces a painful and irresolvable contradiction between man and god and moves it before the gate of every culture, like a huge boulder. The best and highest possession mankind can acquire is obtained by sacrilege and must be paid for with consequences that involve the whole flood of sufferings and sorrows with which the offended divinities have to afflict the nobly aspiring race of men. This is a harsh idea which, by the *dignity* it confers on sacrilege, contrasts strangely with the Semitic myth of the fall in which curiosity, mendacious deception, susceptibility to seduction, lust—in short, a series of pre-eminently feminine affects was considered the origin of evil. What distinguishes the Aryan notion is the sublime view of *active sin* as the characteristically Promethean virtue. With that, the ethical basis for pessimistic tragedy has been found: the justification of human evil, meaning both human guilt and the human suffering it entails.

The misfortune in the nature of things, which the contemplative Aryan is not inclined to interpret away—the contradiction at the heart of the world reveals itself to him as a clash of different worlds, e.g., of a divine and human one, in which each, taken as an individual, has right on its side, but nevertheless has to suffer for its individuation, being merely a single one beside another. In the heroic effort of the individual to attain universality, in the attempt to transcend the curse of individuation and to become the *one* world-being, he suffers in his own person the primordial contradiction that is concealed in things, which means that he commits sacrilege and suffers.

Thus the Aryans understand sacrilege as something masculine,[6] while the Semites understand sin as feminine,[7] just as the

---

terms "Aryan" and "Semitic" more problematic. See, e.g., his note: "Contra Aryan and Semitic. Where races are mixed, there is the source of great cultures" (*Werke, Musarion* edition, vol. XVI, pp. 373f.).

[6] *Der Frevel.*

[7] *Die Sünde.*

original sacrilege is committed by a man, the original sin by a woman. Also, the witches' chorus says:

> *If that is so, we do not mind it:*
> *With a thousand steps the women find it;*
> *But though they rush, we do not care:*
> *With one big jump the men get there.*[8]

Whoever understands this innermost kernel of the Prometheus story—namely, the necessity of sacrilege imposed upon the titanically striving individual—must also immediately feel how un-Apollinian this pessimistic notion is. For Apollo wants to grant repose to individual beings precisely by drawing boundaries between them and by again and again calling these to mind as the most sacred laws of the world, with his demands for self-knowledge and measure.

Lest this Apollinian tendency congeal the form to Egyptian rigidity and coldness, lest the effort to prescribe to the individual wave its path and realm might annul the motion of the whole lake, the high tide of the Dionysian destroyed from time to time all those little circles in which the one-sidedly Apollinian "will" had sought to confine the Hellenic spirit. The suddenly swelling Dionysian tide then takes the separate little wave-mountains of individuals on its back, even as Prometheus' brother, the Titan Atlas, does with the earth. This Titanic impulse to become, as it were, the Atlas for all individuals, carrying them on a broad back, higher and higher, farther and farther, is what the Promethean and the Dionysian have in common.

In this respect, the Prometheus of Aeschylus is a Dionysian mask, while in the aforementioned profound demand for justice Aeschylus reveals to the thoughtful his paternal descent from Apollo, the god of individuation and of just boundaries. So the dual nature of Aeschylus' Prometheus, his nature which is at the same time Dionysian and Apollinian, might be expressed thus in a conceptual formula: "All that exists is just and unjust and equally justified in both."

That is your world! A world indeed!—[9]

---

[8] Goethe's *Faust*, lines 3982–85.
[9] Goethe's *Faust*, line 409.

10

The tradition is undisputed that Greek tragedy in its earliest form had for its sole theme the sufferings of Dionysus and that for a long time the only stage hero was Dionysus himself. But it may be claimed with equal confidence that until Euripides, Dionysus never ceased to be the tragic hero; that all the celebrated figures of the Greek stage—Prometheus, Oedipus, etc.—are mere masks of this original hero, Dionysus. That behind all these masks there is a deity, that is one essential reason for the typical "ideality" of these famous figures which has caused so much astonishment. Somebody, I do not know who, has claimed that all individuals, taken as individuals, are comic and hence untragic—from which it would follow that the Greeks simply *could* not suffer individuals on the tragic stage. In fact, this is what they seem to have felt; and the Platonic distinction and evaluation of the "idea" and the "idol," the mere image, is very deeply rooted in the Hellenic character.

Using Plato's terms we should have to speak of the tragic figures of the Hellenic stage somewhat as follows: the one truly real Dionysus appears in a variety of forms, in the mask of a fighting hero, and entangled, as it were, in the net of the individual will. The god who appears talks and acts so as to resemble an erring, striving, suffering individual. That he *appears* at all with such epic precision and clarity is the work of the dream-interpreter, Apollo, who through this symbolic appearance interprets to the chorus its Dionysian state. In truth, however, the hero is the suffering Dionysus of the Mysteries, the god experiencing in himself the agonies of individuation, of whom wonderful myths tell that as a boy he was torn to pieces by the Titans and now is worshiped in this state as Zagreus. Thus it is intimated that this dismemberment, the properly Dionysian *suffering,* is like a transformation into air, water, earth, and fire, that we are therefore to regard the state of individuation as the origin and primal cause of all suffering, as something objectionable in itself. From the smile of this Dionysus sprang the Olympian gods, from his tears sprang man. In this existence as a dismembered god, Dionysus possesses the dual nature of a cruel, barbarized demon and a mild, gentle ruler. But the hope of the

> *myth of somewhere that we were
> originally separated from one another – +
> search for the other part.*

epopts[1] looked toward a rebirth of Dionysus, which we must now
dimly conceive as the end of individuation. It was for this coming
third Dionysus that the epopts' roaring hymns of joy resounded.
And it is this hope alone that casts a gleam of joy upon the features
of a world torn asunder and shattered into individuals; this is symbolized in the myth of Demeter, sunk in eternal sorrow, who *rejoices* again for the first time when told that she may *once more*
give birth to Dionysus. This view of things already provides us with
all the elements of a profound and pessimistic view of the world,
together with the *mystery doctrine of tragedy:* the fundamental
knowledge of the oneness of everything existent, the conception of
individuation as the primal cause of evil, and of art as the joyous
hope that the spell of individuation may be broken in augury of a
restored oneness.

We have already suggested that the Homeric epos is the poem
of Olympian culture, in which this culture has sung its own song of
victory over the terrors of the war of the Titans. Under the predom-
inating influence of tragic poetry, these Homeric myths are now
born anew; and this metempsychosis reveals that in the meantime
the Olympian culture also has been conquered by a still more profound view of the world. The defiant Titan Prometheus has an-
nounced to his Olympian tormentor that some day the greatest
danger will menace his rule, unless Zeus should enter into an alliance with him in time. In Aeschylus we recognize how the terrified Zeus, fearful of his end, allies himself with the Titan. Thus the
former age of the Titans is once more recovered from Tartarus and
brought to the light.

The philosophy of wild and naked nature beholds with the
frank, undissembling gaze of truth the myths of the Homeric world
as they dance past: they turn pale, they tremble under the piercing
glance of this goddess[2]—till the powerful fist of the Dionysian artist forces them into the service of the new deity. Dionysian truth
takes over the entire domain of myth as the symbolism of *its*
knowledge which it makes known partly in the public cult of tragedy and partly in the secret celebrations of dramatic mysteries, but
always in the old mythical garb.

---

[1] Those initiated into the mysteries.
[2] Truth.

What power was it that freed Prometheus from his vultures and transformed the myth into a vehicle of Dionysian wisdom? It is the Heracleian power of music: having reached its highest manifestation in tragedy, it can invest myths with a new and most profound significance. This we have already characterized as the most powerful function of music. For it is the fate of every myth to creep by degrees into the narrow limits of some alleged historical reality, and to be treated by some later generation as a unique fact with historical claims: and the Greeks were already fairly on the way toward restamping the whole of their mythical juvenile dream sagaciously and arbitrarily into a historico-pragmatical *juvenile history*. For this is the way in which religions are wont to die out: under the stern, intelligent eyes of an orthodox dogmatism, the mythical premises of a religion are systematized as a sum total of historical events; one begins apprehensively to defend the credibility of the myths, while at the same time one opposes any continuation of their natural vitality and growth; the feeling for myth perishes, and its place is taken by the claim of religion to historical foundations. This dying myth was now seized by the new-born genius of Dionysian music; and in these hands it flourished once more with colors such as it had never yet displayed, with a fragrance that awakened a longing anticipation of a metaphysical world. After this final effulgence it collapses, its leaves wither, and soon the mocking Lucians of antiquity catch at the discolored and faded flowers carried away by the four winds. Through tragedy the myth attains its most profound content, its most expressive form; it rises once more like a wounded hero, and its whole excess of strength, together with the philosophic calm of the dying, burns in its eyes with a last powerful gleam.

What did you want, sacrilegious Euripides, when you sought to compel this dying myth to serve you once more? It died under your violent hands—and then you needed a copied, masked myth that, like the ape of Heracles, merely knew how to deck itself out in the ancient pomp. And just as the myth died on you, the genius of music died on you, too. Though with greedy hands you plundered all the gardens of music, you still managed only copied, masked music. And because you had abandoned Dionysus, Apollo abandoned you: rouse all the passions from their resting places and conjure them into your circle, sharpen and whet a sophistical dialectic for the speeches of your heroes—your heroes, too, have only copied, masked passions and speak only copied, masked speeches.

11

Greek tragedy met an end different from that of her older sister-arts: she died by suicide, in consequence of an irreconcilable conflict; she died tragically, while all the others passed away calmly and beautifully at a ripe old age. If it be consonant with a happy natural state to take leave of life easily, leaving behind a fair posterity, the closing period of these older arts exhibits such a happy natural state: slowly they sink from sight, and before their dying eyes stand their fairer progeny, who lift up their heads impatiently, with a bold gesture. But when Greek tragedy died, there rose everywhere the deep sense of an immense void. Just as Greek sailors in the time of Tiberius once heard on a lonesome island the soul-shaking cry, "Great Pan is dead," so the Hellenic world was now pierced by the grievous lament: "Tragedy is dead! Poetry itself has perished with her! Away with you, pale, meager epigones! Away to Hades, that you may for once eat your fill of the crumbs of our former masters!"

When a new artistic genre blossomed forth after all, and revered tragedy as its predecessor and mistress, it was noted with horror that she did indeed bear the features of her mother—but those she had exhibited in her long death-struggle. It was *Euripides* who fought this death struggle of tragedy; the later artistic genre is known as *New Attic Comedy*.[1] In it the degenerate form of tragedy lived on as a monument of its exceedingly painful and violent death.

This connection helps to explain the passionate attachment

---

[1] The chief representative of the so-called Old Comedy was Aristophanes (about 448–380 B.C.). "The New Comedy began to prevail about 336; its characteristic features are the representation of contemporary life by means of imaginary persons drawn from it, the development of plot and character, the substitution of humour for wit, and the introduction of romantic love as a theme. It resembles the tragedy of Euripides (the 'Ion' for example) more than the comedy of Aristophanes. Of the chorus no more remains than a band of musicians and dancers whose performances punctuate intervals in the play. The New Comedy is in fact an obvious progenitor of the modern drama. But the moral standard is surprisingly low. . . ." (*The Oxford Companion to Classical Literature, ed. cit.,* p. 116).

that the poets of the New Comedy felt for Euripides; so that we are no longer surprised at the wish of Philemon, who would have let himself be hanged at once, merely that he might visit Euripides in the lower world—if only he could be certain that the deceased still had possession of his reason. But if we desire, as briefly as possible, and without claiming to say anything exhaustive, to characterize what Euripides has in common with Menander and Philemon, and what appealed to them so strongly as worthy of imitation, it is sufficient to say that Euripides brought the *spectator* onto the stage. He who has perceived the material out of which the Promethean tragic writers prior to Euripides formed their heroes, and how remote from their purpose it was to bring the faithful mask of reality onto the stage, will also be aware of the utterly opposite tendency of Euripides. Through him the everyday man forced his way from the spectators' seats onto the stage; the mirror in which formerly only grand and bold traits were represented now showed the painful fidelity that conscientiously reproduces even the botched outlines of nature.

Odysseus, the typical Hellene of the older art, now sank, in the hands of the new poets, to the figure of the Graeculus, who, as the good-naturedly cunning house-slave, henceforth occupies the center of dramatic interest. What Euripides claims credit for in Aristophanes' *Frogs*,[2] namely, that his nostrums have liberated tragic art from its pompous corpulency, is apparent above all in his tragic heroes. The spectator now actually saw and heard his double on the Euripidean stage, and rejoiced that he could talk so well. But this joy was not all: one could even learn from Euripides how to speak oneself. He prides himself upon this in his contest with Aeschylus: from him the people have learned how to observe, debate, and draw conclusions according to the rules of art and with the cleverest sophistries. Through this revolution in ordinary language, he made the New Comedy possible. For henceforth it was no longer a secret how—and with what maxims—everyday life could be represented on the stage. Civic mediocrity, on which Euripides built all his political hopes, was now given a voice, while heretofore the demigod in tragedy and the drunken satyr, or demiman, in comedy, had deter-

---

[2] Lines 937ff. Aristophanes also lampoons Euripides in *The Acharnians* and in *Thesmophoriazousae*.

mined the character of the language. And so the Aristophanean Euripides prides himself on having portrayed the common, familiar, everyday life and activities of the people, about which all are qualified to pass judgment. If the entire populace now philosophized, managed land and goods, and conducted lawsuits with unheard-of circumspection, he deserved the credit, for this was the result of the wisdom he had inculcated in the people.

It was to a populace thus prepared and enlightened that the New Comedy could address itself: it was Euripides who had taught, as it were, the chorus; only now the chorus of spectators had to be trained. As soon as this chorus was trained to sing in the Euripidean key, there arose that drama which resembles a game of chess—the New Comedy, with its perpetual triumphs of cunning and craftiness. But Euripides—the chorus master—was praised continually: indeed, people would have killed themselves in order to learn still more from him, if they had not known that the tragic poets were quite as dead as tragedy. But with that, the Hellene had given up his belief in immortality; not only his belief in an ideal past, but also his belief in an ideal future. The words of the well-known epitaph, "frivolous and eccentric when an old man," [3] also suit aging Hellenism. The passing moment, wit, levity, and caprice are its highest deities; the fifth estate, that of the slaves, now comes to power, at least in sentiment; and if we may still speak at all of "Greek cheerfulness," it is the cheerfulness of the slave who has nothing of consequence to be responsible for, nothing great to strive for, and who does not value anything in the past or future higher than the present.

It was this semblance of "Greek cheerfulness" which so aroused the profound and formidable natures of the first four centuries of Christianity: this womanish flight from seriousness and terror, this craven satisfaction with easy enjoyment, seemed to them not only contemptible, but a specifically anti-Christian sentiment. And it is due to their influence that the conception of Greek antiquity which endured through the centuries clung with almost unconquerable persistency to that pink hue of cheerfulness—as if there had never been a sixth century with its birth of tragedy, its mysteries, its Py-

---

[3] Quotation from a six-line poem of the young Goethe, entitled "Grabschrift" (epitaph).

thagoras and Heraclitus, as if the works of art of the great period simply did not exist, though these phenomena can hardly be explained as having originated in any such senile and slavish pleasure in existence and cheerfulness, and point to a wholly different conception of the world as the ground of their existence.

The assertion made above, that Euripides brought the spectator onto the stage and thus qualified him to pass judgment on the drama, makes it appear as if the older tragic art had always suffered from bad relations with the spectator; and one might be tempted to extol as an advance over Sophocles the radical tendency of Euripides to produce a proper relation between art and the public. But "public," after all, is a mere word. In no sense is it a homogeneous and constant quantity. Why should the artist be bound to accommodate himself to a power whose strength lies solely in numbers? And if, by virtue of his endowments and aspirations, he should feel himself superior to every one of these spectators, how could he feel greater respect for the collective expression of all these subordinate capacities than for the relatively highest-endowed individual spectator? In truth, if ever a Greek artist throughout a long life treated his public with audacity and self-sufficiency, it was Euripides. When the masses threw themselves at his feet, he openly and with sublime defiance reversed his own tendency, the very tendency with which he had won over the masses. If this genius had had the slightest reverence for the pandemonium of the public, he would have broken down long before the middle of his career, beneath the heavy blows of his failures.

These considerations make it clear that our formula—that Euripides brought the spectator onto the stage in order to make him truly competent to pass judgment—was merely provisional; we must penetrate more deeply to understand his tendency. Conversely, it is well known that Aeschylus and Sophocles during the whole of their lives, and indeed long after, were in complete possession of the people's favor, so there can be no question of a false relation between art and the public in the case of these predecessors of Euripides. What was it then that forcibly drove this artist, so richly endowed, so constantly impelled to production, from the path warmed by the sun of the greatest names in poetry and covered by the cloudless heaven of popular favor? What strange consideration for the spectator led him to oppose the spectator? How could he, out of too great a respect for his public—despise his public?

Euripides—and this is the solution of the riddle just propounded—undoubtedly felt himself, as a poet, superior to the masses in general; but to two of his spectators he did not feel superior. He brought the masses onto the stage; but these two spectators he revered as the only competent judges and masters of his art. Complying with their directions and admonitions, he transferred the entire world of sentiments, passions, and experiences, hitherto present at every festival performance as the invisible chorus on the spectators' benches, into the souls of his stage-heroes. He yielded to their demands, too, when for these new characters he sought out a new language and a new tone. Only in their voices could he hear any conclusive verdict on his work, and also the encouragement that promised eventual success when, as usual, he found himself condemned by the public judgment.

Of these two spectators, one is—Euripides himself, Euripides *as thinker,* not as poet. It might be said of him, as of Lessing, that his extraordinary fund of *critical* talent, if it did not create, at least constantly stimulated his productive *artistic* impulse. With this gift, with all the brightness and dexterity of his critical thinking, Euripides had sat in the theater and striven to recognize in the masterpieces of his great predecessors, as in paintings that have become dark, feature after feature, line after line. And here he had experienced something which should not surprise anyone initiated into the deeper secrets of Aeschylean tragedy. He observed something incommensurable in every feature and in every line, a certain deceptive distinctness and at the same time an enigmatic depth, indeed an infinitude, in the background. Even the clearest figure always had a comet's tail attached to it which seemed to suggest the uncertain, that which could never be illuminated. A similar twilight shrouded the structure of the drama, especially the significance of the chorus. And how dubious the solution of the ethical problems remained to him! How questionable the treatment of the myths! How unequal the distribution of good and bad fortune! Even in the language of the Old Tragedy there was much he found offensive, or at least enigmatic; especially he found too much pomp for simple affairs, too many tropes and monstrous expressions to suit the plainness of the characters. So he sat in the theater, pondering uneasily, and as a spectator he confessed to himself that he did not understand his great predecessors. But if the understanding was for him the real root of all enjoyment and creation, he had to inquire and look around to see whether no one else had the same opinion and also felt this incommensurability. But most people, and among them the finest individuals, had only a suspicious smile for him, and none could explain to him why the great masters were still in the right despite his scruples and objections. And in this state of torment, he found *that other spectator* who did not comprehend tragedy and therefore did not esteem it. Allied with him, he could now venture from his solitude to begin the tremendous struggle against the art of Aeschylus and Sophocles—not with polemical essays, but as a dramatic poet who opposed *his* conception of tragedy to the traditional one.—

12

Before we name this other spectator, let us pause here a moment to recall to our minds our previously described impression of the discordant and incommensurable elements in the nature of Aeschylean tragedy. Let us recall our surprise at the *chorus* and the *tragic hero* of that tragedy, neither of which we could reconcile with our own customs any more than with tradition—till we rediscovered this duality itself as the origin and essence of Greek tragedy, as the expression of two interwoven artistic impulses, *the Apollinian and the Dionysian*.

To separate this original and all-powerful Dionysian element from tragedy, and to reconstruct tragedy purely on the basis of an un-Dionysian art, morality, and world view—this is the tendency of Euripides as it now reveals itself to us in clear illumination.

In the evening of his life, Euripides himself propounded to his contemporaries the question of the value and significance of this tendency, using a myth. Is the Dionysian entitled to exist at all? Should it not be forcibly uprooted from Hellenic soil? Certainly, the poet tells us, if it were only possible: but the god Dionysus is too powerful; his most intelligent adversary—like Pentheus in the *Bacchae*—is unwittingly enchanted by him, and in this enchantment runs to meet his fate. The judgment of the two old men, Cadmus and Tiresias, seems also to be the judgment of the old poet: the reflection of the wisest individuals does not overthrow these old popular traditions, nor the perpetually self-propagating worship of Dionysus; rather it is proper to display a diplomatically cautious interest in the presence of such marvelous forces—although the possibility remains that the god may take offense at such lukewarm participation, and eventually transform the diplomat—like Cadmus—into a dragon. This is what we are told by a poet who opposed Dionysus with heroic valor throughout a long life—and who finally ended his career with a glorification of his adversary and with suicide, like a giddy man who, to escape the horrible vertigo he can no longer endure, casts himself from a tower.

This tragedy was a protest against the practicability of his own tendency; but alas, it had already been put into practice! The marvel had happened: when the poet recanted, his tendency had already triumphed. Dionysus had already been scared from the tragic stage, by a demonic power speaking through Euripides. Even Euripides was, in a sense, only a mask: the deity that spoke through him was neither Dionysus nor Apollo, but an altogether newborn demon, called *Socrates*.

This is the new opposition: the Dionysian and the Socratic—and the art of Greek tragedy was wrecked on this. Though Euripides may seek to comfort us by his recantation, he does not succeed: the most magnificent temple lies in ruins. What does the lamentation of the destroyer profit us, or his confession that it was the most beautiful of all temples? And even if Euripides has been punished by being changed into a dragon by the art critics of all ages—who could be content with so miserable a compensation?

Let us now approach this *Socratic* tendency with which Euripides combated and vanquished Aeschylean tragedy.

We must now ask ourselves, what could be the aim of the Euripidean design, which, in its most ideal form, would wish to base drama exclusively on the un-Dionysian? What form of drama still remained, if it was not to be born of the womb of music, in the mysterious twilight of the Dionysian? Only *the dramatized epos*—but in this Apollinian domain of art the *tragic* effect is certainly unattainable. The subject matter of the events represented is not decisive; indeed, I suggest that it would have been impossible for Goethe in his projected *Nausikaa* to have rendered tragically effective the suicide of this idyllic being, which was to have completed the fifth act. So extraordinary is the power of the epic-Apollinian that before our eyes it transforms the most terrible things by the joy in mere appearance and in redemption through mere appearance. The poet of the dramatized epos cannot blend completely with his images any more than the epic rhapsodist can. He is still that calm, unmoved contemplation which sees the images *before* its wide-open eyes. The actor in this dramatized epos still remains fundamentally a rhapsodist: the consecration of the inner dream lies on all his actions, so that he is never wholly an actor.

How, then, is the Euripidean play related to this ideal of the Apollinian drama? Just as the younger rhapsodist is related to the solemn rhapsodist of old times. In the Platonic *Ion,* the younger rhapsodist describes his own nature as follows: "When I am saying anything sad, my eyes fill with tears; and when I am saying something awful and terrible, then my hair stands on end with fright and my heart beats quickly." Here we no longer remark anything of the epic absorption in mere appearance, or of the dispassionate coolness of the true actor, who precisely in his highest activity is wholly mere appearance and joy in mere appearance. Euripides is the actor whose heart beats, whose hair stands on end; as Socratic thinker he designs the plan, as passionate actor he executes it. Neither in the designing nor in the execution is he a pure artist. Thus the Euripidean drama is a thing both cool and fiery, equally capable of freezing and burning. It is impossible for it to attain the Apollinian effect of the epos, while, on the other hand, it has alienated itself as much as possible from Dionysian elements. Now, in order to be effective at all, it requires new stimulants, which can no longer lie within the sphere of the only two art-impulses, the Apollinian and the Dionysian. These stimulants are cool, paradoxical thoughts, replacing Apollinian contemplation—and fiery *affects,* replacing Dionysian ecstasies; and, it may be added, thoughts and affects copied very realistically and in no sense dipped into the ether of art. (*rational? vrs. feelings?*)

So we see that Euripides did not succeed in basing the drama exclusively on the Apollinian, and his un-Dionysian tendency actually went astray and became naturalistic and inartistic. Now we should be able to come closer to the character of *aesthetic Socratism,* whose supreme law reads roughly as follows, "To be beauti-

ful everything must be intelligible," as the counterpart to the Socratic dictum, "Knowledge is virtue." With this canon in his hands,
Euripides measured all the separate elements of the drama—language, characters, dramaturgic structure, and choric music—and
corrected them according to this principle.

The poetic deficiency and degeneration, which are so often
imputed to Euripides in comparison with Sophocles, are for the
most part products of this penetrating critical process, this audacious reasonableness.

The Euripidean *prologue* may serve as an example of the pro-
ductivity of this rationalistic method. Nothing could be more uncongenial to the technique of our own stage than the prologue in
the drama of Euripides. For a single person to appear at the outset
of the play, telling us who he is, what precedes the action, what has
happened so far, even what will happen in the course of the play,
would be condemned by a modern playwright as a willful, inexcus-
able abandonment of the effect of suspense. We know everything
that is going to happen; who would want to wait till it actually does
happen? After all, we do not even have the exciting relation of a
prophetic dream to a reality that comes to be later on. But Euripides did not think like that at all. The effect of tragedy never de-
pended on epic suspense, on a fascinating uncertainty as to what is
to happen now and afterward, but rather on the great rhetorical-
lyrical scenes in which the passion and dialectic of the protagonist
swelled to a broad and powerful current. Everything laid the
ground for pathos, not for action: and whatever was not directed
toward pathos was considered objectionable. But what interferes
most with the hearer's pleasurable absorption in such scenes is any
missing link, any gap in the texture of the background story. So
long as the spectator has to figure out the meaning of this or that
person, or the presuppositions of this or that conflict of inclinations
and purposes, he cannot become completely absorbed in the activities and sufferings of the chief characters or feel breathless pity and
fear.

Aeschylean-Sophoclean tragedy employed the most ingenious
devices in the initial scenes to place in the spectator's hands, as if
by chance, all the threads necessary for a complete understanding
—a trait proving that noble artistry which, as it were, masks the
necessary formal element and makes it appear accidental. Yet Eu-

ripides thought he observed that during these first scenes the spectator was so anxious to solve the problem of the background history that the poetic beauties and the pathos of the exposition were lost on him. So he put the prologue even before the exposition, and placed it in the mouth of a person who could be trusted: often some deity had to guarantee the plot of the tragedy to the public, to remove every doubt as to the reality of the myth—somewhat as Descartes could prove the reality of the empirical world only by appealing to the truthfulness of God and his inability to utter falsehood. Euripides makes use of this same divine truthfulness once more at the close of his drama, in order to reassure the public as to the future of his heroes; this is the task of the notorious *deus ex machina.* Between this epic preview and epic prospect lies the dramatic-lyric present, the "drama" proper.

Thus Euripides as a poet is essentially an echo of his own conscious knowledge; and it is precisely on this account that he occupies such a remarkable position in the history of Greek art. With reference to his critical-productive activity, he must often have felt as if he had to bring to life for drama the beginning of the essay of Anaxagoras: "In the beginning all things were mixed together; then came the understanding and created order." Anaxagoras with his *"nous"* [1] is said to have appeared among philosophers as the first sober person[2] amid a crowd of drunken ones. Euripides may have conceived his relation to the other tragic poets in terms of a similar image. As long as the sole ruler and disposer of the universe, the *nous,* remained excluded from artistic activity, things were all mixed together in a primeval chaos: this was what Euripides must have thought; and so, as the first "sober" one among them, he had to condemn the "drunken" poets. Sophocles said of Aeschylus that he did what was right, though he did it unconsciously. This was surely not how Euripides saw it. He might have said that Aeschylus, *because* he created unconsciously, did what was *wrong.* The divine Plato, too, almost always speaks only ironically of the creative faculty of the poet, insofar as it is not con-

---

[1] The Greek word is translated as understanding (*Verstand*) in the preceding sentence. The quotation is not to be found in precisely this form in the extant fragments.

[2] Aristotle, *Metaphysics* 984b (A, end of Chapter 3).

scious insight, and places it on a par with the gift of the soothsayer and dream-interpreter: the poet is incapable of composing until he has become unconscious and bereft of understanding. Like Plato, Euripides undertook to show to the world the reverse of the "unintelligent" poet; his aesthetic principle that "to be beautiful everything must be conscious" is, as I have said, the parallel to the Socratic, "to be good everything must be conscious." So we may consider Euripides as the poet of aesthetic Socratism.

Socrates, however, was that *second spectator* who did not comprehend and therefore did not esteem the Old Tragedy; in alliance with him Euripides dared to be the herald of a new art. If it was this of which the older tragedy perished, then aesthetic Socratism was the murderous principle; but insofar as the struggle was directed against the Dionysian element in the older tragedy, we may recognize in Socrates the opponent of Dionysus. He is the new Orpheus who rose against Dionysus, and although he is destined to be torn to pieces by the Maenads of the Athenian court, he still put to flight the powerful god himself—who, as on his flight from Lycurgus the King of Edoni, sought refuge in the depths of the sea, namely the mystical flood of a secret cult which gradually covered the earth.

13

That Socrates was closely related to the tendency of Euripides did not escape the notice of contemporaneous antiquity. The most eloquent expression of this felicitous insight was the story current in Athens that Socrates used to help Euripides write his plays. Whenever an occasion arose to enumerate the demagogues of the day, the adherents of the "good old times" would mention both names in the same breath. To the influence of Socrates and Euripides they attributed the fact that the old Marathonian stalwart fitness of body and soul was being sacrificed more and more to a dubious enlightenment that involved the progressive degeneration of the powers of body and soul. It is in this tone, half indignant, half contemptuous, that Aristophanic comedy used to speak of both of them—to the consternation of modern men, who are quite willing to give up Euripides, but who cannot give sufficient expression to their astonishment that in Aristophanes Socrates should appear as the first and supreme *Sophist,* as the mirror and epitome of all sophistical tendencies. Their only consolation is to pillory Aristophanes himself as a dissolute, mendacious Alcibiades of poetry. Without here defending the profound instinct of Aristophanes against such attacks, I shall continue to show, by means of the sentiments of the time, the close connection between Socrates and Euripides. With this in view, we must remember particularly how Socrates, as an opponent of tragic art, refrained from attending tragedies and appeared among the spectators only when a new play of Euripides was to be performed. Most famous of all, however, is the juxtaposition of the two names by the Delphic oracle, which designated Socrates as the wisest of men and at the same time decided that the second prize in the contest of wisdom belonged to Euripides.

Sophocles was named third in order of rank—he who could boast that, as compared with Aeschylus, he did what was right because he *knew* what was right. Evidently it is precisely the degree of the brightness of this *knowledge* which distinguishes these three men in common as the three "knowing ones" of their time.

The most acute word, however, about this new and unprecedented value set on knowledge and insight was spoken by Socrates when he found that he was the only one who acknowledged to himself that he knew *nothing,* whereas in his critical peregrinations through Athens he had called on the greatest statesmen, orators, poets, and artists, and had everywhere discovered the conceit of knowledge. To his astonishment he perceived that all these celebrities were without a proper and sure insight, even with regard to their own professions, and that they practiced them only by instinct. "Only by instinct": with this phrase we touch upon the heart and core of the Socratic tendency. With it Socratism condemns existing art as well as existing ethics. Wherever Socratism turns its searching eyes it sees lack of insight and the power of illusion; and from this lack it infers the essential perversity and reprehensibility of what exists. Basing himself on this point, Socrates conceives it to be his duty to correct existence: all alone, with an expression of irreverence and superiority, as the precursor of an altogether different culture, art, and morality, he enters a world, to touch whose very hem would give us the greatest happiness.

This is what strikes us as so tremendously problematic whenever we consider Socrates, and again and again we are tempted to fathom the meaning and purpose of this most questionable phenomenon of antiquity. Who is it that may dare single-handed to negate the Greek genius that, as Homer, Pindar, and Aeschylus, as Phidias, as Pericles, as Pythia and Dionysus, as the deepest abyss and the highest height, is sure of our astonished veneration? What demonic power is this that dares to spill this magic potion into dust? What demigod is this to whom the chorus of the noblest spirits of mankind must call out:

> Alas!
> You have shattered
> The beautiful world
> With brazen fist;
> It falls, it is scattered.[1]

We are offered a key to the character of Socrates by the wonderful phenomenon known as "the *daimonion* of Socrates." In exceptional circumstances, when his tremendous intellect wavered, he found secure support in the utterances of a divine voice that spoke up at such moments. This voice, whenever it comes, always *dissuades*. In this utterly abnormal nature, instinctive wisdom appears only in order to *hinder* conscious knowledge occasionally. While in all productive men it is instinct that is the creative-affirmative force, and consciousness acts critically and dissuasively, in Socrates it is instinct that becomes the critic, and consciousness that becomes the creator—truly a monstrosity *per defectum!* Specifically, we observe here a monstrous *defectus* of any mystical disposition, so Socrates might be called the typical *non-mystic*, in whom, through a hypertrophy, the logical nature is developed as excessively as instinctive wisdom is in the mystic. But the logical urge that became manifest in Socrates was absolutely prevented from turning against itself; in its unbridled flood it displays a natural power such as we encounter to our awed amazement only in the very greatest instinctive forces. Anyone who, through the Platonic writings, has experienced even a breath of the divine naïveté and sureness of the Socratic way of life, will also feel how the enormous

---

[1] Goethe's *Faust,* lines 1607–11.

driving-wheel of logical Socratism is in motion, as it were, *behind* Socrates, and that it must be viewed through Socrates as through a shadow.

His own sense of this relationship found expression in the dignified seriousness with which he everywhere, even before his judges, insisted on his divine calling. At bottom, it was as impossible to refute him here as to approve of his instinct-disintegrating influence. In view of this indissoluble conflict, when he had at last been brought before the forum of the Greek state, only one kind of punishment was indicated: exile. Being thoroughly enigmatical, unclassifiable, and inexplicable, he might have been asked to leave the city, and posterity would never have been justified in charging the Athenians with an ignominious deed. But that he was sentenced to death, not exile, Socrates himself seems to have brought about with perfect awareness and without any natural awe of death. He went to his death with the calm with which, according to Plato's description, he leaves the Symposium at dawn, the last of the revelers, to begin a new day, while on the benches and on the earth his drowsy table companions remain behind to dream of Socrates, the true eroticist. *The dying Socrates* became the new ideal, never seen before, of noble Greek youths: above all, the typical Hellenic youth, Plato, prostrated himself before this image with all the ardent devotion of his enthusiastic soul.

14

Let us now imagine the one great Cyclops eye of Socrates fixed on tragedy, an eye in which the fair frenzy of artistic enthusiasm had never glowed. To this eye was denied the pleasure of gazing into the Dionysian abysses. What, then, did it have to see in the "sublime and greatly lauded" tragic art, as Plato called it? Something rather unreasonable, full of causes apparently without effects, and effects apparently without causes; the whole, moreover, so motley and manifold that it could not but be repugnant to a sober mind, and a dangerous tinder for sensitive and susceptible souls. We know the only kind of poetry he comprehended: the *Aesopian fable;* and this he favored no doubt with the smiling accommodation with which the good honest Geller sings the praise of poetry in the fable of the bee and the hen:

Why didn't Soc. understand tragic play — unavailyid?

Poems are useful: they can tell
The truth by means of parable
To those who are not very bright.

But to Socrates it seemed that tragic art did not even "tell the truth"; moreover, it addressed itself to "those who are not very bright," not to the philosopher: a twofold reason for shunning it. Like Plato, he reckoned it among the flattering arts which portray only the agreeable, not the useful; and therefore he required of his disciples abstinence and strict separation from such unphilosophical attractions—with such success that the youthful tragic poet Plato first burned his poems that he might become a student of Socrates. But where unconquerable propensities struggled against the Socratic maxims, their power, together with the impact of his tremendous character, was still great enough to force poetry itself into new and hitherto unknown channels.

An instance of this is Plato, who in condemning tragedy and art in general certainly did not lag behind the naïve cynicism of his master; he was nevertheless constrained by sheer artistic necessity to create an art form that was related to those forms of art which he repudiated. Plato's main objection to the older art—that it is the imitation of a phantom and hence belongs to a sphere even lower than the empirical world—could certainly not be directed against the new art; and so we find Plato endeavoring to transcend reality and to represent the idea which underlies this pseudo-reality. Thus Plato, the thinker, arrived by a detour where he had always been at home as a poet—at the point from which Sophocles and the older art protested solemnly against that objection. If tragedy had absorbed into itself all the earlier types of art, the same might also be said in an eccentric sense of the Platonic dialogue which, a mixture of all extant styles and forms, hovers midway between narrative, lyric, and drama, between prose and poetry, and so has also broken the strict old law of the unity of linguistic form. This tendency was carried still further by the *Cynic* writers, who in the greatest stylistic medley, oscillating between prose and metrical forms, realized also the literary image of the "raving Socrates" whom they represented in real life.

The Platonic dialogue was, as it were, the barge on which the shipwrecked ancient poetry saved herself with all her children:

crowded into a narrow space and timidly submitting to the single
pilot, Socrates, they now sailed into a new world, which never tired
of looking at the fantastic spectacle of this procession. Indeed,
Plato has given to all posterity the model of a new art form, the
model of the *novel*—which may be described as an infinitely en-
hanced Aesopian fable, in which poetry holds the same rank in
relation to dialectical philosophy as this same philosophy held for
many centuries in relation to theology: namely, the rank of *ancilla*.[1] This was the new position into which Plato, under the pressure of the demonic Socrates, forced poetry.

Here *philosophic thought* overgrows art and compels it to
cling close to the trunk of dialectic. The *Apollinian* tendency has
withdrawn into the cocoon of logical schematism; just as in the
case of Euripides we noticed something analogous, as well as a
transformation of the *Dionysian* into naturalistic affects. Socrates,
the dialectical hero of the Platonic drama, reminds us of the kin-
dred nature of the Euripidean hero who must defend his actions
with arguments and counterarguments and in the process often
risks the loss of our tragic pity; for who could mistake the *optimistic* element in the nature of dialectic, which celebrates a triumph
with every conclusion and can breathe only in cool clarity and consciousness—the optimistic element which, having once penetrated
tragedy must gradually overgrow its Dionysian regions and impel it
necessarily to self-destruction—to the death-leap into the bourgeois drama. Consider the consequences of the Socratic maxims:
"Virtue is knowledge; man sins only from ignorance; he who is
virtuous is happy." In these three basic forms of optimism lies
the death of tragedy. For now the virtuous hero must be a dialecti-
cian; now there must be a necessary, visible connection between
virtue and knowledge, faith and morality; now the transcendental
justice of Aeschylus is degraded to the superficial and insolent principle of "poetic justice" with its customary *deus ex machina*.[2]

---

[1] Handmaid.

[2] Aristotle had called Euripides "the most tragic of the poets" (*Poetics*
1453a). Although Nietzsche has more feeling for poetry—and tragedy—
than Aristotle did, this estimate seems fairer than Nietzsche's conception of
Euripides as the most optimistic. Surely, Euripides did not believe that "he
who is virtuous is happy"—on the contrary—and the superabundance of
dialectical fireworks in his tragedies, though it does dissipate the tragic emotion, usually illustrates the futility of reason, its inability to prevent tragedy.

As it confronts this new Socratic-optimistic stage world, how does the *chorus* appear now, and indeed the whole musical-Dionysian substratum of tragedy? As something accidental, a dispensable vestige of the origin of tragedy; while we have seen that the chorus can be understood only as the *cause* of tragedy, and of the tragic in general. This perplexity in regard to the chorus already manifests itself in Sophocles—an important indication that even with him the Dionysian basis of tragedy is beginning to break down. He no longer dares to entrust to the chorus the main share of the effect, but limits its sphere to such an extent that it now appears almost co-ordinate with the actors, just as if it were elevated from the orchestra into the scene; and thus its character is, of course, completely destroyed, even if Aristotle favors precisely this theory of the chorus. This alteration in the position of the chorus, which Sophocles at any rate recommended by his practice and, according to tradition, even by a treatise, is the first step toward the *destruction* of the chorus, whose phases follow one another with alarming rapidity in Euripides, Agathon, and the New Comedy. Optimistic dialectic drives *music* out of tragedy with the scourge of its syllogisms; that is, it destroys the essence of tragedy, which can be interpreted only as a manifestation and projection into images of Dionysian states, as the visible symbolizing of music, as the dream-world of a Dionysian intoxication.

If we must thus assume an anti-Dionysian tendency operating even prior to Socrates, which merely received in him an unprecedentedly magnificent expression, we must not draw back before the question of what such a phenomenon as that of Socrates indicates; for in view of the Platonic dialogues we are certainly not entitled to regard it as a merely disintegrating, negative force. And though there can be no doubt that the most immediate effect of the Socratic impulse tended to the dissolution of Dionysian tragedy, yet a profound experience in Socrates' own life impels us to ask whether there is *necessarily* only an antipodal relation between Socratism and art, and whether the birth of an "artistic Socrates" is altogether a contradiction in terms.

For with respect to art that despotic logician occasionally had the feeling of a gap, a void, half a reproach, a possibly neglected duty. As he tells his friends in prison, there often came to him one and the same dream apparition, which always said the same thing to him: "Socrates, practice music." Up to his very last days he comforts himself with the view that his philosophizing is the highest of the muses, and he finds it hard to believe that a deity should remind him of the "common, popular music." Finally, in prison, in order that he may thoroughly unburden his conscience, he does consent to practice this music for which he has but little respect. And in this mood he writes a prelude to Apollo and turns a few Aesopian fables into verse. It was something akin to the demonic warning voice that urged him to these practices; it was his Apollinian insight that, like a barbaric king, he did not understand the noble image of a god and was in danger of sinning against a deity—through his lack of understanding. The voice of the Socratic dream vision is the only sign of any misgivings about the limits of logic: Perhaps—thus he must have asked himself—what is not intelligible to me is not necessarily unintelligent? Perhaps there is a realm of wisdom from which the logician is exiled? Perhaps art is even a necessary correlative of, and supplement for science?

15

In the spirit of these last suggestive questions it must now be said how the influence of Socrates, down to the present moment and even into all future time, has spread over posterity like a shadow that keeps growing in the evening sun, and how it again and again prompts a regeneration of *art*—of art in the metaphysical, broadest and profoundest sense—and how its own infinity also guarantees the infinity of art.

Before this could be recognized, before the innermost dependence of every art on the Greeks, from Homer to Socrates, was demonstrated conclusively, we had to feel about these Greeks as the Athenians felt about Socrates. Nearly every age and stage of culture has at some time or other sought with profound irritation to free itself from the Greeks, because in their presence everything one has achieved oneself, though apparently quite original and sincerely admired, suddenly seemed to lose life and color and shriveled into a poor copy, even a caricature. And so time after time cordial anger erupts against this presumptuous little people that made bold for all time to designate everything not native as "barbaric." Who are they, one asks, who, though they display only an ephemeral historical splendor, ridiculously restricted institutions, a dubious excellence in their mores, and are marked by ugly vices, yet lay claim to that dignity and pre-eminence among peoples which characterize genius among the masses? Unfortunately, one was not lucky enough to find the cup of hemlock with which one could simply dispose of such a character; for all the poison that envy, calumny, and rancor created did not suffice to destroy that self-sufficient splendor. And so one feels ashamed and afraid in the presence of the Greeks, unless one prizes truth above all things and dares acknowledge even this truth: that the Greeks, as charioteers, hold in their hands the reins of our own and every other culture, but that almost always chariot and horses are of inferior quality and not up to the glory of their leaders, who consider it sport to run such a team into an abyss which they themselves clear with the leap of Achilles.

In order to vindicate the dignity of such a leader's position for Socrates, too, it is enough to recognize in him a type of existence unheard of before him: the type of the *theoretical man* whose significance and aim it is our next task to try to understand. Like the artist, the theoretical man finds an infinite delight in whatever exists, and this satisfaction protects him against the practical ethics of pessimism with its Lynceus eyes[1] that shine only in the dark. Whenever the truth is uncovered, the artist will always cling with rapt gaze to what still remains covering[2] even after such uncovering; but the theoretical man enjoys and finds satisfaction in the discarded covering and finds the highest object of his pleasure in the process of an ever happy uncovering that succeeds through his own efforts.

---

[1] Lynceus, one of the Argonauts, was so sharp-sighted he could see through the earth and distinguish objects almost ten miles away. Although the German word for "lynx" is *Luchs* and Nietzsche writes *Lynkeusaugen*, previous translations say "Lynx eyes."

[2] Previous translations have missed Nietzsche's point. The best commentary on his contrast is found in section 4 of the Preface to *The Gay Science*, reprinted at the end of *Nietzsche contra Wagner* (*Portable Nietzsche*, pp. 681–683). In this beautiful passage Nietzsche takes issue with those who "want by all means to unveil, uncover . . . We no longer believe that truth remains truth when the veils are withdrawn." We have learned "to stop courageously at the surface, the fold, the skin, to adore appearance, to believe in forms, tones, words, in the whole Olympus of appearance. Those Greeks were superficial—*out of profundity.* . . . Are we not, precisely in this respect, Greeks? Adorers of forms, of tones, of words? And therefore—*artists?*"

There would be no science if it were concerned only with that *one* nude goddess and with nothing else. For in that case her devotees would have to feel like men who wanted to dig a hole straight through the earth, assuming that each of them realized that even if he tried his utmost, his whole life long, he would only be able to dig a very small portion of this enormous depth, and even that would be filled in again before his own eyes by the labors of the next in line, so a third person would seem to do well if he picked a new spot for his drilling efforts. Now suppose someone proved convincingly that the goal of the antipodes cannot be reached in this direct manner: who would still wish to go on working in these old depths, unless he had learned meanwhile to be satisfied with finding precious stones or discovering laws of nature?

Therefore Lessing, the most honest theoretical man, dared to announce that he cared more for the search after truth than for truth itself [3]—and thus revealed the fundamental secret of science, to the astonishment, and indeed the anger, of the scientific community. Beside this isolated insight, born of an excess of honesty if not of exuberance, there is, to be sure, a profound *illusion* that first saw the light of the world in the person of Socrates: the unshakable faith that thought, using the thread of logic, can penetrate the deepest abysses of being, and that thought is capable not only of knowing being but even of *correcting* it. This sublime metaphysical illusion accompanies science as an instinct and leads science again and

---

[3] "Not the truth in whose possession any man is, or thinks he is, but the honest effort he has made to find out the truth, is what constitutes the worth of a man. For it is not through the possession but through the inquiry after truth that his powers expand, and in this alone consists his ever growing perfection. Possession makes calm, lazy, proud—

"If God had locked up all truth in his right hand, and in his left the unique, ever-live striving for truth, albeit with the addition that I should always and eternally err, and he said to me, 'Choose!'—I should humbly clasp his left hand, saying: 'Father, give! Pure truth is after all for thee alone!' "

This celebrated passage is found at the end of the first section of *Eine Duplik* (a reply of the accused to the rejoinder of his accuser), 1778. Kierkegaard also admired this passage without feeling that he could follow Lessing's example: see *Concluding Unscientific Postscript*, the final section of Book Two, Part One, and, for some critical discussion, Kaufmann, *From Shakespeare to Existentialism*, rev. ed. (New York, Anchor Books, 1960), pp. 196f.). Nietzsche's treatment of Lessing in his second book, the "Meditation" on *David Friedrich Strauss, the Confessor and Writer* (1873), is discussed at length in Kaufmann, *Nietzsche*, Chapter 4, section 2.

again to its limits at which it must turn into *art—which is really the aim of this mechanism.*

With the torch of this thought in our hands, let us now look at Socrates: he appears to us as the first who could not only live, guided by this instinct of science, but also—and this is far more— die that way. Hence the image of the *dying Socrates,* as the human being whom knowledge and reasons have liberated from the fear of death, is the emblem that, above the entrance gate of science, re- minds all of its mission—namely, to make existence appear com- prehensible and thus justified; and if reasons do not suffice, *myth* has to come to their aid in the end—myth which I have just called the necessary consequence, indeed the purpose, of science.

Once we see clearly how after Socrates, the mystagogue of science, one philosophical school succeeds another, wave upon wave; how the hunger for knowledge reached a never-suspected universality in the widest domain of the educated world, became the real task for every person of higher gifts, and led science onto the high seas from which it has never again been driven alto- gether; how this universality first spread a common net of thought over the whole globe, actually holding out the prospect of the law- fulness of an entire solar system; once we see all this clearly, along with the amazingly high pyramid of knowledge in our own time— we cannot fail to see in Socrates the one turning point and vortex of so-called world history. For if we imagine that the whole incalcu- lable sum of energy used up for this world tendency had been used *not* in the service of knowledge but for the practical, i.e., egoistic aims of individuals and peoples, then we realize that in that case universal wars of annihilation and continual migrations of peoples would probably have weakened the instinctive lust for life to such an extent that suicide would have become a general custom and individuals might have experienced the final remnant of a sense of duty when, like the inhabitants of the Fiji Islands, they had strangled their parents and friends—a practical pessimism that might even have generated a gruesome ethic of genocide[4] moti- vated by pity, and which incidentally is, and was, present in the world wherever art did not appear in some form—especially as

---

[4] *Völkermord.*

religion and science—as a remedy and a preventive for this breath of pestilence.

By contrast with this practical pessimism, Socrates is the prototype of the theoretical optimist who, with his faith that the nature of things can be fathomed, ascribes to knowledge and insight the power of a panacea, while understanding error as the evil *par excellence*. To fathom the depths and to separate true knowledge from appearance and error, seemed to Socratic man the noblest, even the only truly human vocation. And since Socrates, this mechanism of concepts, judgments, and inferences has been esteemed as the highest occupation and the most admirable gift of nature, above all other capacities. Even the most sublime ethical deeds, the stirrings of pity, self-sacrifice, heroism, and that calm sea of the soul, so difficult to attain, which the Apollinian Greek called *sophrosune*,[5] were derived from the dialectic of knowledge by Socrates and his like-minded successors, down to the present, and accordingly designated as teachable.

Anyone who has ever experienced the pleasure of Socratic insight and felt how, spreading in ever-widening circles, it seeks to embrace the whole world of appearances, will never again find any stimulus toward existence more violent than the craving to complete this conquest and to weave the net impenetrably tight. To one who feels that way, the Platonic Socrates will appear as the teacher of an altogether new form of "Greek cheerfulness" and blissful affirmation of existence that seeks to discharge itself in actions—most often in maieutic and educational influences on noble youths, with a view to eventually producing a genius.

But science, spurred by its powerful illusion, speeds irresistibly toward its limits where its optimism, concealed in the essence of logic, suffers shipwreck. For the periphery of the circle of science has an infinite number of points; and while there is no telling how this circle could ever be surveyed completely, noble and gifted men nevertheless reach, e'er half their time[6] and inevitably, such

---

[5] Often rendered, not quite adequately, as temperance.

[6] "Before the middle of his existence" presumably alludes to the beginning of Dante's *Inferno*, not, like my translation, to Milton's sonnet on his blindness.

boundary points[7] on the periphery from which one gazes into what defies illumination. When they see to their horror how logic coils up at these boundaries and finally bites its own tail—suddenly the new form of insight breaks through, *tragic insight* which, merely to be endured, needs art as a protection and remedy.

Our eyes strengthened and refreshed by our contemplation of the Greeks, let us look at the highest spheres of the world around us; then we shall see how the hunger for insatiable and optimistic knowledge[8] that in Socrates appears exemplary has turned into tragic resignation and destitute need for art—while, to be sure, the same hunger on its lower levels can express itself in hostility to art and must particularly detest Dionysian-tragic art, as was illustrated earlier with the fight of Socratism against Aeschylean tragedy.

Here we knock, deeply moved, at the gates of present and future: will this "turning" [9] lead to ever-new configurations of genius and especially of the *Socrates who practices music?* [10] Will the net of art, even if it is called religion or science, that is spread over existence be woven even more tightly and delicately, or is it destined to be torn to shreds in the restless, barbarous, chaotic whirl that now calls itself "the present"?

Concerned but not disconsolate, we stand aside a little while, contemplative men to whom it has been granted to be witnesses of these tremendous struggles and transitions. Alas, it is the magic of these struggles that those who behold them must also take part and fight.[11]

---

[7] *Grenzpunkte.* Jaspers' celebrated *Grenzsituationen* are elaborations of the points here described. And Nietzsche's image of shipwreck (*Scheitern*) also became one of Jaspers' key terms. This passage is as close to Jaspers' existentialism" as section 7 is to Sartre's.

[8] In Nietzsche's text, knowledge is insatiable, not merely the hunger for it.

[9] *Umschlagen.* Cf. "has turned into tragic resignation" in the preceding paragraph.

[10] Even more obviously than the "artistic Socrates" near the end of the preceding section, this is surely an idealized self-portrait: Nietzsche played the piano and composed songs.

[11] The book might well end at this point—as the original version did: Friedrich Nietzsche: *Socrates und die griechische Tragödie: Ursprüngliche Fassung der Geburt der Tragödie aus dem Geiste der Musik* (Socrates and Greek tragedy: original version of *The Birth of Tragedy out of the Spirit of Music*), ed. Hans Joachim Mette (Munich, Beck, 1933). The discussion of the birth

*Music bit
doesn't come through*

16

By this elaborate historical example we have sought to make clear how just as tragedy perishes with the evanescence of the spirit of music, it is only from this spirit that it can be reborn. Lest this assertion seem too strange, it may be well to disclose the origin of this insight by considering the analogous phenomena of our own time; we must enter into the midst of those struggles, which, as I have just said, are being waged in the highest spheres of our contemporary world between insatiable optimistic knowledge and the tragic need of art. In my examination I shall leave out of account all those other antagonistic tendencies which at all times oppose art, especially tragedy, and which now are again extending their triumphant sway to such an extent that of the theatrical arts only the farce and the ballet, for example, put forth their blossoms, which perhaps not everyone cares to smell, in rather rich luxuriance. I will speak only of the noblest *opposition* to the tragic world-conception—and by this I mean science, which is at bottom optimistic, with its ancestor Socrates at its head. A little later on I shall also name those forces which seem to me to guarantee a *rebirth of tragedy*—and perhaps other blessed hopes for the German genius!

Before we plunge into the midst of these struggles, let us array ourselves in the armor of the insights we have acquired. In contrast to all those who are intent on deriving the arts from one exclusive principle, as the necessary vital source of every work of art, I shall keep my eyes fixed on the two artistic deities of the Greeks, Apollo and Dionysus, and recognize in them the living and conspicuous representatives of *two* worlds of art differing in their intrinsic essence and in their highest aims. I see Apollo as the transfiguring genius of the *principium individuationis* through which alone the redemption in illusion is truly to be obtained; while by the mystical triumphant cry of Dionysus the spell of individuation is broken, and the way lies open to the Mothers of Being,[1] to the innermost

---

and death of tragedy is finished in the main, and the following celebration of the rebirth of tragedy weakens the book and was shortly regretted by Nietzsche himself.

[1] An allusion to Goethe's *Faust*, lines 6216ff.

heart of things. This extraordinary contrast, which stretches like a yawning gulf between plastic art as the Apollinian, and music as the Dionysian art,[2] has revealed itself to only one of the great thinkers, to such an extent that, even without this clue to the symbolism of the Hellenic divinities, he conceded to music a character and an origin different from all the other arts, because, unlike them, it is not a copy of the phenomenon, but an immediate copy of the will itself, and therefore complements *everything physical in the world* and every phenomenon by representing *what is metaphysical,* the thing in itself. (Schopenhauer, *Welt als Wille und Vorstellung,* I, p. 310.)

To this most important insight of aesthetics (with which, in the most serious sense, aesthetics properly begins), Richard Wagner, by way of confirmation of its eternal truth, affixed his seal, when he asserted in his *Beethoven* that music must be evaluated according to aesthetic principles quite different from those which apply to all plastic arts, and not, in general, according to the category of beauty; although an erroneous aesthetics, inspired by a mistaken and degenerate art,[3] has, by virtue of the concept of beauty obtaining in the plastic domain, accustomed itself to demand of music an effect similar to that produced by works of plastic art, namely, the arousing of *delight in beautiful forms.* Having recognized this extraordinary contrast, I felt a strong need to approach the essence of Greek tragedy and, with it, the profoundest

---

[2] Nietzsche clearly did not mean to imply that all music is "Dionysian." Yet it did not occur to him at this time to consider Mozart's music as an alternative to Wagner's. Mozart is not mentioned in *The Birth of Tragedy.* He is mentioned elsewhere by the young Nietzsche, and all references express love and admiration. But it was only in 1880, in *The Wanderer and His Shadow* (section 165), after his break with Wagner, that Nietzsche offered a contrast of Wagner and Mozart in one of his books—without mentioning Wagner by name. Eventually, he included this passage and some comparable ones from *Beyond Good and Evil* (1886) in *Nietzsche contra Wagner.* When it occurred to Nietzsche that Mozart's music was not Dionysian, he also realized that Wagner's music was not really "Dionysian" either, but rather "romantic" and "decadent." See *Nietzsche contra Wagner* (in *The Portable Nietzsche,* especially pp. 667ff.) and section 370 of *The Gay Science* (in Kaufmann, *Nietzsche,* Chapter 12, section V).

[3] *Entartete Kunst:* the term was made infamous by the Nazis when they subsumed under it a great deal of modern art which was officially proscribed. But the Nazis wanted "beautiful forms" and raged against art which did not aim at "beauty," while Nietzsche criticizes the assumption that all art must aim at "beautiful forms."

revelation of the Hellenic genius; for I at last thought that I possessed a charm to enable me—far beyond the phraseology of our usual aesthetics—to represent vividly to my mind the fundamental problem of tragedy; whereby I was granted such a surprising and unusual insight into the Hellenic character that it necessarily seemed to me as if our classical-Hellenic science that bears itself so proudly had thus far contrived to subsist mainly on shadow plays and externals.

Perhaps we may touch on this fundamental problem by asking: what aesthetic effect results when the essentially separate art-forces, the Apollinian and the Dionysian, enter into simultaneous activity? Or more briefly: how is music related to image and concept? Schopenhauer, whom Richard Wagner, with special reference to this point, praises for an unsurpassable clearness and clarity of exposition, expresses himself most thoroughly on the subject in the following passage which I shall cite here at full length (*Welt als Wille und Vorstellung*, I, p. 309 [4]): "According to all this, we may regard the phenomenal world, or nature, and music as two different expressions of the same thing,[5] which is therefore itself the only medium of their analogy, so that a knowledge of it is demanded in order to understand that analogy. Music, therefore, if regarded as an expression of the world, is in the highest degree a universal language, which is related indeed to the universality of concepts, much as they are related to the particular things. Its universality, however, is by no means that empty universality of abstraction, but of quite a different kind, and is united with thorough and distinct definiteness. In this respect it resembles geometrical figures and numbers, which are the universal forms of all possible objects of experience and applicable to them all *a priori*, and yet are not abstract but perceptible and thoroughly determinate. All possible efforts, excitements, and manifestations of will, all that goes on in the heart of man and that reason includes in the wide, negative concept of feeling, may be expressed by the infinite number of possible melodies, but always in the universal, in the mere form, with-

---

[4] The reference is Nietzsche's own: see footnote 7, section 1. I have used the R. B. Haldane and J. Kemp translation of this long passage (*World as Will and Idea*, London, Kegan Paul, 1907, I, p. 239) but revised a number of inaccuracies.

[5] The will.

out the material, always according to the thing-in-itself, not the phenomenon, the inmost soul, as it were, of the phenomenon without the body. This deep relation which music has to the true nature of all things also explains the fact that suitable music played to any scene, action, event, or surrounding seems to disclose to us its most secret meaning, and appears as the most accurate and distinct commentary upon it. This is so truly the case that whoever gives himself up entirely to the impression of a symphony, seems to see all the possible events of life and the world take place in himself; yet if he reflects, he can find no likeness between the music and the things that passed before his mind. For, as we have said, music is distinguished from all the other arts by the fact that it is not a copy of the phenomenon, or, more accurately, of the adequate objectivity of the will, but an immediate copy of the will itself, and therefore complements everything physical in the world and every phenomenon by representing what is metaphysical, the thing in itself. We might, therefore, just as well call the world embodied music as embodied will; and this is the reason why music makes every painting, and indeed every scene of real life and of the world, at once appear with higher significance, certainly all the more, in proportion as its melody is analogous to the inner spirit of the given phenomenon. Therefore we are able to set a poem to music as a song, or a visible representation as a pantomime, or both as an opera. Such particular pictures of human life, set to the universal language of music, are never bound to it or correspond to it with stringent necessity; but they stand to it only in the relation of an example chosen at will to a general concept. In the determinateness of the real, they represent that which music expresses in the universality of mere form. For melodies are to a certain extent, like general concepts, an abstraction from the actual. This actual world, then, the world of particular things, affords the object of perception, the special and individual, the particular case, both to the universality of the concepts and to the universality of the melodies. But these two universalities are in a certain respect opposed to each other; for the concepts contain particulars only as the first forms abstracted from perception, as it were, the separated shell of things; thus they are, strictly speaking, *abstracta:* music, on the other hand, gives the inmost kernel which precedes all forms, or the heart of things. This relation may be very well expressed in the language of the schoolmen, by saying, the concepts are the *universalia post rem,* but music gives the *universalia ante rem,* and the real world the *universalia in re.* But that in general a relation is possible between a composition and a visible representation rests, as we have said, upon the fact that both are simply different expressions of the same inner being of the world. When now, in the particular case, such a relation is actually given, that is to say, when the composer has been able to express in the universal language of music the stirrings of will which constitute the heart of an event, then the melody of the song, the music of the opera, is expressive. But the analogy discovered by the composer between the two must have proceeded from the direct knowledge of the nature of the world unknown to his reason, and must not be an imitation produced with conscious intention by means of concepts, otherwise the music does not express the inner nature, the will itself, but merely gives an inadequate imitation of its phenomenon. All truly imitative music does this."

According to the doctrine of Schopenhauer, therefore, we understand music as the immediate language of the will, and we feel our fancy stimulated to give form to this invisible and yet so actively stirred spirit-world which speaks to us, and we feel prompted to embody it in an analogous example. On the other hand, image and concept, under the influence of a truly corresponding music, acquire a higher significance. Dionysian art therefore is wont to exercise two kinds of influences on the Apollinian art faculty: music incites to the *symbolic intuition* of Dionysian universality, and music allows the symbolic image to emerge *in its highest significance.* From these facts, intelligible in themselves and not inaccessible to a more penetrating examination, I infer the capacity of music to give birth to *myth* (the most significant example), and particularly the *tragic* myth: the myth which expresses Dionysian knowledge in symbols. In the phenomenon of the lyrist, I have shown how music strives to express its nature in Apollinian images. If now we reflect that music at its highest stage must seek to attain also to its highest objectification in images, we must deem it possible that it also knows how to find the symbolic expression for its unique Dionysian wisdom; and where shall we seek for this expression if not in tragedy and, in general, in the conception of the tragic?

From the nature of art as it is usually conceived according to the single category of appearance and beauty, the tragic cannot honestly be deduced at all; it is only through the spirit of music that we can understand the joy involved in the annihilation of the individual. For it is only in particular examples of such annihilation that we see clearly the eternal phenomenon of Dionysian art, which gives expression to the will in its omnipotence, as it were, behind the *principium individuationis,* the eternal life beyond all phenomena, and despite all annihilation. The metaphysical joy in the tragic is a translation of the instinctive unconscious Dionysian wisdom into the language of images: the hero, the highest manifestation of the will, is negated for our pleasure, because he is only phenomenon, and because the eternal life of the will is not affected by his annihilation. "We believe in eternal life," exclaims tragedy; while music is the immediate idea of this life. Plastic art has an altogether different aim: here Apollo overcomes the suffering of the individual by the radiant glorification of the *eternity of the phenomenon:* here beauty triumphs over the suffering inherent in life; pain is obliterated by lies from the features of nature. In Dionysian art and its tragic symbolism the same nature cries to us with its true, undissembled voice: "Be as I am! Amid the ceaseless flux of phenomena I am the eternally creative primordial mother, eternally impelling to existence, eternally finding satisfaction in this change of phenomena!"

17

Dionysian art, too, wishes to convince us of the eternal joy of existence: only we are to seek this joy not in phenomena, but behind them. We are to recognize that all that comes into being must be ready for a sorrowful end; we are forced to look into the terrors of the individual existence—yet we are not to become rigid with fear: a metaphysical comfort tears us momentarily from the bustle of the changing figures. We are really for a brief moment primordial being itself, feeling its raging desire for existence and joy in existence; the struggle, the pain, the destruction of phenomena, now appear necessary to us, in view of the excess of countless forms of existence which force and push one another into life, in view of the exuberant fertility of the universal will. We are pierced by the maddening sting of these pains just when we have become, as it were, one with the infinite primordial joy in existence, and when we anticipate, in Dionysian ecstasy, the indestructibility and eternity of this joy. In spite of fear and pity, we are the happy living beings, not as individuals, but as the *one* living being, with whose creative joy we are united.

The history of the rise of Greek tragedy now tells us with luminous precision how the tragic art of the Greeks was really born of the spirit of music. With this conception we believe we have done justice for the first time to the primitive and astonishing significance of the chorus. At the same time, however, we must admit that the meaning of tragic myth set forth above never became clear in transparent concepts to the Greek poets, not to speak of the Greek philosophers: their heroes speak, as it were, more superficially than they act; the myth does not at all obtain adequate objectification in the spoken word. The structure of the scenes and the visual images reveal a deeper wisdom than the poet himself can put into words and concepts: the same is also observable in Shakespeare, whose Hamlet, for instance, similarly, talks more superficially than he acts, so that the previously mentioned lesson of Hamlet is to be deduced, not from his words, but from a profound contemplation and survey of the whole.

With respect to Greek tragedy, which of course presents itself to us only as word-drama, I have even intimated that the lack of congruity between myth and expression might easily lead us to regard it as shallower and less significant than it really is, and accordingly to attribute to it a more superficial effect than it must have had according to the testimony of the ancients: for how easily one forgets that what the word-poet did not succeed in doing, namely, attain the highest spiritualization and ideality of the myth, he might very well succeed in doing every moment as creative musician! To be sure, we are almost forced to construct for ourselves by scholarly research the superior power of the musical effect in order to experience something of the incomparable comfort which must have been characteristic of true tragedy. Even this musical superiority, however, would only have been felt by us had we been Greeks; for in the entire development of Greek music—as compared with the infinitely richer music known and familiar to us—we imagine we hear only the youthful song of the musical genius modestly intoned. The Greeks, as the Egyptian priests say, are eternal children, and in tragic art too they are only children who do not know what a sublime plaything originated in their hands and—was quickly demolished.

That striving of the spirit of music toward visual and mythical objectification, which increases from the beginnings of lyric poetry up to Attic tragedy, suddenly breaks off after attaining a luxuriant development, and disappears, as it were, from the surface of Hellenic art; while the Dionysian world view born of this striving lives on in the mysteries and, in its strangest metamorphoses and debasements, does not cease to attract serious natures. Will it not some day rise once again out of its mystic depths as art?

Here we are detained by the question, whether the power, by virtue of whose opposing influence tragedy perished, has for all time sufficient strength to prevent the artistic reawakening of tragedy and the tragic world view. If ancient tragedy was diverted from its course by the dialectical desire for knowledge and the optimism of science, this fact might lead us to believe that there is an eternal conflict between *the theoretic* and *the tragic world view;* and only after the spirit of science has been pursued to its limits, and its claim to universal validity destroyed by the evidence of these limits may we hope for a rebirth of tragedy—a form of culture for which we should have to use the symbol *of the music-practicing Socrates* in the sense spoken of above.[1] In this contrast, I understand by the spirit of science the faith that first came to light in the person of Socrates—the faith in the explicability of nature and in knowledge as a panacea.

He who recalls the immediate consequences of this restlessly progressing spirit of science will realize at once that *myth* was annihilated by it, and that, because of this annihilation, poetry was driven like a homeless being from her natural ideal soil. If we have been right in assigning to music the power of again giving birth to myth, we may similarly expect to find the spirit of science on the path where it inimically opposes this mythopoeic power of music. This takes place in the development of the *New Attic Dithyramb,* the music of which no longer expressed the inner essence, the will itself, but only rendered the phenomenon inadequately, in an imitation by means of concepts. From this intrinsically degenerate music

---

[1] Section 15, text for note 10.

the genuinely musical natures turned away with the same repugnance that they felt for the art-destroying tendency of Socrates. The unerring instinct of Aristophanes was surely right when .it included Socrates himself, the tragedy of Euripides, and the music of the New Dithyrambic poets in the same feeling of hatred, recognizing in all three phenomena the signs of a degenerate culture.

In this New Dithyramb, music is outrageously manipulated so as to be the imitative counterfeit of a phenomenon, for instance, of a battle or a storm at sea; and thus, of course, it has been utterly robbed of its mythopoeic power. For if it seeks to arouse pleasure only by impelling us to seek external analogies between a vital or natural process and certain rhythmical figures and characteristic sounds of music; if our understanding is to content itself with the perception of these analogies; we are reduced to a frame of mind which makes impossible any reception of the mythical; for the myth wants to be experienced vividly as a unique example of a universality and truth that gaze into the infinite. The truly Dionysian music presents itself as such a general mirror of the universal will: the vivid event refracted in this mirror expands at once for our consciousness to the copy of an external truth. Conversely, such a vivid event is at once divested of every mythical character by the tone-painting of the New Dithyramb; music now becomes a wretched copy of the phenomenon, and therefore infinitely poorer than the phenomenon itself. And through this poverty it still further reduces the phenomenon for our consciousness, so that now, for example, a musically imitated battle of this sort exhausts itself in marches, signal sounds, etc., and our imagination is arrested precisely by these superficialities. Tone-painting is thus in every respect the opposite of true music with its mythopoeic power: through it the phenomenon, poor in itself, is made still poorer, while through Dionysian music the individual phenomenon is enriched and expanded into an image of the world. It was a great triumph for the un-Dionysian spirit when, by the development of the New Dithyramb, it had estranged music from itself and reduced it to be the slave of phenomena. Euripides, who, though in a higher sense, must be considered a thoroughly unmusical nature, is for this very reason a passionate adherent of the New Dithyrambic Music, and with the liberality of a robber makes use of all its effective tricks and mannerisms.

Plato's – other world – how related?

In another direction also we see at work the power of this un-Dionysian myth-opposing spirit, when we turn our attention to the prevalence of *character representation* and psychological refinement in tragedy from Sophocles onward. The character must no longer be expanded into an eternal type, but, on the contrary, must develop individually through artistic subordinate traits and shadings, through the nicest precision of all lines, in such a manner that the spectator is in general no longer conscious of the myth, but of the vigorous truth to nature and the artist's imitative power. Here also we observe the victory of the phenomenon over the universal, and the delight in a unique, almost anatomical preparation; we are already in the atmosphere of a theoretical world, where scientific knowledge is valued more highly than the artistic reflection of a universal law.

The movement in the direction of character delineation proceeds rapidly: while Sophocles still portrays complete characters and employs myth for their refined development, Euripides already draws only prominent individual traits of character, which can express themselves in violent bursts of passion. In the New Attic Comedy, however, there are only masks with *one* expression: frivolous old men, duped panders, and cunning slaves, recurring incessantly. Where now is the mythopoeic spirit of music? What still remains of music is either excitatory or reminiscent music, that is, either a stimulant for dull and faded nerves, or tone-painting. As regards the former, it hardly matters about the text set to it: as soon as his heroes and choruses begin to sing, everything becomes pretty slovenly in Euripides; to what pass must things have come with his impertinent successors?

The new un-Dionysian spirit, however, reveals itself most plainly in the *dénouements* of the new dramas. In the Old Tragedy one could sense at the end that metaphysical comfort without which the delight in tragedy cannot be explained at all. The reconciling tones from another world sound purest, perhaps, in the *Oedipus at Colonus*. Now that the genius of music has fled from tragedy, tragedy, strictly speaking, is dead: for from what source shall we now draw this metaphysical comfort? The new spirit, therefore, sought for an earthly resolution of the tragic dissonance. The hero, after being sufficiently tortured by fate, earned a well-deserved reward through a splendid marriage or tokens of divine favor. The hero had turned gladiator on whom, after he had been nicely beaten and covered with wounds, freedom was occasionally bestowed. The *deus ex machina* took the place of metaphysical comfort.

I will not say that the tragic world view was everywhere completely destroyed by this intruding un-Dionysian spirit: we only know that it had to flee from art into the underworld as it were, in the degenerate form of a secret cult. Over the widest extent of the Hellenic character, however, there raged the consuming blast of this spirit, which manifests itself in the form of "Greek cheerfulness," which we have already spoken of as a senile, unproductive love of existence. This cheerfulness stands opposed to the splendid "naïveté" of the earlier Greeks, which, according to the characterization given above, must be conceived as the blossom of the Apollinian culture springing from a dark abyss, as the victory which the Hellenic will, through its mirroring of beauty, obtains over suffering and the wisdom of suffering.

The noblest manifestation of that other form of "Greek cheerfulness," the Alexandrian, is the cheerfulness of the *theoretical man*. It exhibits the same characteristic symptoms that I have just deduced from the spirit of the un-Dionysian: it combats Dionysian wisdom and art, it seeks to dissolve myth, it substitutes for a metaphysical comfort an earthly consonance, in fact, a *deus ex machina* of its own, the god of machines and crucibles, that is, the powers of the spirits of nature recognized and employed in the service of a higher egoism; it believes that it can correct the world by knowledge, guide life by science, and actually confine the individual within a limited sphere of solvable problems, from which he can cheerfully say to life: "I desire you; you are worth knowing."

18

It is an eternal phenomenon: the insatiable will always find a way to detain its creatures in life and compel them to live on, by means of an illusion spread over things. One is chained by the Socratic love of knowledge and the delusion of being able thereby to heal the eternal wound of existence; another is ensnared by art's seductive veil of beauty fluttering before his eyes; still another by the metaphysical comfort that beneath the whirl of phenomena eternal life flows on indestructibly—to say nothing of the more vulgar and almost more powerful illusions which the will always has at hand. These three stages of illusion are actually designed only for the more nobly formed natures, who actually feel profoundly the weight and burden of existence, and must be deluded by exquisite stimulants into forgetfulness of their displeasure. All that we call culture is made up of these stimulants; and, according to the proportion of the ingredients, we have either a dominantly *Socratic* or *artistic* or *tragic* culture; or, if historical exemplifications are permitted, there is either an Alexandrian or a Hellenic or a Buddhistic culture.[1]

Our whole modern world is entangled in the net of Alexandrian[2] culture. It proposes as its ideal the theoretical man equipped with the greatest forces of knowledge, and laboring in the service of science, whose archetype and progenitor is Socrates. All our educational methods originally have this ideal in view: every other form of existence must struggle on laboriously beside it, as something tolerated, but not intended. In an almost alarming manner the cultured man was for a long time found only in the form of the scholar: even our poetical arts have been forced to evolve from scholarly imitations, and in the main effect, that of rhyme, we still recognize the origin of our poetic form from artificial experiments with a nonindigenous, really scholarly language. How unintelligible

---

[1] All editions published by Nietzsche himself contain these words, and Wilamowitz cited this passage both in 1872 (p. 6) and in 1873 (p. 6). The standard editions of Nietzsche's collected works substitute "an Indian (Brahmanic) culture" for "Buddhistic culture." According to volume I (p. 599) of the so-called Grossoktav edition of Nietzsche's *Werke* (1905), this change is based on "a penciled correction in Nietzsche's own hand in his copy of the *second* version." It would seem that both "Buddhistic" and "Brahmanic" depend on some misconception; neither seems to make much sense.

[2] It is not uncommon to distinguish the Alexandrian period of Greek literature from the immediately preceding Attic period. The great tragic poets, as well as Thucydides, Plato, and Aristotle are associated with Athens and belong to the immensely creative fifth and fourth centuries, along with Phidias and Praxiteles. The glories of Alexandria, the intellectual capital of the Hellenic world from about 300 to 30 B.C., include no remotely comparable creative achievements but are its immense library, which far surpassed any previous collection, and its often exceedingly erudite scholars. To be sure, one still wrote poetry and vast amounts of prose, but on the whole the achievements of the scientists and scholars were more remarkable. Nietzsche is plainly suggesting that nineteenth-century Germany is in important respects strikingly similar to Alexandrian civilization.

must *Faust,* the modern cultured man, who is in himself intelligible, have appeared to a true Greek—Faust, storming unsatisfied through all the faculties, devoted to magic and the devil from a desire for knowledge; Faust, whom we have but to place beside Socrates for the purpose of comparison, in order to see that modern man is beginning to divine the limits of this Socratic love of knowledge and yearns for a coast in the wide waste of the ocean of knowledge. When Goethe on one occasion said to Eckermann with reference to Napoleon: "Yes, my good friend, there is also a productiveness of deeds," he reminded us in a charmingly naïve manner that the nontheorist is something incredible and astounding to modern man; so that we again have need of the wisdom of Goethe to discover that such a surprising form of existence is not only comprehensible, but even pardonable.

Now we must not hide from ourselves what is concealed in the womb of this Socratic culture: optimism, with its delusion of limitless power. We must not be alarmed if the fruits of this optimism ripen—if society, leavened to the very lowest strata by this kind of culture, gradually begins to tremble with wanton agitations and desires, if the belief in the earthly happiness of all, if the belief in the possibility of such a general intellectual culture changes into the threatening demand for such an Alexandrian earthly happiness, into the conjuring up of a Euripidean *deus ex machina.*

Let us mark this well: the Alexandrian culture, to be able to exist permanently, requires a slave class, but with its optimistic view of life it denies the necessity of such a class, and consequently, when its beautifully seductive and tranquillizing utterances about the "dignity of man" and the "dignity of labor" are no longer effective, it gradually drifts toward a dreadful destruction. There is nothing more terrible than a class of barbaric slaves who have learned to regard their existence as an injustice, and now prepare to avenge, not only themselves, but all generations. In the face of such threatening storms, who dares to appeal with any confidence to our pale and exhausted religions, the very foundations of which have degenerated into scholarly religions? Myth, the necessary prerequisite of every religion, is already paralyzed everywhere, and even in this domain the optimistic spirit, which we have just designated as the germ of destruction in our society, has attained the mastery.

While the disaster slumbering in the womb of theoretical culture gradually begins to frighten modern man, and he anxiously ransacks the stores of his experience for means to avert the danger, though he has no great faith in these means; while he, therefore, begins to divine the consequences of his situation—great men, universally gifted, have contrived, with an incredible amount of thought, to make use of the paraphernalia of science itself, to point out the limits and the relativity of knowledge generally, and thus to deny decisively the claim of science to universal validity and universal aims. And their demonstration diagnosed for the first time the illusory notion which pretends to be able to fathom the innermost essence of things with the aid of causality. The extraordinary courage and wisdom of *Kant* and *Schopenhauer* have succeeded in gaining the most difficult victory, the victory over the optimism concealed in the essence of logic—an optimism that is the basis of our culture. While this optimism, resting on apparently unobjectionable *aeternae veritates*,[3] had believed that all the riddles of the universe could be known and fathomed, and had treated space, time, and causality as entirely unconditional laws of the most universal validity, Kant showed that these really served only to elevate the mere phenomenon, the work of *māyā,* to the position of the sole and highest reality, as if it were the innermost and true essence of things, thus making impossible any knowledge of this essence or, in Schopenhauer's words, lulling the dreamer still more soundly asleep.

With this insight a culture is inaugurated that I venture to call a tragic culture. Its most important characteristic is that wisdom takes the place of science as the highest end—wisdom that, uninfluenced by the seductive distractions of the sciences, turns with unmoved eyes to a comprehensive view of the world, and seeks to grasp, with sympathetic feelings of love, the eternal suffering as its own.

Let us imagine a coming generation with such intrepidity of vision, with such a heroic penchant for the tremendous; let us imagine the bold stride of these dragon-slayers, the proud audacity with which they turn their back on all the weaklings' doctrines of optim-

---

[3] Eternal verities.

ism in order to "live resolutely" in wholeness and fullness:[4] would it not be necessary for the tragic man of such a culture, in view of his self-education for seriousness and terror, to desire a new art, the art of metaphysical comfort, to desire tragedy as his own proper Helen, and to exclaim with Faust:

> *Should not my longing overleap the distance*
> *And draw the fairest form into existence?* [5]

But now that the Socratic culture can only hold the scepter of its infallibility with trembling hands; now that it has been shaken from two directions—once by the fear of its own consequences which it at length begins to surmise, and again because it no longer has its former naïve confidence in the eternal validity of its foundation—it is a sad spectacle to see how the dance of its thought rushes longingly toward ever-new forms, to embrace them, and then, shuddering, lets them go suddenly as Mephistopheles does the seductive Lamiae.[6] It is certainly the sign of the "breach" of which everyone speaks as the fundamental malady of modern culture, that the theoretical man, alarmed and dissatisfied at his own consequences, no longer dares entrust himself to the terrible icy current of existence: he runs timidly up and down the bank. So thoroughly has he been pampered by his optimistic views that he no longer wants to have anything whole, with all of nature's cruelty attaching to it. Besides, he feels that a culture based on the principles of science must be destroyed when it begins to grow *illogical,* that is, to retreat before its own consequences. Our art reveals this universal distress: in vain does one depend imitatively on all the great productive periods and natures; in vain does one accumulate the entire "world-literature" around modern man for his comfort; in vain does one place oneself in the midst of the art styles and artists of all ages, so that one may give names to them as Adam did to the

---

[4] The quotation is from Goethe's poem *"Generalbeichte"* (general confession), written in 1802—an exuberant anti-Philistine manifesto.

[5] This whole paragraph is ridiculed by Nietzsche himself in the final section of his "Attempt at a Self-Criticism," printed as a preface to the "new edition" of 1886 and included above in the present English version. The quotation is from Goethe's *Faust,* Part II, lines 7438ff.

[6] In Goethe's *Faust,* Part II, lines 7769ff. (in the classical Walpurgis Night).

beasts: one still remains eternally hungry, the "critic" without joy and energy, the Alexandrian man, who is at bottom a librarian and corrector of proofs, and wretchedly goes blind from the dust of books and from printers' errors.

19

We cannot indicate the innermost modern content of this Socratic culture more distinctly than by calling it *the culture of the opera:* for it is in this department that this culture has expressed its aims and perceptions with special naïveté, which is surprising when we compare the genesis of the opera and the facts of operatic development with the eternal truths of the Apollinian and Dionysian. I recall first of all the origin of the *stilo rappresentativo*[1] and the recitative. Is it credible that this thoroughly externalized operatic music, incapable of devotion, could be received and cherished with enthusiastic favor, as a rebirth, as it were, of all true music, by the very age in which had appeared the ineffably sublime and sacred music of Palestrina? And who, on the other hand, would think of making only the diversion-craving luxuriousness of those Florentine circles and the vanity of their dramatic singers responsible for the love of the opera which spread with such rapidity? That in the same age, even among the same people, this passion for a half-musical mode of speech should awaken alongside of the vaulted structure of Palestrina harmonies which all medieval Christendom had been building up, I can explain to myself only by a cooperating, *extra-artistic tendency* in the essence of the recitative.

The listener who insists on distinctly hearing the words under the music has his desire fulfilled by the singer in that the latter speaks rather than sings, intensifying the pathetic expression of the words by means of this half-song. By this intensification of the pathos he facilitates the understanding of the words and overcomes the remaining half of the music. The specific danger now threatening him is that in some unguarded moment he may stress the music unduly, which would immediately entail the destruction of the pathos of the speech and the distinctness of the words; while, on the other hand, he feels himself continually impelled to musical

---

[1] Representational style.

discharge and a virtuoso exhibition of his vocal talent. Here the "poet" comes to his aid, who knows how to provide him with abundant opportunities for lyrical interjections, repetitions of words and sentences, etc.—at which places the singer, now in the purely musical element, can rest himself without paying any attention to the words. This alternation of emotionally impressive speech which, however, is only half sung, with interjections which are wholly sung, an alternation characteristic of the *stilo rappresentativo,* this rapidly changing endeavor to affect now the concepts and imagination of the hearer, now his musical sense, is something so utterly unnatural and likewise so intrinsically contradictory both to the Apollinian and Dionysian artistic impulses, that one has to infer an origin of the recitative lying outside all artistic instincts. According to this description, the recitative must be defined as a mixture of epic and lyric delivery, not by any means as an intrinsically stable mixture, a state not to be attained in the case of such totally disparate elements, but as an entirely superficial mosaic conglutination, such as is totally unprecedented in the domain of nature and experience. *But this was not the opinion of the inventors of the recitative:* they themselves, together with their age, believed rather that the mystery of antique music has been solved by this *stilo rappresentativo,* in which, so they thought, was to be found the only explanation of the enormous influence of an Orpheus, an Amphion, and even of Greek tragedy. The new style was looked upon as the reawakening of the most effective music, ancient Greek music: indeed, in accordance with the universal and popular conception of the Homeric *as the primitive world,* they could abandon themselves to the dream of having descended once more into the paradisiacal beginnings of mankind, where music also must have had that unsurpassed purity, power, and innocence of which the poets, in their pastoral plays, could give such touching accounts. Here we can see into the innermost development of this thoroughly modern variety of art, the opera: art here responds to a powerful need, but it is a nonaesthetic need: the yearning for the idyllic, the faith in the primordial existence of the artistic and good man. The recitative was regarded as the rediscovered language of this primitive man; opera as the rediscovered country of this idyllically or heroically good creature, who simultaneously with every action follows a natural artistic impulse, who accomplishes his speech with a little singing, in order that he may immediately break forth into full song at the slightest emotional excitement.

It is now a matter of indifference to us that the humanists of the time combated the old ecclesiastical conception of man as inherently corrupt and lost, with this newly created picture of the paradisiacal artist: so that opera is to be understood as the opposition dogma of the good man, but may also, at the same time, provide a consolation for that pessimism which, owing to the frightful uncertainty of all conditions of life, attracted precisely the serious-minded men of the time. For us, it is enough to have perceived that the essential charm, and therefore the genesis, of this new art form lies in the gratification of an altogether nonaesthetic need, in the optimistic glorification of man as such, in the conception of the primitive man as the man naturally good and artistic—a principle of the opera that has gradually changed into a threatening and terrible *demand* which, in face of contemporary socialistic movements, we can no longer ignore. The "good primitive man" wants his rights: what paradisiacal prospects!

Besides this I place another equally obvious confirmation of my view that opera is based on the same principles as our Alexandrian culture. Opera is the birth of the theoretical man, the critical layman, not of the artist: one of the most surprising facts in the history of all the arts. It was the demand of thoroughly unmusical hearers that before everything else the words must be understood, so that according to them a rebirth of music is to be expected only when some mode of singing has been discovered in which text-word lords it over counterpoint like master over servant. For the words, it is argued, are as much nobler than the accompanying harmonic system as the soul is nobler than the body.

It was in accordance with the laically unmusical crudeness of these views that the combination of music, image, and words was effected in the beginnings of the opera. In the spirit of this aesthetic the first experiments were made in the leading amateur circles of Florence by the poets and singers patronized there. The man incapable of art creates for himself a kind of art precisely because he is the inartistic man as such. Because he does not sense the Dionysian depth of music, he changes his musical taste into an appreciation of the understandable word-and-tone-rhetoric of the passions in the *stilo rappresentativo,* and into the voluptuousness of the arts of song. Because he is unable to behold a vision, he forces the machinist and the decorative artist into his service. Because he cannot comprehend the true nature of the artist, he conjures up the "artistic primitive man" to suit his taste, that is, the man who sings and recites verses under the influence of passion. He dreams himself back into a time when passion sufficed to generate songs and poems; as if emotion had ever been able to create anything artistic.

The premise of the opera is a false belief concerning the artistic process: the idyllic belief that every sentient man is an artist. This belief would make opera the expression of the taste of the laity in art, dictating their laws with the cheerful optimism of the theoretical man.

Should we desire to combine the two conceptions that have just been shown to have influenced the origin of opera, it would merely remain for us to speak of an *idyllic tendency of the opera.* In this connection we need only avail ourselves of the expressions and explanation of Schiller. Nature and the ideal, he says, are either objects of grief, when the former is represented as lost, the latter unattained; or both are objects of joy, in that they are represented as real. The first case furnishes the elegy in its narrower signification, the second the idyll in its widest sense.

Here we must at once call attention to the common characteristic of these two conceptions in the genesis of opera, namely, that in them the ideal is not felt as unattained or nature as lost. This sentiment supposes that there was a primitive age of man when he lay close to the heart of nature, and, owing to this naturalness, had at once attained the ideal of mankind in a paradisiacal goodness and artistry. From this perfect primitive man all of us were supposed to be descended. We were even supposed to be faithful copies of him; only we had to cast off a few things in order to recognize ourselves once more as this primitive man, on the strength of a voluntary renunciation of superfluous learnedness, of superabundant culture. It was to such a concord of nature and the ideal, to an idyllic reality, that the cultured Renaissance man let himself be led back by his operatic imitation of Greek tragedy. He made use of this tragedy as Dante made use of Vergil, in order to be conducted to the gates of paradise; while from this point he continued unassisted and passed over from an imitation of the highest Greek art-form to a "restoration of all things," to an imitation of man's original art-

world. What a cheerful confidence there is about these daring endeavors, in the very heart of theoretical culture!—solely to be explained by the comforting belief, that "man-in-himself" is the
eternally virtuous hero of the opera, the eternally piping or singing
shepherd, who must always in the end rediscover himself as such,
should he ever at any time have really lost himself; to be considered solely as the fruit of that optimism, which here rises like a
sweetishly seductive column of vapor from the depth of the Socratic world view.

Therefore, the features of the opera do not by any means exhibit the elegiac sorrow of an eternal loss, but rather the cheerfulness of eternal rediscovery, the comfortable delight in an idyllic
reality which one can at least always imagine as real. But in this
process one may some day grasp the fact that this supposed reality
is nothing but a fantastically silly dawdling, at which everyone who
could judge it by the terrible seriousness of true nature, and compare it with actual primitive scenes of the beginnings of mankind,
would be impelled to call out, nauseated: Away with the phantom!

Nevertheless, it would be a mistake to imagine that it is possible merely by a vigorous shout to frighten away such a playful
thing as the opera, as if it were a specter. He who would destroy the
opera must take up the struggle against Alexandrian cheerfulness,
which expresses itself so naïvely in opera concerning its favorite
idea. Indeed, opera is its specific form of art. But what may art
itself expect from the operation of an art form whose beginnings lie
entirely outside of the aesthetic province and which has stolen over
from a half-moral sphere into the artistic domain, deceiving us only
occasionally about its hybrid origin? By what sap is this parasitic
opera nourished, if not by that of true art? Must we not suppose
that the highest and, indeed, the truly serious task of art—to save
the eye from gazing into the horrors of night and to deliver the
subject by the healing balm of illusion from the spasms of the agitations of the will—must degenerate under the influence of its idyllic
seductions and Alexandrian flatteries to become an empty and
merely distracting diversion? What will become of the eternal
truths of the Dionysian and Apollinian when the styles are mixed in
this fashion, as I have shown to be the essence of the *stilo rappresentativo?* A style in which music is regarded as the servant, the
text as the master, where music is compared with the body, the text

with the soul? where at best the highest aim will be directed toward a paraphrastic tone-painting, just as formerly in the New Attic Dithyramb? where music is completely alienated from its true dignity as the Dionysian mirror of the world, so that the only thing left to it, as the slave of phenomena, is to imitate the formal character of phenomena, and to arouse a superficial pleasure in the play of lines and proportions. Closely observed, this fatal influence of the opera on music is seen to coincide exactly with the universal development of modern music; the optimism lurking in the genesis of the opera and in the character of the culture thereby represented, has, with alarming rapidity, succeeded in divesting music of its Dionysian-cosmic mission and impressing on it a playfully formal and pleasurable character: a change comparable to the metamorphosis of the Aeschylean man into the cheerful Alexandrian.

If, however, in the exemplification here indicated, we have rightly associated the disappearance of the Dionysian spirit with a most striking, but hitherto unexplained, transformation and degeneration of the Hellenic man—what hopes must revive in us when the most certain auspices guarantee *the reverse process, the gradual awakening of the Dionysian spirit* in our modern world! It is impossible that the divine strength of Herakles should languish for ever in ample bondage to Omphale.[2] Out of the Dionysian root of the German spirit a power has arisen which, having nothing in common with the primitive conditions of Socratic culture, can neither be explained nor excused by it, but which is rather felt by this culture as something terribly inexplicable and overwhelmingly hostile—*German music* as we must understand it, particularly in its vast solar orbit from Bach to Beethoven, from Beethoven to Wagner.

Even under the most favorable circumstances what can the knowledge-craving Socratism of our days do with this demon rising from unfathomable depths? Neither by means of the flourishes and arabesques of operatic melody, nor with the aid of the arithmetical counting board of fugue and contrapuntal dialectic is the formula to be found by whose thrice-powerful light one might subdue this

---

[2] A queen of Lydia by whom Herakles claimed to have been detained for a year of bondage, according to Sophocles, *Trachiniae,* lines 248ff. In Ovid's *Heroïdes,* 9.53ff., the story is elaborated.

Wish I could have the differences in music right here to experience!

demon and compel it to speak. What a spectacle, when our latter-day aestheticians, with a net of "beauty" peculiar to themselves, pursue and clutch at the genius of music whirling before display activities which are not to be judged by the standard of eternal beauty any more than by the standard of the sublime. Let us but observe these patrons of music at close range, as they really are, indefatigably crying: "Beauty! beauty!" Do they really bear the stamp of nature's darling children who are fostered and nourished at the breast of the beautiful, or are they not rather seeking a mendacious cloak for their own coarseness, an aesthetical pretext for their own insensitive sobriety; here I am thinking of Otto Jahn, for example.[3] But let the liar and the hypocrite beware of German music: for amid all our culture it is really the only genuine, pure, and purifying fire-spirit from which and toward which, as in the teaching of the great Heraclitus of Ephesus, all things move in a double orbit: all that we now call culture, education, civilization, must some day appear before the unerring judge, Dionysus.

Let us recollect further that Kant and Schopenhauer made it possible for the spirit of *German philosophy,* streaming from similar sources, to destroy scientific Socratism's complacent delight in existence by establishing its boundaries; how through this delimitation was introduced an infinitely profounder and more serious view

---

[3] Otto Jahn was born in 1813, like Nietzsche's father, Richard Wagner, and Kierkegaard, and died in 1869. He was a professor of classical philology at Bonn, first a friend and later a foe of Nietzsche's teacher Ritschl. His many publications included articles on Greek tragedies and on ancient sculptures and vase paintings, a life of Mozart, and essays on music. To explain the above remark, it may be relevant to recall a passage in one of Nietzsche's letters to Rohde, October 8, 1868: "Recently I have also read . . . Jahn's essays on music, including those on Wagner. It requires some enthusiasm to do justice to such a man, while Jahn has an instinctive aversion and listens only with ears that are half plugged. Nevertheless I agree with him on many points; especially insofar as he considers Wagner the representative of a modern dilettantism that absorbs and digests all artistic interests. But precisely from this point of view one can hardly be astonished enough at how imposing every single artistic talent is in this man, and what inexhaustible energy is here coupled with such many-sided artistic talents, while 'education,' the more motley and comprehensive it is, usually appears with weak eyes, feeble legs, and unnerved loins. Moreover, Wagner has a dimension of feelings that remains altogether hidden from O. Jahn: Jahn simply remains a . . . healthy man for whom the myth of Tannhäuser and the atmosphere of Lohengrin remain a closed world. What I like about Wagner is what I like about Schopenhauer: the ethical air, the Faustian fragrance, cross, death, and tomb, etc."

of ethical problems and of art, which we may designate as Diony-sian wisdom comprised in concepts. To what then does the mystery of this oneness of German music and philosophy point if not to a new form of existence, concerning whose character we can only inform ourselves by surmise from Hellenic analogies? For to us who stand on the boundary line between two different forms of existence, the Hellenic prototype retains this immeasurable value, that all these transitions and struggles are imprinted upon it in a classically instructive form; except that we, as it were, pass through the chief epochs of the Hellenic genius, analogically in *reverse* order, and seem now, for instance, to be passing backward from the Alexandrian age to the period of tragedy. At the same time we have the feeling that the birth of a tragic age simply means a return to itself of the German spirit, a blessed self-rediscovery after pow-erful intrusive influences had for a long time compelled it, living as it did in a helpless and unchaste barbarism, to servitude under their form. Now at last, upon returning to the primitive source of its being, it may venture to stride along boldly and freely before the eyes of all nations without being attached to the lead strings of a Romanic civilization; if only it can learn constantly from one peo-ple—the Greeks, from whom to be able to learn at all is itself a high honor and a rare distinction. And when were we in greater need of these highest of all teachers than at present, when we are experiencing a *rebirth of tragedy* and are in danger alike of not knowing whence it comes and of being unable to make clear to ourselves whither it tends?

20

Some day, before an impartial judge, it may be decided in what time and in what men the German spirit has so far striven most resolutely to learn from the Greeks; and if we confidently as-sume that this unique praise must be accorded to the noblest intel-lectual efforts of Goethe, Schiller, and Winckelmann, we should certainly have to add that since their time and the more immediate consequences of their efforts, the endeavor to attain to culture and to the Greeks on the same path has grown incomprehensibly fee-bler and feebler. That we may not despair utterly of the German spirit, must we not conclude that, in some essential matter, even these champions did not penetrate into the core of the Hellenic nature, to establish a permanent alliance between German and Greek culture? So an unconscious recognition of this shortcoming may have prompted the disheartening doubt, even in very serious people, whether after such predecessors they could possibly advance further on this path of culture or could reach the goal at all. Accordingly, we see that opinions concerning the value of the Greeks for education have been degenerating in the most alarming manner since that time. Expressions of compassionate condescension may be heard in the most varied camps of the spirit—and of lack of spirit. Elsewhere, ineffectual rhetoric plays with the phrases "Greek harmony," "Greek beauty," "Greek cheerfulness." And those very circles whose dignified task it might be to draw indefatigably from the Greek reservoir for the good of German culture, the teachers of the higher educational institutions, have learned best to come to terms with the Greeks easily and in good time, often by skeptically abandoning the Hellenic ideal and completely perverting the true purpose of antiquarian studies. Whoever in these circles has not completely exhausted himself in his endeavor to be a dependable corrector of old texts or a linguistic microscopist who apes natural history is probably trying to assimilate Greek antiquity "historically," along with other antiquities, at any rate according to the method and with the supercilious airs of our present cultured historiography.

The cultural power of our higher educational institutions has perhaps never been lower or feebler than at present. The "journalist," the paper slave of the day, triumphs over the professor in all matters pertaining to culture; and nothing remains to the latter but the metamorphosis, often experienced by now, of fluttering also like a cheerful cultured butterfly, with the "light elegance" peculiar to this sphere, employing the journalist's style. In what painful confusion must the cultured class of such a period gaze at the phenomenon which perhaps is to be comprehended analogically only by means of the profoundest principle of the hitherto unintelligible Hellenic genius—the phenomenon of the reawakening of the Dionysian spirit and the rebirth of tragedy?

There has never been another period in the history of art in which so-called culture and true art have been so estranged and opposed as we may observe them to be at present. We can understand why so feeble a culture hates true art; it fears destruction from its hands. But has not an entire cultural form, namely, the Socratic-Alexandrian, exhausted itself after culminating in such a daintily tapering point as our present culture? If heroes like Goethe and Schiller could not succeed in breaking open the enchanted gate which leads into the Hellenic magic mountain; if with their most dauntless striving they could not go beyond the longing gaze which Goethe's Iphigenia casts from barbaric Tauris to her home across the ocean, what could the epigones of such heroes hope for—unless, amid the mystic tones of reawakened tragic music, the gate should open for them suddenly of its own accord, from an entirely different side, quite overlooked in all previous cultural endeavors.

Let no one try to blight our faith in a yet-impending rebirth of Hellenic antiquity; for this alone gives us hope for a renovation and purification of the German spirit through the fire magic of music.[1] What else could we name that might awaken any comforting expectations for the future in the midst of the desolation and exhaustion of contemporary culture? In vain we look for a single vigorously developed root, for a spot of fertile and healthy soil: everywhere there is dust and sand; everything has become rigid and languishes. One who is disconsolate and lonely could not choose a better symbol than the knight with death and devil, as Dürer has drawn him for us, the armored knight with the iron, hard look, who knows how to pursue his terrible path, undeterred by his gruesome companions, and yet without hope, alone with his horse and dog. Our Schopenhauer was such a Dürer knight; he lacked all hope, but he desired truth. He has no peers.

But how suddenly the desert of our exhausted culture, just described in such gloomy terms, is changed when it is touched by the Dionysian magic! A tempest seizes everything that has outlived itself, everything that is decayed, broken, and withered, and, whirling, shrouds it in a cloud of red dust to carry it into the air like a vulture. Confused, our eyes look after what has disappeared; for what they see has been raised as from a depression into golden light, so full and green, so amply alive, immeasurable and full of yearning. Tragedy is seated amid this excess of life, suffering, and

---

[1] This request that no one should trouble our faith because it alone gives us hope, contrasts very sharply with Nietzsche's later attitude toward faith.

pleasure, in sublime ecstasy, listening to a distant melancholy song that tells of the mothers of being whose names are: Delusion, Will, Woe.[2]

Yes, my friends, believe with me in Dionysian life and the rebirth of tragedy. The age of the Socratic man is over; put on wreaths of ivy, put the thyrsus into your hand, and do not be surprised when tigers and panthers lie down, fawning, at your feet. Only dare to be tragic men; for you are to be redeemed. You shall accompany the Dionysian pageant from India to Greece. Prepare yourselves for hard strife, but believe in the miracles of your god.

21

Returning from these hortatory tones to the mood befitting contemplation, I repeat that we can learn only from the Greeks what such an almost miraculously sudden awakening of tragedy means for the innermost life ground of a people. It is the people of the tragic mysteries that fights the battles against the Persians; and the people that fought these wars in turn needs tragedy as a necessary potion to recover. Who would have supposed that precisely this people, after it had been deeply agitated through several generations by the strongest spasms of the Dionysian demon, should still have been capable of such a uniformly vigorous effusion of the simplest political feeling, the most natural patriotic instincts, and original manly desire to fight? After all, one feels in every case in which Dionysian excitement gains any significant extent how the Dionysian liberation from the fetters of the individual finds expression first of all in a diminution of, in indifference to, indeed, in hostility to, the political instincts. Just as certainly, Apollo who forms states is also the genius of the *principium individuationis,* and state and patriotism cannot live without an affirmation of the individual personality. But from orgies a people can take one path only, the path to Indian Buddhism, and in order that this may be endurable at all with its yearning for the nothing, it requires these rare ecstatic states with their elevation above space, time, and the individual. These states in turn demand a philosophy

---

[2] *Wahn, Wille, Wehe.* This passage reads like a parody of Wagner, but certainly was not meant to be satirical.

that teaches men how to overcome by the force of an idea the indescribable displeasure of the states that lie between. Where the political drives are taken to be absolutely valid, it is just as necessary that a people should go the path toward the most extreme secularization whose most magnificent but also most terrifying expression may be found in the Roman *imperium*.

Placed between India and Rome, and pushed toward a seductive choice, the Greeks succeeded in inventing a third form, in classical purity—to be sure, one they did not long use themselves, but one that precisely for that reason gained immortality. For that the favorites of the gods die early, is true in all things; but it is just as certain that they then live eternally with the gods. After all, one should not demand of what is noblest of all that it should have the durable toughness of leather. That staunch perseverance which characterized, for example, the national instincts of the Romans, probably does not belong among the necessary predicates of perfection. But let us ask by means of what remedy it was possible for the Greeks during their great period, in spite of the extraordinary strength of their Dionysian and political instincts, not to exhaust themselves either in ecstatic brooding or in a consuming chase after worldly power and worldly honor, but rather to attain that splendid mixture which resembles a noble wine in making one feel fiery and contemplative at the same time. Here we must clearly think of the tremendous power that stimulated, purified, and discharged the whole life of the people: *tragedy*. We cannot begin to sense its highest value until it confronts us, as it did the Greeks, as the quintessence of all prophylactic powers of healing, as the mediator that worked among the strongest and in themselves most fatal qualities of the people.

Tragedy absorbs the highest ecstasies of music, so that it truly brings music, both among the Greeks and among us, to its perfection; but then it places the tragic myth and the tragic hero next to it, and he, like a powerful Titan, takes the whole Dionysian world upon his back and thus relieves us of this burden. On the other hand, by means of the same tragic myth, in the person of the tragic hero, it knows how to redeem us from the greedy thirst for this existence, and with an admonishing gesture it reminds us of another existence and a higher pleasure for which the struggling hero prepares himself by means of his destruction, not by means of his triumphs. Between the universal validity of its music and the listener, receptive in his Dionysian state, tragedy places a sublime parable, the myth, and deceives the listener into feeling that the music is merely the highest means to bring life into the vivid world of myth. Relying on this noble deception, it may now move its limbs in dithyrambic dances and yield unhesitatingly to an ecstatic feeling of freedom in which it could not dare to wallow as pure music without this deception. The myth protects us against the music, while on the other hand it alone gives music the highest freedom. In return, music imparts to the tragic myth an intense and convincing metaphysical significance that word and image without this singular help could never have attained. And above all, it is through music that the tragic spectator is overcome by an assured premonition of a highest pleasure[1] attained through destruction and negation, so he feels as if the innermost abyss of things spoke to him perceptibly.

If these last sentences have perhaps managed to give only a preliminary expression to these difficult ideas and are immediately intelligible only to few, I nevertheless may not desist at this point from trying to stimulate my friends to further efforts and must ask them to use a single example of our common experience in order to prepare themselves for a general insight. In giving this example, I must not appeal to those who use the images of what happens on the stage, the words and emotions of the acting persons, in order to approach with their help the musical feeling; for these people do not speak music as their mother tongue and, in spite of this help, never get beyond the entrance halls of musical perception, without ever being able to as much as touch the inner sanctum. Some of them, like Gervinus,[2] do not even reach the entrance halls. I must appeal only to those who, immediately related to music, have in it, as it were, their motherly womb, and are related to things almost exclusively through unconscious musical relations. To these genuine musicians I direct the question whether they can imagine a human being who would be able to perceive the third act of *Tristan and Isolde,* without any aid of word and image, purely as a tremen-

---

[1] An allusion to Faust's last words in lines 11,585f. of Goethe's play.
[2] G. G. Gervinus, author of *Shakespeare,* 2 vols., Leipzig, 1850, 3rd ed., 1862; English tr., *Shakespeare Commentaries,* 1863.

dous symphonic movement, without expiring in a spasmodic un-harnessing of all the wings of the soul?

Suppose a human being has thus put his ear, as it were, to the heart chamber of the world will and felt the roaring desire for exist-ence pouring from there into all the veins of the world, as a thun-dering current or as the gentlest brook, dissolving into a mist—how could he fail to break suddenly? How could he endure to perceive the echo of innumerable shouts of pleasure and woe in the "wide space of the world night," enclosed in the wretched glass capsule of the human individual, without inexorably fleeing toward his pri-mordial home, as he hears this shepherd's dance of metaphysics? But if such a work could nevertheless be perceived as a whole, without denial of individual existence; if such a creation could be created without smashing its creator—whence do we take the solu-tion of such a contradiction?

Here the tragic myth and the tragic hero intervene between our highest musical emotion and this music—at botton only as symbols of the most universal facts, of which only music can speak so directly. But if our feelings were those of entirely Dionysian beings, myth as a symbol would remain totally ineffective and un-noticed, and would never for a moment keep us from listening to the re-echo of the *universalia ante rem*.[3] Yet here the *Apollinian* power erupts to restore the almost shattered individual with the healing balm of blissful illusion: suddenly we imagine we see only Tristan, motionless, asking himself dully: "The old tune, why does it wake me?" And what once seemed to us like a hollow sigh from the core of being now merely wants to tell us how "desolate and empty the sea." [4] And where, breathless, we once thought we were being extinguished in a convulsive distention of all our feelings, and little remained to tie us to our present existence, we now hear and see only the hero wounded to death, yet not dying, with his despair-ing cry: "Longing! Longing! In death still longing! for very longing not dying!" And where, formerly after such an excess and super-abundance of consuming agonies, the jubilation of the horn cut through our hearts almost like the ultimate agony, the rejoicing

---

[3] The universals before (antedating) the thing.

[4] *Wie "öd und leer das Meer,"* also quoted from *Tristan und Isolde* by T. S. Eliot in *The Waste Land* (1922), line 42.

Kurwenal now stands between us and this "jubilation in itself," his face turned toward the ship which carries Isolde. However powerfully pity affects us, it nevertheless saves us in a way from the primordial suffering of the world, just as the symbolic image of the myth saves us from the immediate perception of the highest world-idea, just as thought and word save us from the uninhibited effusion of the unconscious will. The glorious Apollinian illusion makes it appear as if even the tone world confronted us as a sculpted world, as if the fate of Tristan and Isolde had been formed and molded in it, too, as in an exceedingly tender and expressive material.

Thus the Apollinian tears us out of the Dionysian universality and lets us find delight in individuals; it attaches our pity to them, and by means of them it satisfies our sense of beauty which longs for great and sublime forms; it presents images of life to us, and incites us to comprehend in thought the core of life they contain. With the immense impact of the image, the concept, the ethical teaching, and the sympathetic emotion, the Apollinian tears man from his orgiastic self-annihilation and blinds him to the universality of the Dionysian process, deluding him into the belief that he is seeing a single image of the world (*Tristan and Isolde,* for instance), and that, *through music,* he is merely supposed to *see* it still better and more profoundly. What can the healing magic of Apollo not accomplish when it can even create the illusion that the Dionysian is really in the service of the Apollinian and capable of enhancing its effects—as if music were essentially the art of presenting an Apollinian content?

By means of the pre-established harmony between perfect drama and its music, the drama attains a superlative vividness unattainable in mere spoken drama. In the independently moving lines of the melody all the living figures of the scene simplify themselves before us to the distinctness of curved lines, and the harmonies of these lines sympathize in a most delicate manner with the events on the stage. These harmonies make the relations of things immediately perceptible to us in a sensuous, by no means abstract manner, and thus we perceive that it is only in these relations that the essence of a character and of a melodic line is revealed clearly. And while music thus compels us to see more and more profoundly than usual, and we see the action on the stage as a delicate web, the world of the stage is expanded infinitely and illuminated for our spiritualized eye. How could a word-poet furnish anything analogous, when he strives to attain this internal expansion and illumination of the visible stage-world by means of a much more imperfect mechanism, indirectly, proceeding from word and concept? Although musical tragedy also avails itself of the word, it can at the same time place beside it the basis and origin of the word, making the development of the word clear to us, from the inside.

Concerning the process just described, however, we may still say with equal assurance that it is merely a glorious appearance, namely, the aforementioned Apollinian *illusion* whose influence aims to deliver us from the Dionysian flood and excess. For, at bottom, the relation of music to drama is precisely the reverse: music is the real idea of the world, drama is but the reflection of this idea, a single silhouette of it. The identity between the melody and the living figure, between the harmony and the character relations of that figure, is true in a sense opposite to what one would suppose on the contemplation of musical tragedy. Even if we agitate and enliven the figure in the most visible manner, and illuminate it from within, it still remains merely a phenomenon from which no bridge leads us to true reality, into the heart of the world. But music speaks out of this heart; and though countless phenomena of the kind were to accompany this music, they could never exhaust its essence, but would always be nothing more than its externalized copies.

As for the intricate relationship of music and drama, nothing can be explained, while everything may be confused, by the popular and thoroughly false contrast of soul and body; but the unphilosophical crudeness of this contrast seems to have become—who knows for what reasons—a readily accepted article of faith among our aestheticians, while they have learned nothing of the contrast of the phenomenon and the thing-in-itself—or, for equally unknown reasons, have not cared to learn anything about it.

Should our analysis have established that the Apollinian element in tragedy has by means of its illusion gained a complete victory over the primoridal Dionysian element of music, making music subservient to its aims, namely, to make the drama as vivid as possible—it would certainly be necessary to add a very important qualification: at the most essential point this Apollinian illusion is broken and annihilated. The drama that, with the aid of music, unfolds itself before us with such inwardly illumined distinctness in all its movements and figures, as if we saw the texture coming into being on the loom as the shuttle flies to and fro—attains as a whole an effect that transcends *all Apollinian artistic effects*. In the total effect of tragedy, the Dionysian predominates once again. Tragedy closes with a sound which could never come from the realm of Apollinian art. And thus the Apollinian illusion reveals itself as what it really is—the veiling during the performance of the tragedy of the real Dionysian effect; but the latter is so powerful that it ends by forcing the Apollinian drama itself into a sphere where it begins to speak with Dionysian wisdom and even denies itself and its Apollinian visibility. Thus the intricate relation of the Apollinian and the Dionysian in tragedy may really be symbolized by a fraternal union of the two deities: Dionysus speaks the language of Apollo; and Apollo, finally the language of Dionysus; and so the highest goal of tragedy and of all art is attained.

22

Let the attentive friend imagine the effect of a true musical tragedy purely and simply, as he knows it from experience. I think I have so portrayed the phenomenon of this effect in both its phases that he can now interpret his own experiences. For he will recollect how with regard to the myth which passed in front of him, he felt himself exalted to a kind of omniscience, as if his visual faculty were no longer merely a surface faculty but capable of penetrating into the interior, and as if he now saw before him, with the aid of music, the waves of the will, the conflict of motives, and the swelling flood of the passions, sensuously visible, as it were, like a multitude of vividly moving lines and figures; and he felt he could dip into the most delicate secrets of unconscious emotions. While he thus becomes conscious of the highest exaltation of his instincts for clarity and transfiguration, he nevertheless feels just as definitely that this long series of Apollinian artistic effects still does *not* generate that blessed continuance in will-less contemplation which the plastic artist and the epic poet, that is to say, the strictly Apollinian artists, evoke in him with their artistic productions: to wit, the justification of the world of the *individuatio* attained by this contemplation—which is the climax and essence of Apollinian art. He beholds the transfigured world of the stage and nevertheless denies it. He sees the tragic hero before him in epic clearness and beauty, and nevertheless rejoices in his annihilation. He comprehends the action deep down, and yet likes to flee into the incomprehensible. He feels the actions of the hero to be justified, and is nevertheless still more elated when these actions annihilate their agent. He shudders at the sufferings which will befall the hero, and yet anticipates in them a higher, much more overpowering joy. He sees more extensively and profoundly than ever, and yet wishes he were blind.

How must we derive this curious internal bifurcation, this blunting of the Apollinian point, if not from the *Dionysian* magic that, though apparently exciting the Apollinian emotions to their highest pitch, still retains the power to force into its service his excess of Apollinian force?

The *tragic myth* is to be understood only as a symbolization of Dionysian wisdom through Apollinian artifices. The myth leads the world of phenomena to its limits where it denies itself and seeks to flee back again into the womb of the true and only reality, where it then seems to commence its metaphysical swansong, like Isolde:

> *In the rapture ocean's*
> *billowing roll,*
> *in the fragrance waves'*
> *ringing sound,*
> *in the world breath's*
> *wafting whole—*
> *to drown, to sink—*
> *unconscious—highest joy!* [1]

---

[1]   In des Wonnemeeres
       wogendem Schwall,
       in der Duft-Wellen
       tönendem Schall,
       in des Weltathems
       wehendem All—
       ertrinken—versinken—
           unbewusst—höchste Lust!

Thus we use the experiences of the truly aesthetic listener to bring to mind the tragic artist himself as he creates his figures like a fecund divinity of individuation (so his work can hardly be understood as an "imitation of nature") and as his vast Dionysian impulse then devours his entire world of phenomena, in order to let us sense beyond it, and through its destruction, the highest artistic primal joy, in the bosom of the primordially One. Of course, our aestheticians have nothing to say about this return to the primordial home, or the fraternal union of the two art-deities, nor of the excitement of the hearer which is Apollinian as well as Dionysian; but they never tire of characterizing the struggle of the hero with fate, the triumph of the moral world order, or the purgation of the emotions through tragedy, as the essence of the tragic. And their indefatigability makes me think that perhaps they are not aesthetically sensitive at all, but react merely as moral beings when listening to a tragedy.

Never since Aristotle has an explanation of the tragic effect been offered from which aesthetic states or an aesthetic activity of the listener could be inferred. Now the serious events are supposed to prompt pity and fear to discharge themselves in a way that relieves us; now we are supposed to feel elevated and inspired by the triumph of good and noble principles, at the sacrifice of the hero in the interest of a moral vision of the universe. I am sure that for countless men precisely this, and only this, is the effect of tragedy, but it plainly follows that all these men, together with their interpreting aestheticians, have had no experience of tragedy as a supreme *art*.

The pathological discharge, the catharsis of Aristotle, of which philologists are not sure whether it should be included among medical or moral phenomena, recalls a remarkable notion of Goethe's. "Without a lively pathological interest," he says, "I, too, have never yet succeeded in elaborating a tragic situation of any kind, and hence I have rather avoided than sought it. Can it perhaps have been yet another merit of the ancients that the deepest pathos was with them merely aesthetic play, while with us the truth of nature must co-operate in order to produce such a work?"

We can now answer this profound final question in the affirmative after our glorious experiences, having found to our astonishment that the deepest pathos can indeed be merely aesthetic play in the case of musical tragedy. Therefore we are justified in believing that now for the first time the primal phenomenon of the tragic can be described with some degree of success. Anyone who still persists in talking only of those vicarious effects proceeding from extra-aesthetic spheres, and who does not feel that he is above the pathological-moral process, should despair of his aesthetic nature: should we recommend to him as an innocent equivalent the interpretation of Shakespeare after the manner of Gervinus and the diligent search for poetic justice? [2]

Thus the aesthetic *listener* is also reborn with the rebirth of tragedy. In his place in the theater, a curious *quid pro quo*[3] used to sit with half moral and half scholarly pretensions—the "critic." Everything in his sphere so far has been artificial and merely whitewashed with an appearance of life. The performing artist was really at a loss how to deal with a listener who comported himself so critically; so he, as well as the dramatist or operatic composer who inspired him, searched anxiously for the last remains of life in a being so pretentiously barren and incapable of enjoyment. So far, however, such "critics" have constituted the audience: the student, the schoolboy, even the most innocuous female had been unwittingly prepared by education and newspapers for this kind of perception of works of art. Confronted with such a public, the nobler natures among the artists counted upon exciting their moral-religious emotions, and the appeal to the moral world-order intervened vicariously where some powerful artistic magic ought to enrapture the genuine listener. Or some more imposing, or at all events exciting, trend of the contemporary political and social world was so vividly presented by the dramatist that the listener could forget his critical exhaustion and abandon himself to emotions similar to those felt in patriotic or warlike moments, or before the tribune of parliament, or at the condemnation of crime and vice—an alienation from the true aims of art that sometimes had to result in an outright cult of tendentiousness. But what happened next is what has always happened to all artificial arts: a rapid degeneration of such tendentiousness. The attempt, for example, to use the theater as an institution for the moral education of the peo-

---

[2] See section 21, note 2.
[3] One thing in place of another.

ple, still taken seriously in Schiller's time, is already reckoned among the incredible antiques of a dated type of education. While the critic got the upper hand in the theater and concert hall, the journalist in the schools, and the press in society, art degenerated into a particularly lowly topic of conversation, and aesthetic criticism was used as a means of uniting a vain, distracted, selfish, and moreover piteously unoriginal sociability whose character is suggested by Schopenhauer's parable of the porcupines.[4] As a result, art has never been so much talked about and so little esteemed. But is it still possible to have intercourse with a person capable of conversing about Beethoven or Shakespeare?[5] Let each answer this question according to his own feelings: he will at any rate show by his answer his conception of "culture," provided he at least tries to answer the question, and has not already become dumfounded with astonishment.

On the other hand, many a being more nobly and delicately endowed by nature, though he may have gradually become a critical barbarian in the manner described, might have something to say about the unexpected as well as totally unintelligible effect that a successful performance of *Lohengrin,* for example, had on him— except that perhaps there was no helpful interpreting hand to guide him; so the incomprehensibly different and altogether incomparable sensation that thrilled him remained isolated and, like a mys-

---

[4] The parable is found at the end of Schopenhauer's *Parerga und Paralipomena,* vol. II (1851), section 396: "On a cold winter day, a group of porcupines huddled together closely to save themselves by their mutual warmth from freezing. But soon they felt the mutual quills and drew apart. Whenever the need for warmth brought them closer together again, this second evil was repeated, so that they were tossed back and forth between these two kinds of suffering until they discovered a moderate distance that proved most tolerable.— Thus the need for company, born of the emptiness and monotony inside them, drives men together; but their many revolting qualities and intolerable faults repel them again. The medium distance that they finally discover and that makes association possible is politeness and good manners. Whoever does not keep this distance is told, among the British: keep your distance!— To be sure, this only permits imperfect satisfaction of the need for mutual warmth, but it also keeps one from feeling the prick of the quills.— But whoever possesses much inner warmth of his own will prefer to avoid company lest he cause or suffer annoyance." I have quoted this parable in its entirety; *keep your distance* is English in the original.
[5] Cf. T. S. Eliot's "Love Song of J. Alfred Prufrock": "In the room the women come and go/Talking of Michelangelo."

terious star, became extinct after a short period of brilliance. But it was then that he had an inkling of what an aesthetic listener is.

23

Whoever wishes to test rigorously to what extent he himself is related to the true aesthetic listener or belongs to the community of the Socratic-critical persons needs only to examine sincerely the feeling with which he accepts miracles represented on the stage: whether he feels his historical sense, which insists on strict psychological causality, insulted by them, whether he makes a benevolent concession and admits the miracle as a phenomenon intelligible to childhood but alien to him, or whether he experiences anything else. For in this way he will be able to determine to what extent he is capable of understanding *myth* as a concentrated image of the world that, as a condensation of phenomena, cannot dispense with miracles. It is probable, however, that almost everyone, upon close examination, finds that the critical-historical spirit of our culture has so affected him that he can only make the former existence of myth credible to himself by means of scholarship, through intermediary abstractions. But without myth every culture loses the healthy natural power of its creativity: only a horizon defined by myths completes and unifies a whole cultural movement. Myth alone saves all the powers of the imagination and of the Apollinian dream from their aimless wanderings. The images of the myth have to be the unnoticed omnipresent demonic guardians, under whose care the young soul grows to maturity and whose signs help the man to interpret his life and struggles. Even the state knows no more powerful unwritten laws than the mythical foundation that guarantees its connection with religion and its growth from mythical notions.

By way of comparison let us now picture the abstract man, untutored by myth; abstract education; abstract morality; abstract law; the abstract state; let us imagine the lawless roving of the artistic imagination, unchecked by any native myth; let us think of a culture that has no fixed and sacred primordial site but is doomed to exhaust all possibilities and to nourish itself wretchedly on all other cultures—there we have the present age, the result of that

First take on new meaning.

Socratism which is bent on the destruction of myth. And now the mythless man stands eternally hungry, surrounded by all past ages, and digs and grubs for roots, even if he has to dig for them among the remotest antiquities. The tremendous historical need of our unsatisfied modern culture, the assembling around one of countless other cultures, the consuming desire for knowledge—what does all this point to, if not to the loss of myth, the loss of the mythical home, the mythical maternal womb? Let us ask ourselves whether the feverish and uncanny excitement of this culture is anything but the greedy seizing and snatching at food of a hungry man—and who would care to contribute anything to a culture that cannot be satisfied no matter how much it devours, and at whose contact the most vigorous and wholesome nourishment is changed into "history and criticism"?

We should also have to regard our German character with sorrowful despair, if it had already become inextricably entangled in, or even identical with, its culture, as we may observe to our horror in the case of civilized France. What for a long time was the great advantage of France and the cause of her vast superiority, namely, this very identity of people and culture, might compel us in view of this sight to congratulate ourselves that this so questionable culture of ours has as yet nothing in common with the noble core of our people's character.[1] On the contrary, all our hopes stretch out longingly toward the perception that beneath this restlessly palpitating cultural life and convulsion there is concealed a glorious, intrinsically healthy, primordial power that, to be sure, stirs vigorously only at intervals in stupendous moments, and then continues to dream of a future awakening. It is from this abyss that the German Reformation came forth; and in its chorales the future tune of German music resounded for the first time. So deep, courageous, and spiritual, so exuberantly good and tender did this chorale of

---

[1] This pro-German and anti-French passage echoes Wagner and is utterly at odds with Nietzsche's later works. Indeed, even his second book, the essay on *David Strauss* (1873), published the year after the first edition of *The Birth,* begins with "the bad and dangerous consequences of the war" of 1870–71; and the first paragraph ends with the prospect of *"the defeat—yes, the extirpation of the German spirit in favor of the 'German Reich.'"* After his break with Wagner, Nietzsche expressed his admiration for the French again and again; and no major German writer has ever equaled Nietzsche's stringent criticisms of his own people.

Luther sound—as the first Dionysian luring call breaking forth from dense thickets at the approach of spring. And in competing echoes the solemnly exuberant procession of Dionysian revelers responded, to whom we are indebted for German music—and to whom we shall be indebted for *the rebirth of German myth*.

I know that I must now lead the sympathizing and attentive friend to an elevated position of lonely contemplation, where he will have but few companions, and I call out encouragingly to him that we must hold fast to our luminous guides, the Greeks. To purify our aesthetic insight, we have previously borrowed from them the two divine figures who rule over separate realms of art, and concerning whose mutual contact and enhancement we have acquired some notion through Greek tragedy. It had to appear to us that the demise of Greek tragedy was brought about through a remarkable and forcible dissociation of these two primordial artistic drives. To this process there corresponded a degeneration and transformation of the character of the Greek people, which calls for serious reflection on how necessary and close the fundamental connections are between art and the people, myth and custom, tragedy and the state. This demise of tragedy was at the same time the demise of myth. Until then the Greeks had felt involuntarily impelled to relate all their experiences immediately to their myths, indeed to understand them only in this relation. Thus even the immediate present had to appear to them right away *sub specie aeterni*[2] and in a certain sense as timeless.

But the state no less than art dipped into this current of the timeless to find rest in it from the burden and the greed of the moment. And any people—just as, incidentally, also any individual—is worth only as much as it is able to press upon its experiences the stamp of the eternal; for thus it is, as it were, desecularized and shows its unconscious inward convictions of the relativity of time and of the true, that is metaphysical, significance of life. The opposite of this happens when a people begins to comprehend itself historically and to smash the mythical works that surround it. At that point we generally find a decisive secularization, a break with the unconscious metaphysics of its previous existence, together with all its ethical consequences. Greek

_____

[2] Under the aspect of the eternal.

art and pre-eminently Greek tragedy delayed above all the destruction of myth. One had to destroy tragedy, too, in order to be able to live away from the soil of home, uninhibited, in the wilderness of thought, custom, and deed. Even now this metaphysical drive still tries to create for itself a certainly attenuated form of transfiguration, in the Socratism of science that strives for life; but on the lower steps, this same drive led only to a feverish search that gradually lost itself in a pandemonium of myths and superstitions that were collected from all over and piled up in confusion: nevertheless the Greek sat among them with an unstilled heart until he learned to mask this fever with Greek cheerfulness and Greek frivolity, becoming a *Graeculus*,[3] or he numbed his mind completely in some dark Oriental superstition.

Since the reawakening of Alexandrian-Roman antiquity in the fifteenth century we have approximated this state in the most evident manner, after a long interlude that is difficult to describe. On the heights we encounter the same overabundant lust for knowledge, the same unsatisfied delight in discovery, the same tremendous secularization, and beside it a homeless roving, a greedy crowding around foreign tables, a frivolous deification of the present, or a dully dazed retreat—everything *sub specie saeculi*,[4] of the "present age." And these same symptoms allow us to infer the same lack at the heart of this culture, the destruction of myth. It scarcely seems possible to be continually successful at transplanting a foreign myth without irreparably damaging the tree by this transplantation. In one case it may perhaps be strong and healthy enough to eliminate this foreign element in a terrible fight; usually, however, it must consume itself, sick and withered or in diseased superfoetation.

We think so highly of the pure and vigorous core of the German character that we dare to expect of it above all others this elimination of the forcibly implanted foreign elements, and consider it possible that the German spirit will return to itself. Some may suppose that this spirit must begin its fight with the elimination of everything Romanic. If so they may recognize an external preparation and encouragement in the victorious fortitude and bloody

---

[3] A contemptuous term for a Greek. See section 11.
[4] Under the aspect of the times, or the spirit of the age.

glory of the last war; but one must still seek the inner necessity in the ambition to be always worthy of the sublime champions on this way, Luther as well as our great artists and poets. But let him never believe that he could fight similar fights without the gods of his house, or his mythical home, without "bringing back" all German things! And if the German should hesitantly look around for a leader who might bring him back again into his long lost home whose ways and paths he scarcely knows anymore, let him merely listen to the ecstatically luring call of the Dionysian bird that hovers above him and wants to point the way for him.

24

Among the peculiar art effects of musical tragedy we had to emphasize an Apollinian *illusion* by means of which we were supposed to be saved from the immediate unity with Dionysian music, while our musical excitement could discharge itself in an Apollinian field and in relation to a visible intermediary world that had been interposed. At the same time we thought that we had observed how precisely through this discharge the intermediary world of the action on the stage, and the drama in general, had been made visible and intelligible from the inside to a degree that in all other Apollinian art remains unattained. Where the Apollinian receives wings from the spirit of music and soars, we thus found the highest intensification of its powers, and in this fraternal union of Apollo and Dionysus we had to recognize the apex of the Apollinian as well as the Dionysian aims of art.

To be sure, the Apollinian projection that is thus illuminated from inside by music does not achieve the peculiar effect of the weaker degrees of Apollinian art. What the epic or the animated stone can do, compelling the contemplative eye to find calm delight in the world of individuation, that could not be attained here, in spite of a higher animation and clarity. We looked at the drama and with penetrating eye reached its inner world of motives—and yet we felt as if only a parable passed us by, whose most profound meaning we almost thought we could guess and that we wished to draw away like a curtain in order to behold the primordial image behind it. The brightest clarity of the image did not suffice us, for this seemed to wish just as much to reveal something as to conceal something. Its revelation, being like a parable, seemed to summon us to tear the veil and to uncover the mysterious background; but at the same time this all-illuminated total visibility cast a spell over the eyes and prevented them from penetrating deeper.

Those who have never had the experience of having to see at the same time that they also longed to transcend all seeing will scarcely be able to imagine how definitely and clearly these two processes coexist and are felt at the same time, as one contemplates the tragic myth. But all truly aesthetic spectators will confirm that among the peculiar effects of tragedy this coexistence is the most remarkable. Now transfer this phenomenon of the aesthetic spectator into an analogous process in the tragic artist, and you will have understood the genesis of the *tragic myth*. With the Apollinian art sphere he shares the complete pleasure in mere appearance and in seeing, yet at the same time he negates this pleasure and finds a still higher satisfaction in the destruction of the visible world of mere appearance.

The content of the tragic myth is, first of all, an epic event and the glorification of the fighting hero. But what is the origin of this enigmatic trait that the suffering and the fate of the hero, the most painful triumphs, the most agonizing oppositions of motives, in short, the exemplification of this wisdom of Silenus, or, to put it aesthetically, that which is ugly and disharmonic, is represented ever anew in such countless forms and with such a distinct preference—and precisely in the most fruitful and youthful period of a people? Surely a higher pleasure must be perceived in all this.

That life is really so tragic would least of all explain the origin of an art form—assuming that art is not merely imitation of the reality of nature but rather a metaphysical supplement of the reality of nature, placed beside it for its overcoming. The tragic myth, too, insofar as it belongs to art at all, participates fully in this metaphysical intention of art to transfigure. But what does it transfigure when it presents the world of appearance in the image of the suffering hero? Least of all the "reality" of this world of appearance, for it says to us: "Look there! Look closely! This is your life, this is the hand on the clock of your existence."

And the myth should show us this life in order to thus transfigure it for us? But if not, in what then lies the aesthetic pleasure with which we let these images, too, pass before us? I ask about the

Zorba the Greek — dance — (Dio?)

aesthetic pleasure, though I know full well that many of these images also produce at times a moral delight, for example, under the form of pity or moral triumph. But those who would derive the effect of the tragic solely from these moral sources—which, to be sure, has been the custom in aesthetics all too long—should least of all believe that they have thus accomplished something for art, which above all must demand purity in its sphere. If you would explain the tragic myth, the first requirement is to seek the pleasure that is peculiar to it in the purely aesthetic sphere, without transgressing into the region of pity, fear, or the morally sublime. How can the ugly and the disharmonic, the content of the tragic myth, stimulate aesthetic pleasure?

Here it becomes necessary to take a bold running start and leap into a metaphysics of art, by repeating the sentence written above,[1] that existence and the world seem justified only as an aesthetic phenomenon. In this sense, it is precisely the tragic myth that has to convince us that even the ugly and disharmonic are part of an artistic game that the will in the eternal amplitude of its pleasure plays with itself. But this primordial phenomenon of Dionysian art is difficult to grasp, and there is only one direct way to make it intelligible and grasp it immediately: through the wonderful significance of *musical dissonance*. Quite generally, only music, placed beside the world, can give us an idea of what is meant by the justification of the world as an aesthetic phenomenon. The joy aroused by the tragic myth has the same origin as the joyous sensation of dissonance in music. The Dionysian, with its primordial joy experienced even in pain, is the common source of music and tragic myth.

Is it not possible that by calling to our aid the musical relation of dissonance we may meanwhile have made the difficult problem of the tragic effect much easier? For we now understand what it means to wish to see tragedy and at the same time to long to get beyond all seeing: referring to the artistically employed dissonances, we should have to characterize the corresponding state by saying that we desire to hear and at the same time long to get beyond all hearing. That striving for the infinite, the wing-beat of longing that accompanies the highest delight in clearly perceived reality, reminds us that in both states we must recognize a Diony-

[1] Section 5.

sian phenomenon: again and again it reveals to us the playful construction and destruction of the individual world as the overflow of a primordial delight. Thus the dark Heraclitus compares the world-building force to a playing child that places stones here and there and builds sand hills only to overthrow them again.

In order, then, to form a true estimate of the Dionysian capacity of a people, we must think not only of their music, but also just as necessarily of their tragic myth, as the second witness of this capacity. Considering this extremely close relationship between music and myth, one must suppose that a degeneration and depravation of the one will involve a deterioration of the other, if the weakening of the myth really expresses a weakening of the Dionysian capacity. Concerning both, however, a glance at the development of the German character should not leave us in any doubt. In the opera, just as in the abstract character of our mythless existence, in an art degenerated to mere entertainment as well as in a life guided by concepts, the inartistic as well as life-consuming nature of Socratic optimism had revealed itself to us. Yet we were comforted by indications that nevertheless in some inaccessible abyss the German spirit still rests and dreams, undestroyed, in glorious health, profundity, and Dionysian strength, like a knight sunk in slumber; and from this abyss the Dionysian song rises to our ears to let us know that this German knight is still dreaming his primordial Dionysian myth in blissfully serious visions. Let no one believe that the German spirit has forever lost its mythical home when it can still understand so plainly the voices of the birds that tell of that home. Some day it will find itself awake in all the morning freshness following a tremendous sleep: then it will slay dragons, destroy vicious dwarfs,[2] wake Brünnhilde—and even Wotan's spear will not be able to stop its course!

My friends, you who believe in Dionysian music, you also know what tragedy means to us. There we have tragic myth reborn from music—and in this myth we can hope for everything and forget what is most painful. What is most painful for all of us, how-

---

[2] In his otherwise immensely perceptive and interesting interpretation, in the chapter on *The Birth of Tragedy* in *Ecce Homo*, Nietzsche claims at the end of section 1 that the "vicious dwarfs" (see also the next paragraph) represent "Christian priests." The imagery, of course, is taken from the Siegfried myth.

ever, is—the prolonged degradation in which the German genius has lived, estranged from house and home, in the service of vicious dwarfs. You understand my words—as you will also, in conclusion, understand my hopes.

25

Music and tragic myth are equally expressions of the Dionysian capacity of a people, and they are inseparable.[1] Both derive from a sphere of art that lies beyond the Apollinian; both transfigure a region in whose joyous chords dissonance as well as the terrible image of the world fade away charmingly; both play with the sting of displeasure, trusting in their exceedingly powerful magic arts; and by means of this play both justify the existence of even the "worst world." Thus the Dionysian is seen to be, compared to the Apollinian, the eternal and original artistic power that first calls the whole world of phenomena into existence—and it is only in the midst of this world that a new transfiguring illusion[2] becomes necessary in order to keep the animated world of individuation alive.

If we could imagine dissonance become man—and what else is man?—this dissonance, to be able to live, would need a splendid illusion[3] that would cover dissonance with a veil of beauty. This is the true artistic aim of Apollo in whose name we comprehend all those countless illusions of the beauty of mere appearance[4] that at every moment make life worth living at all and prompt the desire to live on in order to experience the next moment.

Of this foundation of all existence—the Dionysian basic ground of the world—not one whit more may enter the consciousness of the human individual than can be overcome again by this Apollinian power of transfiguration. Thus these two art drives must unfold their powers in a strict proportion, according to the law of eternal justice. Where the Dionysian powers rise up as impetuously as we experience them now, Apollo, too, must already have de-

---

[1] The rhapsody on Wagner continues, heedless of Mozart and Beethoven, Handel and Haydn, and scores of others.

[2] *Verklärungsschein* could also mean a transfiguring halo.

[3] *Illusion.*

[4] *Illusionen des schönen Scheins.*

scended among us, wrapped in a cloud; and the next generation will probably behold his most ample beautiful effects.

That this effect should be necessary, everybody should be able to feel most assuredly by means of intuition, provided he has ever felt, if only in a dream, that he was carried back into an ancient Greek existence. Walking under lofty Ionic colonnades, looking up toward a horizon that was cut off by pure and noble lines, finding reflections of his transfigured shape in the shining marble at his side, and all around him solemnly striding or delicately moving human beings, speaking with harmonious voices and in a rhythmic language of gestures—in view of this continual influx of beauty, would he not have to exclaim, raising his hand to Apollo: "Blessed people of Hellas! How great must Dionysus be among you if the god of Delos considers such magic necessary to heal your dithyrambic madness!"

To a man in such a mood, however, an old Athenian, looking up at him with the sublime eyes of Aeschylus, might reply: "But say this, too, curious stranger: how much did this people have to suffer to be able to become so beautiful! But now follow me to witness a tragedy, and sacrifice with me in the temple of both deities!"

THE
CASE OF WAGNER

A Musicians' Problem

Translator's Introduction

Although it is well known that Nietzsche and Wagner were friends for a while and then broke with each other, this essay has not received the attention it deserves. In English it has so far been available only in the old eighteen-volume edition of the *Collected Works*. An earlier version, done for the same collection, was discarded.

This is not the place to review the relation of the two men in detail, or to discuss and evaluate the literature on the subject. A rapid sketch of the background of this book must suffice.

Wagner, born in 1813—the same year as Nietzsche's father, as well as Verdi and Kierkegaard—was the only great genius whom Nietzsche ever knew intimately. The friendship was never even remotely symmetrical: apart from the difference in age, Nietzsche was still a student in November 1868 when, at twenty-four, he first met Wagner who, at fifty-five, had completed the bulk of his work. That winter Nietzsche was appointed to a chair of classical philology at the University of Basel, in Switzerland, within easy reach of Tribschen, also in Switzerland, where Wagner was then living. For Wagner, who had many detractors, it was nice to have a brilliant young professor as an ally; and when *The Birth of Tragedy* appeared, he wrote Nietzsche: "I have never yet read anything more beautiful than your book." What he liked best was, of course, the worst part of the book, the lengthy last part with its effusive appreciation of Wagner. Nor did he have anything but praise for those stylistic qualities which Nietzsche himself later criticized in his preface to the edition of 1886. Such imitation of his own manner and such acceptance of his image of himself at face value were the tribute Wagner exacted. Indeed, he asked for revisions in the endings of *The Birth* and, a little later, of the third "Untimely Meditation" on *Schopenhauer as Educator;* and he was displeased that in the second "meditation," *On the Use and Disadvantage of History for Life,* there was no explicit reference to him. He had no sense of Nietzsche's distinctive genius and mission: the younger man was to be his apostle—and a friend who could be asked to do the master's Christmas shopping and to help with other such chores.

No doubt there were many factors that helped to maintain the friendship for almost ten years. Not the least of these was a common enthusiasm for Schopenhauer, who had only recently begun to gain recognition as a major philospher. But as far as Nietzsche was concerned, the major consideration was surely that, for all his faults and foibles, Wagner was a great artist and incomparably more fascinating than anybody else Nietzsche knew. To be close personally to such a man, to be able to listen to him discoursing freely about his work and ideas, to belong to the master's inner circle—all that was not merely a privilege but seemed the best thing that had ever happened to the young professor. Not only was he able to try out his own ideas on a man of genius; he had found a second home. Nietzsche's father had died in 1849, before the boy was five, and his mother's narrow piety and lack of education had made his own home quite devoid of intellectual stimulation. Nietzsche had several good friends his own age, and some of these shared his enthusaism for Wagner—notably Erwin Rohde, the classical philologist, and Gustav Krug, who had tried to convert his friends to Wagner in the early eighteen-sixties.[1]

That Wagner was demanding and irritable, and that many of his emphatic opinions were very dubious, was obvious but seemed a small price for the benefits of such a friendship. Even Ernest Newman, who yields to none in his admiration and enthusiasm for Wagner, while he lacks any solid first-hand knowledge of Nietzsche and, on the basis of the "masterly epitome of Nietzsche's thinking"[2] written by one of the worst Nazi hacks, gives a thoroughly

---

[1] See Frederick R. Love's monograph on *Young Nietzsche and the Wagnerian Experience* (Chapel Hill, University of North Carolina Press, 1963). Love's most original contribution is that he shows how "the record of Nietzsche's compositions clearly provides a basis for modifying the widely held view of the philosopher as a passionate devotee of Wagnerian music" (p. viii). He also argues that "Wagner's music remained for Nietzsche an unsolved problem from first to last, a problem that was temporarily suppressed during the period of his closest association with the composer" (p. 80), and that "Nietzsche's infatuation with Wagnerian music . . . may indeed be regarded as an aberration" (p. 82). In other words, in 1878 Nietzsche did not break faith with himself, as the Wagnerians have claimed, but began to find himself.

[2] Ernest Newman, *The Life of Richard Wagner* (New York, Alfred A. Knopf), vol. IV, p. 335. The reference is to Alfred Bäumler's notorious

TRANSLATOR'S INTRODUCTION   149

misleading picture of Nietzsche, speaks of Wagner's "insatiable lust
for domination," admits that he wanted to be "an undisputed dic-
tator," [3] and describes how Wagner "worked himself into a parox-
ysm over Bismarck's tolerance towards the Jews." [4] In short, to
come fully into his own, Nietzsche had to break with Wagner.

As long as he lived at Tribschen, a lonely genius, Wagner's
impassioned faith in the superiority of the Germans and the inferi-
ority of other peoples, especially the French and the Jews, could
perhaps be decently ignored; but when Wagner came to terms with
the new German Empire and set up a great cultural center in Bayreuth, the time for a clear stand was at hand—and Nietzsche disso-
ciated himself from what Bayreuth symbolized.[5] Two further factors contributed to the break.

Nietzsche did not take Christianity lightly. His father, whose
memory he revered, had been a minister; so had both of his grand-
fathers; and his mother was a devout Christian. The significance of
Schopenhauer for Nietzsche and Wagner had been tied to Schopenhauer's frank atheism. In January 1878, when Wagner sent Nietzsche his *Parsifal,* with a humorous and friendly inscription, this
opera struck Nietzsche as shameless: Wagner was exploiting Christianity for theatrical effect, and the self-styled modern Aeschylus
was celebrating the anti-Greek ideal of what Wagner himself called
"pure foolishness." But what sealed the break was not even *Parsifal,* nor Nietzsche's reaction to Wagner. It was rather Nietzsche's
emergence into independence and Wagner's reaction to that.

In May 1878 Nietzsche sent Wagner his own new book, *Human,
All-Too-Human,* with a motto from Descartes and a dedication to
Voltaire. He was done with silence in the face of anti-French
outbursts. He had developed from Schopenhauer to Voltaire, and
from romantic essays to aphorisms influenced by French models.
He repudiated nationalism emphatically and proposed the ideal of
the "good European." All this was much more unforgivable in
Wagner's eyes than even *Parsifal* had been in Nietzsche's, and in

---

Nietzsche, der Philosoph und Politiker (1931), which led the Nazis to call
Bäumler to Berlin as Professor of Philosophy.

[3] *Ibid.,* p. 297.

[4] *Ibid.,* p. 598.

[5] Newman is thus more right than he himself realizes when he admits that
the break was precipitated "not by Wagner's art, but by Bayreuth" (p. 525).

August of that year Wagner attacked his erstwhile friend in the *Bayreuther Blätter*.

In 1874, when he was still working on the fourth "meditation," a eulogy of Wagner, Nietzsche had also jotted down in his notebooks a great many critical observations. *The Birth* had appeared in 1872, the first "meditation" in 1873, the second and third both in 1874, but the fourth gave Nietzsche a great deal of trouble and was not published until 1876. In *Human, All-Too-Human* (1878) Wagner's name does not appear—it is found in the preface added to the new edition of 1886—but the chapter on the souls of artists and writers contains observations and reflections prompted by Wagner. With this book Nietzsche came into his own.

In his later works Wagner is occasionally mentioned, but it was not until 1888, when his inhibitions had decreased drastically, that he published a small volume devoted entirely to "The Case of Wagner." That this book on Wagner troubled him, too, is evident even from its form: there is a postscript of considerable length, then a second postscript, and finally an epilogue.

Wagner was dead by then, and the problem that confronted Nietzsche was in part similar to that which Heine had resolved when he had published one of his best books, *Ludwig Börne* (1840), after Börne's death. The book had been greeted by a storm of indignation, but much later Thomas Mann was to say that of Heine's "works I have long loved the book on Börne most. . . . His psychology of the Nazarene type anticipates Nietzsche. . . . And incidentally this book contains the most superb German prose before Nietzsche. Incidentally? Ah, only those who understand the blissfully distracted smile with which he answered his friends when they warned him, presenting to him the human, personal, political offensiveness of the book, 'But isn't it expressed beautifully?'— only those comprehend what a memorable phenomenon this artist Jew has been among Germans!" [6]

After the storm broke in 1888, Nietzsche, who had meanwhile completed *Twilight of the Idols* and *The Antichrist,* divided his time between *Ecce Homo* and his final effort, *Nietzsche contra Wagner,* which he finished Christmas 1888, only a few days before

---

[6] Thomas Mann, "Notiz über Heine" (1908) in *Rede und Antwort* (1922: speech and response—an early collection of his non-fiction), p. 382.

his total collapse. This last book consists of passages "selected . . . from my older writings—some go back all the way to 1877— perhaps clarified here and there, above all, shortened." [7] The book was designed to show that *The Case of Wagner* had not been inspired by sudden malice, and that Nietzsche had long taken similar stands. Nietzsche sometimes wrote in relative haste, though the difference between the books he prepared for publication and the notes others published after his death remains very considerable. *Nietzsche contra Wagner* is perhaps his most beautiful book, and those seeking a commentary to *The Case of Wagner* would surely have been referred to the later, still briefer book, had they asked the author.

The present commentary consists of three parts: the translator's introduction, a number of footnotes to the translation, and a selection of pertinent passages from Nietzsche's correspondence of 1888. A weightier commentary does not seem necessary—and would not be in the spirit of this very short and elegant work.

W. K.

---

[7] Preface. A complete translation is included in *The Portable Nietzsche*, ed. and tr. by Walter Kaufmann.

THE
CASE OF WAGNER

———❖———

Turinese Letter of May 1888

ridendo dicere severum[1]—

---

[1] "Through what is laughable say what is somber." A variation of Horace's *ridentem dicere verum, quid vetat* ("What forbids us to tell the truth, laughing?") *Satires* I.24.

Preface

I have granted myself some small relief. It is not merely pure malice when I praise Bizet in this essay at the expense of Wagner. Interspersed with many jokes, I bring up a matter that is no joke. To turn my back on Wagner was for me a fate; to like anything at all again after that, a triumph. Perhaps nobody was more dangerously attached to—grown together with—Wagnerizing; nobody tried harder to resist it; nobody was happier to be rid of it. A long story! — You want a word for it?— If I were a moralist, who knows what I might call it? Perhaps self-overcoming.— But the philosopher has no love for moralists. Neither does he love pretty words.

What does a philosopher demand of himself first and last? To overcome his time in himself, to become "timeless." With what must he therefore engage in the hardest combat? With whatever marks him as the child of his time. Well, then! I am, no less than Wagner, a child of this time; that is, a decadent: but I comprehended this, I resisted it. The philosopher in me resisted.

Nothing has preoccupied me more profoundly than the problem of decadence—I had reasons. "Good and evil" is merely a variation of that problem. Once one has developed a keen eye for the symptoms of decline, one understands morality, too—one understands what is hiding under its most sacred names and value formulas: impoverished life, the will to the end, the great weariness. Morality negates life.

For such a task I required a special self-discipline: to take sides against everything sick in me, including Wagner, including Schopenhauer, including all of modern "humaneness."— A profound estrangement, cold, sobering up—against everything that is of this time, everything timely—and most desirable of all, the eye of Zarathustra, an eye that beholds the whole fact of man at a tremendous distance—below. For such a goal—what sacrifice wouldn't be fitting? what "self-overcoming"? what "self-denial"?

My greatest experience was a recovery. Wagner is merely one of my sicknesses.

Not that I wish to be ungrateful to this sickness. When in this essay I assert the proposition that Wagner is harmful, I wish no less to assert for whom he is nevertheless indispensable—for the philosopher. Others may be able to get along without Wagner; but the philosopher is not free to do without Wagner. He has to be the bad conscience of his time:[1] for that he needs to understand it best. But confronted with the labyrinth of the modern soul, where could he find a guide more initiated, a more eloquent prophet of the soul, than Wagner? Through Wagner modernity speaks most intimately, concealing neither its good nor its evil—having forgotten all sense of shame. And conversely: one has almost completed an account of the value of what is modern once one has gained clarity about what is good and evil in Wagner.

I understand perfectly when a musician says today: "I hate Wagner, but I can no longer endure any other music." But I'd also understand a philosopher who would declare: "Wagner sums up modernity. There is no way out, one must first become a Wagnerian."

---

[1] Cf. *Beyond Good and Evil,* section 212.

1

Yesterday I heard—would you believe it?—Bizet's master-piece, for the twentieth time. Again I stayed there with tender de-votion; again I did not run away. This triumph over my impatience surprises me. How such a work makes one perfect! One becomes a "masterpiece" oneself.

Really, every time I heard *Carmen* I seemed to myself more of a philosopher, a better philosopher, than I generally consider my-self: so patient do I become, so happy, so Indian, so settled.— To sit five hours: the first stage of holiness!

May I say that the tone of Bizet's orchestra is almost the only one I can still endure? That other orchestral tone which is now the fashion, Wagner's, brutal, artificial, and "innocent" at the same time—thus it speaks all at once to the three senses of the modern soul—how harmful for me is this Wagnerian orchestral tone! I call it *sirocco*. I break out into a disagreeable sweat. *My* good weather is gone.

This music seems perfect to me. It approaches lightly, sup-plely, politely. It is pleasant, it does not *sweat*. "What is good is light; whatever is divine moves on tender feet": first principle of my aesthetics. This music is evil, subtly fatalistic: at the same time it re-mains popular—its subtlety belongs to a race, not to an individual. It is rich. It is precise. It builds, organizes, finishes: thus it consti-tutes the opposite of the polyp in music, the "infinite melody." Have more painful tragic accents ever been heard on the stage? How are they achieved? Without grimaces. Without counterfeit. Without the *lie* of the great style.

Finally, this music treats the listener as intelligent, as if him-self a musician—and is in this respect, too, the counterpart of Wagner, who was, whatever else he was, at any rate the most *impo-lite* genius in the world (Wagner treats us as if——he says some-thing so often—till one despairs—till one believes it).

Once more: I become a better human being when this Bizet speaks to me. Also a better musician, a better *listener*. Is it even possible to listen better?— I actually bury my ears under this music to hear its causes. It seems to me I experience its genesis—I tremble before dangers that accompany some strange risk; I am delighted by strokes of good fortune of which Bizet is innocent.— And, oddly, deep down I don't think of it, or don't know how much I think about it. For entirely different thoughts are meanwhile running through my head.

Has it been noticed that music liberates the spirit? gives wings to thought? that one becomes more of a philosopher the more one becomes a musician?— The gray sky of abstraction rent as if by lightning; the light strong enough for the filigree of things; the great problems near enough to grasp; the world surveyed as from a mountain.— I have just defined the pathos of philosophy.— And unexpectedly answers drop into my lap, a little hail of ice and wisdom, of *solved* problems.— Where am I?— Bizet makes me fertile. Whatever is good makes me fertile. I have no other gratitude, nor do I have any other proof for what is good.

2

This work, too, redeems; Wagner is not the only "redeemer." With this work one takes leave of the damp north, of all the steam of the Wagnerian ideal. Even the plot spells redemption from that. From Mérimée it still has the logic in passion, the shortest line, the harsh necessity; above all, it has what goes with the torrid zone: the dryness of the air, the *limpidezza*[1] in the air. In every respect, the climate is changed. Another sensuality, another sensibility speaks here, another cheerfulness. This music is cheerful, but not in a French or German way. Its cheerfulness is African; fate hangs over it; its happiness is brief, sudden, without pardon. I envy Bizet for having had the courage for this sensibility which had hitherto had no language in the cultivated music of Europe—for this more southern, brown, burnt sensibility.— How the yellow afternoons of its happiness do us good! We look into the distance as we listen: did we ever find the sea smoother?— And how soothingly the Moorish dance speaks to us? How even our insatiability for once gets to know satiety in this lascivious melancholy!

Finally, love—love translated back into nature. Not the love of a "higher virgin"! No Senta-sentimentality![2] But love as *fatum*,

---

[1] Limpidity, clarity
[2] Senta is the heroine of Wagner's *Flying Dutchman*.

as fatality, cynical, innocent, cruel—and precisely in this a piece of nature. That love which is war in its means, and at bottom the deadly hatred of the sexes!— I know no case where the tragic joke that constitutes the essence of love is expressed so strictly, translated with equal terror into a formula, as in Don José's last cry, which concludes the work:

> "Yes. I have killed her,
> I—my adored Carmen!"

Such a conception of love (the only one worthy of a philosopher) is rare: it raises a work of art above thousands.[3] For on the average, artists do what all the world does, even worse—they misunderstand love. Wagner, too, misunderstood it. They believe one becomes selfless in love because one desires the advantage of another human being, often against one's own advantage. But in return for that they want to *possess* the other person.—Even God does not constitute an exception at this point. He is far from thinking, "What is it to you if I love you?" [4]—he becomes terrible when one does not love him in return. L'amour—this saying remains true among gods and men—est de tous les sentiments le plus égoïste, et par conséquent, lorsqu'il est blessé, le moins généreux. (B. Constant.) [5]

3

You begin to see how much this music improves me?— Il faut méditerraniser la musique:[1] I have reasons for this formula (Beyond Good and Evil, Aph. 255). The return to nature, health,

---

[3] Compare Nietzsche's admiration for Shakespeare's characterization of Brutus in Julius Caesar (discussed with quotations in Kaufmann's Nietzsche—see Index, under Brutus), and Oscar Wilde's Ballad of Reading Gaol (1898): "For all men kill the thing they love . . ."

[4] Goethe, Wahrheit und Dichtung, Book 14; cf. Wilhelm Meisters Lehrjahre, IV.9 (Theatralische Sendung, VI.4), where the wording is ever so slightly different. In his autobiography Goethe links these words with Spinoza's famous dictum: "Whoever loves God cannot will that God should love him in return" (Ethics, V.19).

[5] "Love is of all sentiments the most egoistic, and, as a consequence, when it is wounded, the least generous."

[1] "Music should be Mediterranized."

cheerfulness, youth, *virtue!*— And yet I was one of the most corrupted Wagnerians.— I was capable of taking Wagner seriously.—
Ah, this old magician, how much he imposed upon us! The first
thing his art offers us is a magnifying glass: one looks through it,
one does not trust one's own eyes—everything looks big, *even
Wagner.*— What a clever rattlesnake! It has filled our whole life
with its rattling about "devotion," about "loyalty," about "purity";
and with its praise of chastity it withdrew from the corrupted
world.— And we believed it in all these things.—

But you do not hear me? You, too, prefer Wagner's problem
to Bizet's? I, too, do not underestimate it; it has its peculiar magic.
The problem of redemption is certainly a venerable problem. There
is nothing about which Wagner has thought more deeply than redemption: his opera is the opera of redemption. Somebody or other
always wants to be redeemed in his work: sometimes a male, sometimes a little female—this is *his* problem.— And how richly he
varies his leitmotif! What rare, what profound dodges! Who if not
Wagner would teach us that innocence prefers to redeem interesting sinners? (The case in *Tannhäuser.*) Or that even the Wandering Jew is redeemed, settles down, when he marries? (The case in
The Flying Dutchman.) Or that old corrupted females prefer to be
redeemed by chaste youths? (The case of Kundry.[2]) Or that beautiful maidens like best to be redeemed by a knight who is a Wagnerian? (The case in *Die Meistersinger.*) Or that married women, too,
enjoy being redeemed by a knight? (The case of Isolde.) Or that
"the old God," after having compromised himself morally in every
respect, is finally redeemed by a free spirit and immoralist? (The
case in the *Ring.*) Do admire this final profundity above all! Do
you understand it? I—beware of understanding it.

That yet other lessons may be learned from the works just
named I'd sooner demonstrate than deny. That a Wagnerian ballet
may drive one to despair—and virtue! (Again the case of *Tannhäuser.*) That it may have the direst consequences if one doesn't go
to bed at the right time. (Once more the case of *Lohengrin.*) That
one should never know too precisely whom exactly one has married. (For the third time, the case of *Lohengrin.*)

---

[2] In *Parsifal.*

Tristan and Isolde glorifies the perfect spouse who in a certain case has only the single question: "But why didn't you tell me this before? Nothing simpler than that!" Answer:

> *"That I may not tell you;*
>   *and what you ask*
>   *you may never know."*

Lohengrin contains a solemn excommunication of inquiry and questioning. Wagner thus represents the Christian concept, "you ought to and must *believe."* It is a crime against what is highest and holiest to be scientific.

The Flying Dutchman preaches the sublime doctrine that woman makes even the most restless man stable; in Wagnerian terms, she "redeems" him. Here we permit ourselves a question. Supposing this were true, would it also be desirable?

What becomes of the "Wandering Jew" [3] whom a woman adores and makes stable? He mercly ceases to be eternal; he gets married, he is of no further concern to us.

Translated into reality: the danger for artists, for geniuses— and who else is the "Wandering Jew"?—is woman: adoring women confront them with corruption. Hardly any of them have character enough not to be corrupted—or "redeemed"—when they find themselves treated like gods: soon they condescend to the level of the women.— Man is a coward, confronted with the Eternal-Feminine[4]—and the females know it.— In many cases of feminine love, perhaps including the most famous ones above all, love is merely a more refined form of parasitism, a form of nestling down in another soul, sometimes even in the flesh of another—alas, always decidedly at the expense of "the host"!

One knows Goethe's fate in moraline-sour, old-maidish Germany. He always seemed offensive to Germans; he had honest admirers only among Jewesses. Schiller, the "noble" Schiller, who lambasted the ears of the Germans with big words—*he* was after their hearts. What did they hold against Goethe? The "mount of

---

[3] In German, literally the "Eternal Jew."

[4] Goethe's *Faust* ends: "The Eternal-Feminine / Lures us to perfection." But the classical representative of the attitude toward marriage expressed in the sentences about the "Wandering Jew" was nevertheless Goethe.

Venus"; and that he had written *Venetian Epigrams*. Klopstock[5] already felt called upon to deliver a moral sermon to him; there was a time when Herder[6] liked to use the word "Priapus" whenever he spoke of Goethe. Even *Wilhelm Meister* was considered merely a symptom of decline, "going to the dogs" as far as morals go. Niebuhr,[7] for example, was enraged by the "menagerie of tame animals" and the "worthlessness" of the hero, and finally he broke out into the lament, fit to be sung by Biterolf:[8] "Nothing could easily make a more painful impression than a great spirit who deprives himself of his wings and seeks virtuosity in something much inferior, *renouncing what is higher.*"— Above all, however, the higher virgins were indignant: all the petty courts, every kind of "Wartburg"[9] in Germany crossed themselves against Goethe, against the "unclean spirit" in Goethe.

This is the story Wagner put into music. He *redeems* Goethe, that goes without saying; but in such a way that at the same time he himself sides shrewdly with the higher virgin. Goethe is saved: a prayer saves him, a higher virgin *lures him to perfection.*

What Goethe might have thought of Wagner?— Goethe once asked himself what danger threatened all romantics: the fatality of romanticism. His answer was: "suffocating of the rumination of moral and religious absurdities." In brief: *Parsifal.*

The philosopher adds an epilogue to this: *Holiness*—perhaps

---

[5] Friedrich Gottlieb Klopstock (1724–1803), twenty-five years older than Goethe, was the most renowned German poet of his generation.

[6] Johann Gottfried von Herder (1744–1803) studied under Kant and became one of Germany's most influential writers. His major works include the first great collection of folk poetry, *Stimmen der Völker in Liedern* (voices of peoples in songs), 1778–79, and *Ideen zur Philosophie der Geschichte der Menschheit* (ideas on the philosophy of the history of humanity), 1784–91. He was a friend of, and major influence on, the young Goethe, and in 1776 he became general superintendent and court preacher in Weimar.

[7] Barthold Georg Niebuhr (1776–1831) was a statesman and historian. "Niebuhr's *Roman History* counts among epoch-making histories both as marking an era in the study of its special subject and for its momentous influence on the general conception of history" (*Encyclopaedia Britannica*, 11th ed., vol. XIX, p. 668).

[8] Biterolf is one of the knights in Wagner's *Tannhäuser.*

[9] Luther translated the Bible on the Wartburg, and on one of the walls tourists are shown an inkspot which originated, according to tradition, when Luther threw his inkwell at the devil who had appeared to him.

the last thing the people and women still get to see of higher values, the horizon of the ideal for all who are by nature myopic. But among philosophers this is, like every horizon, a mere case of lack of understanding, a sort of shutting the gate at the point where *their* world only begins—*their* danger, their ideal, their desideratum.— To say it more politely: *la philosophie ne suffit pas au grand nombre. Il lui faut la sainteté.*—[10]

<h1 style="text-align:center">4</h1>

I shall still relate the story of the *Ring*. It belongs here. It, too, is a story of redemption: only this time it is Wagner who is redeemed.—

Half his life, Wagner believed in the Revolution as much as ever a Frenchman believed in it. He searched for it in the runic writing of myth, he believed that in Siegfried he had found the typical revolutionary.

"Whence comes all misfortune in the world?" Wagner asked himself. From "old contracts," he answered, like all revolutionary ideologists. In plain: from customs, laws, moralities, institutions, from everything on which the old world, the old society rests. "How can one rid the world of misfortune? How can one abolish the old society?" Only by declaring war against "contracts" (tradition, morality). *That is what Siegfried does.* He starts early, very early: his very genesis is a declaration of war against morality—he comes into this world through adultery, through incest.— It is not the saga but Wagner who invented this radical trait; at this point he revised the saga.

Siegfried continues as he has begun: he merely follows his first impulse, he overthrows everything traditional, all reverence, all *fear*. Whatever displeases him he stabs to death. Without the least respect, he tackles old deities. But his main enterprise aims *to emancipate woman*—"to redeem Brunhilde."— Siegfried and Brunhilde; the sacrament of free love; the rise of the golden age; the twilight of the gods for the old morality—*all ill has been abolished*.

For a long time, Wagner's ship followed *this* course gaily. No

---

[10] "Philosophy is not suited for the masses. What they need is holiness."

doubt, this was where Wagner sought his highest goal.— What happened? A misfortune. The ship struck a reef; Wagner was stuck. The reef was Schopenhauer's philosophy; Wagner was stranded on a *contrary* world view. What had he transposed into music? Optimism. Wagner was ashamed. Even an optimism for which Schopenhauer had coined an evil epithet—*infamous*[1] optimism. He was ashamed a second time. He reflected for a long while, his situation seemed desperate.— Finally, a way out dawned on him: the reef on which he was shipwrecked—what if he interpreted it as the *goal,* as the secret intent, as the true significance of his voyage? To be shipwrecked *here*—that was a goal, too. *Bene navigavi, cum naufragium feci.*[2]

So he translated the *Ring* into Schopenhauer's terms. Everything goes wrong, everything perishes, the new world is as bad as the old: the *nothing,* the Indian Circe beckons.

Brunhilde was initially supposed to take her farewell with a song in honor of free love, putting off the world with the hope for a socialist utopia in which "all turns out well"—but now gets something else to do. She has to study Schopenhauer first; she has to transpose the fourth book of *The World as Will and Representation* into verse. *Wagner was redeemed.*

In all seriousness, this *was* a redemption. The benefit Schopenhauer conferred on Wagner is immeasurable. Only the *philosopher of decadence* gave to the artist of decadence—*himself.*

5

To *the artist of decadence:* there we have the crucial words. And here my seriousness begins. I am far from looking on guilelessly while this decadent corrupts our health—and music as well. Is Wagner a human being at all? Isn't he rather a sickness? He makes sick whatever he touches—*he has made music sick*—

A typical decadent who has a sense of necessity in his corrupted taste, who claims it as a higher taste, who knows how to get his corruption accepted as law, as progress, as fulfillment.

And he is not resisted. His seductive force increases tremen-

---

[1] *Ruchlos.*
[2] "When I suffer shipwreck, I have navigated well."

dously, smoke clouds of incense surround him, the misunderstandings about him parade as "gospel"—he hasn't by any means con-
verted only the *poor in spirit*.

I feel the urge to open the windows a little. Air! More air!—[1]

That people in Germany should deceive themselves about Wagner does not surprise me. The opposite would surprise me. The
Germans have constructed a Wagner for themselves whom they
can revere: they have never been psychologists; their gratitude consists in misunderstanding. But that people in Paris, too, deceive
themselves about Wagner, though there they are hardly anything
anymore except psychologists! And in St. Petersburg, where they
guess things that aren't guessed even in Paris! How closely related
Wagner must be to the whole of European decadence to avoid being experienced by them as a decadent. He belongs to it: he is its
protagonist, its greatest name.— One honors oneself when raising
him to the clouds.

For that one does not resist him, this itself is a sign of decadence. The instincts are weakened. What one ought to shun is
found attractive. One puts to one's lips what drives one yet faster
into the abyss.

Is an example desired? One only need observe the regimen
that those suffering from anemia or gout or diabetes prescribe for
themselves. Definition of a vegetarian: one who requires a corrob-
orant diet. To sense that what is harmful is harmful, to be *able* to
forbid oneself something harmful, is a sign of youth and vitality.
The exhausted are *attracted* by what is harmful: the vegetarian by
vegetables.[2] Sickness itself can be a stimulant to life: only one has
to be healthy enough for this stimulant.[3]

---

[1] *Luft! Mehr Luft!* Goethe's last words are said to have been: *Licht! Mehr Licht!* "Light! More light!"

[2] Wagner was a doctrinaire vegetarian, and Nietzsche's brother-in-law, Bern-
hard Förster, copied Wagner's vegetarianism along with his anti-Semitic
ideology; so did Hitler. Nietzsche wrote his mother about Förster: "For my
personal taste such an agitator is something impossible for closer acquaint-
ance. . . . Vegetarianism, as Dr. Förster wants it, makes such natures only
still more petulant" (*Briefe an Mutter und Schwester* [letters to mother and
sister, Leipzig, 1909] no. 409; for further quotations from letters about
Förster see Kaufmann's *Nietzsche,* Chapter 1, section III).

[3] For parallel passages in Nietzsche's other works, see the last three pages
of Chapter 4, section I, in Kaufmann's *Nietzsche.*

Wagner increases exhaustion: that is why he attracts the weak and exhausted. Oh, the rattlesnake-happiness of the old master when he always saw precisely "the little children" coming unto him! [4]

I place this perspective at the outset: Wagner's art is sick. The problems he presents on the stage—all of them problems of hysterics—the convulsive nature of his affects, his overexcited sensibility, his taste that required ever stronger spices, his instability which he dressed up as principles, not least of all the choice of his heroes and heroines—consider them as physiological types (a pathological gallery)!—all of this taken together represents a profile of sickness that permits no further doubt. *Wagner est une névrose.*[5] Perhaps nothing is better known today, at least nothing has been better studied, than the Protean character of degeneration that here conceals itself in the chrysalis of art and artist. Our physicians and physiologists confront their most interesting case in Wagner, at least a very complete case. Precisely because nothing is more modern than this total sickness, this lateness and overexcitement of the nervous mechanism, Wagner is *the modern artist par excellence,* the Cagliostro of modernity. In his art all that the modern world requires most urgently is mixed in the most seductive manner: the three great *stimulantia* of the exhausted—the *brutal,* the *artificial,* and the *innocent* (idiotic).[6]

Wagner represents a great corruption of music. He has guessed that it is a means to excite weary nerves—and with that he has made music sick. His inventiveness is not inconsiderable in the art of goading again those who are weariest, calling back into life those who are half dead. He is a master of hypnotic tricks, he manages to throw down the strongest like bulls. Wagner's *success*—his success with nerves and consequently women—has turned the whole world of ambitious musicians into disciples of his secret art. And not only the ambitious, the *clever,* too.— Only sick music makes money today; our big theaters subsist on Wagner.

---

[4] Allusion to Matthew 19:14, Mark 10:14, Luke 18:16.

[5] "Wagner is a neurosis."

[6] The words "idiot" and "idiotic" occur frequently in Nietzsche's writings—after his discovery of Dostoevsky early in 1887. See Kaufmann's *Nietzsche,* Chapter 12, note 2, where the relevant passages are cited.

6

I permit myself some exhilaration again. Suppose it were the case that Wagner's *success* became incarnate, took human form and, dressed up as a philanthropic music scholar, mixed with young artists. How do you suppose he would talk?

My friends, he would say, let us have a few words among ourselves. It is easier to write bad music than good. What if it were more profitable, too? more effective, persuasive, inspiring, reliable—*Wagnerian?*—*Pulchrum est paucorum hominum.*[1] Bad enough. We understand Latin; perhaps we also understand our own advantage. What is beautiful has a fly in its ointment: we know that. Why, then, have beauty? Why not rather that which is great, sublime, gigantic—that which moves *masses?*— Once more: it is easier to be gigantic than to be beautiful; we know that.

We know the masses, we know the theater. The best among those who sit there—German youths, horned Siegfrieds, and other Wagnerians—require the sublime, the profound, the overwhelming. That much we are capable of. And the others who also sit there—the culture *crétins,* the petty snobs, the eternally feminine, those with a happy digestion, in sum, the *people*—also require the sublime, the profound, the overwhelming. They all have the same logic. "Whoever throws us is strong; whoever elevates us is divine; whoever leads us to have intimations is profound."— Let us make up our minds, honored musicians: we want to throw them, we want to elevate them, we want to lead them to have intimations. That much we are capable of.

Regarding the matter of inducing intimations: this is the point of departure for our concept of "style." Above all, no thought! Nothing is more compromising than a thought. Rather the state preceding thought, the throng of yet unborn thoughts, the promise of future thoughts, the world as it was before God created it—a recrudescence of chaos.— Chaos induces intimations.

To speak in the language of the master: infinity, but without melody.

Secondly, as far as throwing people is concerned, this really

---

[1] "What is beautiful belongs to the few."

belongs partly in physiology. Let us study the instruments above all. Some of them persuade even the intestines (they *open* the gates, as Handel put it); others bewitch the marrow of the spine. The color of the tone is decisive; what it is that resounds is almost a matter of indifference. This is the point to refine. Why squander ourselves? Regarding the tone, let us be characteristic to the point of folly. People will give credit to our spirit if our tones seem to pose many riddles. Let us agitate the nerves, let us slay them, let us handle lightning and thunder—that will throw them.—

Above all, however, *passion* throws people.— Let us reach an understanding about passion. Nothing is cheaper than passion. One can dispense with all the virtues of counterpoint, one need not have learned a thing—passion is one ability we always have. Beauty is difficult: beware of beaufy!— And *melody!* Slander, my friends, let us slander, if we are at all serious about our ideal, let us slander melody! Nothing is more dangerous than a beautiful melody. Nothing corrupts taste more surely. We are lost, my friends, once beautiful melodies are loved again!—

Principle: melody is immoral. *Proof:* Palestrina. *Practical application: Parsifal.* The lack of melody even sanctifies.—

And this is the definition of passion. Passion—or the gymnastics of what is ugly on the rope of enharmonics.— Let us dare, my friends, to be ugly. Wagner has dared it. Let us dauntlessly roll in front of us the mud of the most contrary harmonies. Let us not spare our hands. Only thus will we become *natural.*

A final bit of advice! Perhaps it includes everything else. *Let us be idealists!* This is, if not the cleverest thing we can do at least the wisest. To elevate[2] men one has to be sublime[3] oneself. Let us walk on clouds, let us harangue the infinite, let us surround ourselves with symbols! *Sursum! Bumbum!*—there is no better advice. The "swelled bosom" shall be our argument, the beautiful sentiment our advocate. Virtue prevails even over counterpoint. "Whoever makes us better cannot fail to be good himself": thus mankind has always inferred. So let us improve mankind![4] Thus one be-

---

[2] *Erheben.*

[3] *Erhaben.*

[4] Nietzsche's next book, *Twilight of the Idols,* contains a chapter with the sarcastic title, "The 'Improvers' of Mankind."

comes good (thus one even becomes a "classic" [5]—Schiller became a "classic"). The hunt for low excitement of the senses, for so-called beauty, has enervated the Italians: let us remain German! Even Mozart's attitude to music was—as Wagner said to comfort *us*—at bottom frivolous.

Let us never admit that music "serves recreation"; that it "exhilarates"; that it "gives pleasure." *Let us never give pleasure!* We are lost as soon as art is again thought of hedonistically.— That is bad eighteenth century.— Nothing on the other hand should be more advisable than a dose of—*hypocrisy, sit venia verbo.*[6] That lends dignity.— And let us choose the hour when it is decent to look black, to heave sighs publicly, to heave Christian sighs, to make an exhibition of great Christian pity. "Man is corrupt: who redeems him? *what redeems him?*"— Let us not answer. Let us be cautious. Let us resist our ambition which would found religions. But nobody may doubt that *we* redeem him, that *our* music alone saves.— (Wagner's essay, *Religion and Art.*)

7

Enough! Enough! My cheerful strokes, I fear, may have revealed sinister reality all too clearly—the picture of a decay of art, a decay of the artists as well. The latter, the decay of a character, could perhaps find preliminary expression in this formula: the musician now becomes an actor, his art develops more and more as a talent to *lie*. I shall have an opportunity (in a chapter of my main work, entitled "Toward a Physiology of Art" [1]) to show in more detail how this over-all change of art into histrionics is no less an expression of physiological degeneration (more precisely, a form of hystericism) than every single corruption and infirmity of the art inaugurated by Wagner: for example, the visual restlessness which requires one continually to change one's position. One doesn't understand a thing about Wagner as long as one finds in him merely an arbitrary play of nature, a whim, an accident. He was no

---

[5] *Klassiker,* a term pre-eminently associated with Goethe and Schiller.
[6] "May this word be forgiven."
[1] This was not actually written, but notes for it were included in the posthumously published *Will to Power,* in Book 3, Part 4.

"fragmentary," "hapless," or "contradictory" genius, as people have said. Wagner was something *perfect,* a typical decadent in whom there is no trace of "free will" and in whom every feature is necessary. If anything in Wagner is interesting it is the logic with which a physiological defect makes move upon move and takes step upon step as practice and procedure, as innovation in principles, as a crisis in taste.

For the present I merely dwell on the question of *style.*— What is the sign of every *literary decadence?* That life no longer dwells in the whole. The word becomes sovereign and leaps out of the sentence, the sentence reaches out and obscures the meaning of the page, the page gains life at the expense of the whole—the whole is no longer a whole.[2] But this is the simile of every style of *decadence*: every time, the anarchy of atoms, disgregation of the will, "freedom of the individual," to use moral terms—expanded into a political theory, "*equal* rights for all." Life, *equal* vitality, the vibration and exuberance of life pushed back into the smallest forms; the rest, *poor* in life. Everywhere paralysis, arduousness, torpidity *or* hostility and chaos: both more and more obvious the higher one ascends in forms of organization. The whole no longer lives at all: it is composite, calculated, artificial, and artifact.—

Wagner begins from a hallucination—not of sounds but of gestures. Then he seeks the sign language of sounds for them. If one would admire him, one should watch him at work at this point: how he separates, how he gains small units, how he animates these, severs them, and makes them visible. But this exhausts his strength: the rest is no good. How wretched, how embarrassed, how amateurish is his manner of "development," his attempt to at least interlard what has not grown out of each other. His manners recall those of the *frères* de Goncourt,[3] who are quite generally pertinent to Wagner's style: one feels a kind of compassion for so much distress. That Wagner disguised as a principle his incapacity

---

[2] To those who know Nietzsche's own books only superficially, this may seem to be a perfect description of *his* style. But see the second paragraph of his preface to *The Case of Wagner,* and Kaufmann's *Nietzsche,* Chapter 2, section I.

[3] Cf. *Twilight of the Idols* (in *Portable Nietzsche*), p. 517 ("Skirmishes of an Untimely Man," section 7).

for giving organic form, that he establishes a "dramatic style" where we merely establish his incapacity for any style whatever, this is in line with a bold habit that accompanied Wagner through his whole life: he posits a principle where he lacks a capacity (— very different in this respect, incidentally, from the old Kant who preferred another boldness: wherever he lacked a principle he posited a special human capacity).[4]

Once more: Wagner is admirable and gracious only in the invention of what is smallest, in spinning out the details. Here one is entirely justified in proclaiming him a master of the first rank, as our greatest *miniaturist* in music who crowds into the smallest space an infinity of sense and sweetness. His wealth of colors, of half shadows, of the secrecies of dying light spoils one to such an extent that afterward almost all other musicians seem too robust.

If one would believe me one should have to derive the highest conception of Wagner not from what is liked about him today. That has been invented to persuade the masses; from that we recoil as from an all too impudent fresco.[5] Of what concern to *us* is the *agaçant*[6] brutality of the *Tannhäuser* Overture. Or the circus of *Walküre?* Whatever of Wagner's music has become popular also apart from the theater shows dubious taste and corrupts taste. The *Tannhäuser* March I suspect of *bonhommerie;*[7] the overture of *The Flying Dutchman* is noise about nothing;[8] the *Lohengrin* Prelude furnished the first example, only too insidious, only too successful, of hypnotism by means of music (—I do not like whatever music has no ambition beyond persuasion of the nerves). But quite apart from the *magnétiseur*[9] and fresco-painter Wagner, there is another Wagner who lays aside small gems: our greatest melancholiac in music, full of glances, tendernesses, and comforting words in which nobody has anticipated him, the master in tones of a heavy-hearted and drowsy happiness.

---

[4] Cf. *Beyond Good and Evil,* section 11.

[5] *Einem allzufrechen Affresko.*

[6] *Provocative.*

[7] *Biedermännerei.*

[8] *Ein Lärm um nichts.* The German version of Shakespeare's *Much Ado About Nothing* is entitled *Viel Lärmen um Nichts.*

[9] Hypnotist.

A lexicon of Wagner's most intimate words, all of them short things of five to fifteen measures, all of it music *nobody knows*.— Wagner had the virtue of decadents: pity.

8

"Very good. But how *can* one lose a taste for this decadent if one does not happen to be a musician, if one does not happen to be a decadent oneself?"

On the contrary, how can one *fail* to do it? Just try it.— You do not know who Wagner is: a first-rate actor. Is a more profound, a *weightier* effect to be found in the theater? Just look at these youths —rigid, pale, breathless! These are the Wagnerians: they understand nothing about music—and yet Wagner becomes master over them.— Wagner's art has the pressure of a hundred atmospheres: stoop! what else can one do?

The actor Wagner is a tyrant; his pathos topples every taste, every resistance.— Who equals the persuasive power of these gestures? Who else envisages gestures with such assurance, so clearly from the start? The way Wagner's pathos holds its breath, refuses to let go an extreme feeling, achieves a terrifying *duration* of states when even a moment threatens to strangle us—

Was Wagner a musician at all? At any rate, there was something else that he was more: namely, an incomparable *histrio*,[1] the greatest mime, the most amazing genius of the theater ever among Germans, our *scenic artist par excellence*. He belongs elsewhere, not in the history of music: one should not confuse him with the genuine masters of that. Wagner *and* Beethoven—that is blasphemy and really wrongs even Wagner.— As a musician, too, he was only what he was in general: he *became* a musician, he *became* a poet because the tyrant within him, his actor's genius, compelled him. One cannot begin to figure out Wagner until one figures out his dominant instinct.

Wagner was *not* a musician by instinct. He showed this by abandoning all lawfulness and, more precisely, all style in music in order to turn it into what he required, theatrical rhetoric, a means of expression, of underscoring gestures, of suggestion, of the psy-

---

[1] Actor.

chologically picturesque. Here we may consider Wagner an inventor
and innovator of the first rank—*he has increased music's capacity
for language to the point of making it immeasurable:* he is the
Victor Hugo of music as language. Always presupposing that one
first allows that under certain circumstances music may be not music but language, instrument, *ancilla*[2] *dramaturgica*. Wagner's music, if not shielded by theater taste, which is a very tolerant taste, is
simply bad music, perhaps the worst ever made. When a musician
can no longer count up to three he becomes "dramatic," he becomes "Wagnerian."

Wagner almost discovered how much magic is still possible
with music that has been dissolved and, as it were, made *elementary*. His consciousness of that is downright uncanny, no less than
his instinctive realization that he simply did not require the higher
lawfulness, *style*. What is elementary is *sufficient*—sound, movement, color, in brief the sensuousness of music. Wagner never cal-
culates as a musician, from some sort of musician's conscience:
what he wants is effect, nothing but effect. And he knows those on
whom he wants to achieve his effects.— At this point he is as free
from qualms as Schiller was, as every man of the theater is, and he
also has the same contempt for the world which he prostrates at his
feet.— One is an actor by virtue of being ahead of the rest of mankind in one insight: what is meant to have the effect of truth must
not be true. The proposition was formulated by Talma;[3] it contains
the whole psychology of the actor; it also contains—we need not
doubt it—his morality. Wagner's music is never true.

But *it is taken for true;* and thus it is in order.

As long as we are still childlike, and Wagnerians as well, we
consider Wagner himself rich, even as a paragon of a squanderer,
even as the owner of huge estates in the realm of sound. He is
admired for what young Frenchmen admire in Victor Hugo, "the
royal largesse." Later one comes to admire both of them for the
opposite reasons: as masters and models of economy, as *shrewd*
hosts. Nobody equals their talent for presenting a princely table at
modest expense.

The Wagnerian, with his believer's stomach, actually feels

---

[2] Handmaiden.
[3] François Joseph Talma (1763–1826) was a celebrated French actor.

sated by the fare his master's magic evokes for him. The rest of us, demanding *substance* above all else, in books as well as in music, are scarcely taken care of by merely "represented" tables and hence are much worse off. To say it plainly: Wagner does not give us enough to chew on. His *recitativo*—little meat, rather more bone, and a lot of broth—I have called *"alla genovese"*—without the least intention of flattering the Genoese, but rather the *older recitativo,* the *recitativo secco.*[4]

Finally, as far as the Wagnerian "leitmotif" is concerned, I lack all culinary understanding for that. If pressed, I might possibly concede it the status of an ideal toothpick, as an opportunity to get rid of *remainders* of food. There remain the "arias" of Wagner.— And now I shall not say another word.

9

In projecting his plot, too, Wagner is above all an actor. What he envisages first is a scene whose effectiveness is absolutely safe, a genuine *actio** with an *hautrelief* of gestures, a scene that *throws* people—this he thinks through in depth, and from this he then derives the characters. All the rest follows from this, in accordance with a technical economy that has no reasons for being subtle. It is *not* the public of Corneille of whom Wagner has to be considerate, but mere nineteenth century. About "the one thing needful" Wagner would think approximately the way any other actor today thinks about it: a series of strong scenes, one stronger than the other—and in between much *shrewd* stupidity. To begin with, he tries to guarantee the effectiveness of his work to himself; he starts with the third act; he *proves* his work to himself by means of its ultimate effect. With such a sense of the theater for one's guide, one

---

[4] Dry.

* [Nietzsche's] *Note.* It has been a real misfortune for aesthetics that the word *drama* has always been translated "action" [*Handlung*]. It is not Wagner alone who errs at this point, the error is world-wide and extends even to the philologists who ought to know better. Ancient drama aimed at scenes of great *pathos*—it precluded action (moving it *before* the beginning or *behind* the scene). The word *drama* is of Doric origin, and according to Doric usage it means "event," "story"—both words in the hieratic sense. The most ancient drama represented the legend of the place, the "holy story" on which the foundation of the cult rested (not a doing but a happening: *dran* in Doric actually does not mean "do").

is in no danger of unexpectedly creating a drama. Drama requires *rigorous* logic: but what did Wagner ever care about logic? To say it once more: it was *not* the public of Corneille of whom Wagner had to be considerate—but mere Germans.

We know which technical problem requires all of the dramatist's powers and often makes him sweat blood: making the *knot* necessary, and the resolution as well, so both will be possible in one way only while giving the impression of freedom (the principle of the least exertion of energy). That, however, leads Wagner least of all to sweat blood; it is certain that he exerted the least energy on the knot and its resolution. Take any of Wagner's "knots" and examine it under the microscope—and you'll have to laugh, I promise you. Nothing is more amusing than the knot of *Tristan,* unless it is the knot of the *Meistersinger*.

Wagner is *no* dramatist; don't be imposed upon! He loved the word "drama"—that's all; he always loved pretty words. The word "drama" in his writings is nevertheless a mere misunderstanding (and a bit of shrewdness: Wagner always affected superiority over the word "opera")—much the way the word "spirit" in the New Testament is a mere misunderstanding.

For one thing, he was not enough of a psychologist for drama; instinctively, he avoided psychological motivation—how? by always putting idiosyncrasy in its place.— Very modern, isn't it? Very Parisian. Very *decadent*.

Incidentally, the *knots* that Wagner really could resolve with the aid of dramatic inventions were of an entirely different nature. I offer an example. Assume a case in which Wagner requires a female voice. An entire act *without* a female voice—impossible! But none of the "heroines" are free at the moment. What does Wagner do? He emancipates the oldest woman of the world, Erda: "Come up, old grandmother! You have to sing." Erda sings. Wagner's purpose is realized. Immediately he abolishes the old lady again. "Why ever did you come? Beat it. Go on sleeping."— *In summa:* a scene full of mythological shivers which gives Wagnerians *intimations*.—

"But the *content* of the Wagnerian texts! their mythic content! their eternal content!"— Question: how can we test this content, this eternal content?— The chemist replies: translate Wagner into reality, into the modern—let us be even crueler—into the bourgeois! What becomes of Wagner then?— Among ourselves, I have tried it. Nothing is more entertaining, nothing to be recommended more highly for walks, than retelling Wagner in *more youthful* proportions: for example, Parsifal as a candidate for a theological degree, with secondary school education (the latter being indispensable for *pure foolishness*). What surprises one encounters in the process! Would you believe it? All of Wagner's heroines, without exception, as soon as they are stripped of their heroic skin, become almost indistinguishable from Madame Bovary! And conversely one understands that Flaubert *could have* translated his heroine into Scandinavian or Carthaginian terms and then offered her, mythologized, to Wagner as a libretto. Indeed, transposed into hugeness, Wagner does not seem to have been interested in any problems except those which now preoccupy the little decadents of Paris. Always five steps from the hospital. All of them entirely modern, entirely *metropolitan* problems. Don't doubt it.

Have you ever noticed (it belongs with this association of ideas) that Wagner's heroines never have children?— They *can't*.— The despair with which Wagner tackled the problem of having Siegfried born at all shows *how* modern his feelings were at this point.— Siegfried "emancipates woman"—but without any hope of progeny.— One fact, finally, which leaves us dumfounded: Parsifal is the father of Lohengrin. How did he do it?— Must one remember at this point that "chastity works *miracles*"?—

Wagnerus dixit princeps in castitate auctoritas.[1]

10

Incidentally, a word about Wagner's writings: they offer, among other things, a course in *shrewdness*. The system of procedures that Wagner handles is applicable to a hundred other cases: let him who has ears hear. Perhaps I shall be entitled to public gratitude if I formulate the three most valuable procedures with some precision.

Everything Wagner can *not* do is reprehensible.

There is much else Wagner could do: but he doesn't want to, from rigorism in principle.

Everything Wagner *can* do, nobody will be able to do after

---

[1] "Said by Wagner, the foremost authority on chastity."

him, nobody has done before him, nobody *shall* do after him.—
Wagner is divine.

These three propositions are the quintessence of Wagner's literature; the rest is—mere "literature."

Not every music so far has required a literature: one ought to
look for a sufficient reason here. Is it that Wagner's music is too
difficult to understand? Or is he afraid of the opposite, that it might
be understood too easily—that one will *not* find it *difficult enough*
to understand?

As a matter of fact, he repeated a single proposition all his life
long: that his music did not mean mere music. But more. But infinitely more.— *"Not mere* music"—no musician would say that. To
say it once more, Wagner was unable to create from a totality; he
had no choice, he had to make patchwork, "motifs," gestures, formulas, doing things double and even a hundredfold—he remained
an orator even as a musician—he therefore had to move his "it
means" into the foreground as a matter of principle. "Music is always a mere means": that was his theory, that above all the only
practice open to him. But no musician would think that way.

Wagner required literature to persuade all the world to take
his music seriously, to take it as profound "because its *meaning*
was infinite"; he was his life long the commentator of the "idea."—
What is the meaning of Elsa? But there is no doubt about that:
Elsa is "the unconscious *spirit of the people"* (—"realizing this, I
necessarily became a complete revolutionary").

Let us remember that Wagner was young at the time Hegel
and Schelling seduced men's spirits; that he guessed, that he
grasped with his very hands the only thing the Germans take seriously—"the idea," which is to say, something that is obscure, uncertain, full of intimations; that among Germans clarity is an objection, logic a refutation. Harshly, Schopenhauer accused the epoch
of Hegel and Schelling of dishonesty—harshly, also wrongly: he
himself, the old pessimistic counterfeiter,[1] was not a whit more
"honest" than his more famous contemporaries. Let us keep morals out of this: Hegel is a *taste.*— And not merely a German but a

---

[1] This is one of many passages in which Nietzsche uses this term in exactly
the same sense in which André Gide (1869–1951) later used it, in 1926, as
the title of his greatest novel: *Les Faux-monnayeurs.* Gide had earlier used
another Nietzschean term in another book title: *The Immoralist* (1902).

European taste.— A taste Wagner comprehended—to which he felt equal—which he immortalized.— He merely applied it to music—he invented a style for himself charged with "infinite meaning"—he became the *heir of Hegel*.— Music as "idea."—

And how Wagner was understood!— The same human type that raved about Hegel, today raves about Wagner; in his school they even *write* Hegelian.— Above all, German youths understood him. The two words "infinite" and "meaning" were really sufficient: they induced a state of incomparable well-being in young men. It was not with his music that Wagner conquered them, it was with the "idea"—it is the enigmatic character of his art, its playing hide-and-seek behind a hundred symbols, its polychromy of the ideal that leads and lures these youths to Wagner; it is Wagner's genius for shaping clouds, his whirling, hurling, and twirling through the air, his everywhere and nowhere—the very same means by which Hegel formerly seduced and lured them!

In the midst of Wagner's multiplicity, abundance, and arbitrariness they feel as if justified in their own eyes—"redeemed." Trembling, they hear how the *great symbols* approach from foggy distances to resound in his art with muted thunder; they are not impatient when at times things are gray, gruesome, and cold. After all, they are, without exception, like Wagner himself, *related* to such bad weather, German weather! Wotan is their god: but Wotan is the god of bad weather.

They are quite right, these German youths, considering what they are like: how *could* they miss what we others, *we halcyons,* miss in Wagner—*la gaya scienza;*[2] light feet, wit, fire, grace; the great logic; the dance of the stars; the exuberant spirituality; the southern shivers of light; the *smooth* sea—perfection.—

11

I have explained where Wagner belongs—*not* in the history of music. What does he signify nevertheless in that history? *The emer-*

---

[2] These three words form the subtitle of Nietzsche's book, *Die Fröhliche Wissenschaft* (the gay science; 1882), translated into English under the title *Joyful Wisdom*. The concept of "gay science" goes back to the fourteenth century, when it was used to refer to the art of the troubadours. Cf. also *Beyond Good and Evil,* end of section 260.

gence of the actor in music: a capital event that invites thought, perhaps also fear. In a formula: "Wagner and Liszt."

Never yet has the integrity of musicians, their "authenticity," been put to the test so dangerously. One can grasp it with one's very hands: great success, success with the masses no longer sides with those who are authentic—one has to be an actor to achieve that.

Victor Hugo and Richard Wagner—they signify the same thing: in declining cultures, wherever the decision comes to rest with the masses, authenticity becomes superfluous, disadvantageous, a liability. Only the actor still arouses *great* enthusiasm.

Thus the *golden age* dawns for the actor—for him and for everything related to his kind. Wagner marches with drums and pipes at the head of all artists of delivery, of presentation, of virtuosity; the conductors, machinists, and stage singers were the first he convinced. Not to forget the orchestra musicians—these he "redeemed" from boredom.

The movement Wagner created even reaches over into the field of knowledge: gradually, relevant sciences emerge from centuries of scholasticism. To give an example, I single out for special commendation the merits of *Riemann*[1] regarding rhythmics: he was the first to establish the validity of the central concept of punctuation for music, too (unfortunately, he used an ugly term, *Phrasierung* [phrasing]).

All of these are, as I own gratefully, the best among Wagner's admirers, those most deserving of our respect—they are simply right to admire Wagner. They share the same instinct, they recognize in him the highest representative of their type, they feel changed into a power, even a great power, ever since he kindled them with his own ardor. For here, if anywhere, Wagner's influence has really been *beneficial*. Never yet has so much been thought, desired, and worked in this area. Wagner has given all of these artists a new conscience. What they now demand of themselves, *get* from themselves, they never demanded of themselves before Wagner came along—formerly, they were too modest. A new spirit pre-

---

[1] Karl Wilhelm Julius Hugo Riemann (1849–1919; pseudonym, Hugibert Ries) wrote extensively on musical theory and published a musical dictionary that went into many editions.

vails in the theater since Wagner's spirit prevails there: one demands what is most difficult, one censures severely, one praises rarely—what is good, even excellent, is considered the rule. Taste is no longer required; not even a voice. Wagner is sung only with a ruined voice: the effect is "dramatic." Even talent is precluded. *Espressivo* at any cost, as demanded by the Wagnerian ideal, the ideal of decadence, does not get along well with talent. It merely requires *virtue*—meaning training, automatism, "self-denial." Neither taste, nor voice, nor talent: Wagner's stage requires one thing only—*Teutons!*— Definition of the Teuton: obedience and long legs.—

It is full of profound significance that the arrival of Wagner coincides in time with the arrival of the *"Reich":* both events prove the very same thing: obedience and long legs.— Never has obedience been better, never has commanding. Wagnerian conductors in particular are worthy of an age that posterity will call one day, with awed respect, *the classical age of war.* Wagner understood how to command; in this, too, he was the great teacher. He commanded as the inexorable will to himself, as lifelong self-discipline: Wagner who furnishes perhaps the greatest example of self-violation in the history of art (—even Alfieri,[2] otherwise his closest relative, stands surpassed. Note by a Turinese).

12

The insight that our actors are more deserving of admiration than ever does not imply that they are any less dangerous.— But who could still doubt what I want—what are the *three demands* for which my wrath, my concern, my love of art has this time opened my mouth?

> *That the theater should not lord it over the arts.*
> *That the actor should not seduce those who are authentic.*
> *That music should not become an art of lying.*
>
> FRIEDRICH NIETZSCHE

---

[2] Count Vittorio Alfieri (1749–1803), a dramatist, spent much of his life in Turin.

Postscript

The seriousness of the last words permits me to publish at this point a few sentences from an as yet unprinted essay. At least they should leave no room for doubt about my seriousness in this matter. This essay bears the title: *The Price We Are Paying for Wagner*.

One pays heavily for being one of Wagner's disciples. An obscure recognition of this fact is still encountered even today. Wagner's success, his *triumph*, has not eradicated it. But formerly it was strong, it was terrible, it was like a dark hatred—through almost three quarters of Wagner's life. The resistance he encountered among us Germans cannot be esteemed too highly or honored too much. He was resisted like a sickness—not with reasons—one does not refute a sickness—but with inhibition, mistrust, vexation, and disgust, with a gloomy seriousness, as if he represented some great creeping danger. Our honored aestheticians have compromised themselves when, coming from three schools of German philosophy, they waged an absurd war against Wagner's principles with "if" and "for"—as if he cared about principles, even his own!

The Germans themselves had reason enough in their instincts to rule out any "if" and "for." An instinct is weakened when it rationalizes itself: for *by* rationalizing itself it weakens itself. If there are any signs that, in spite of the total character of European decadence, the German character still possesses some degree of health, some instinctive sense for what is harmful and dangerous, this *dim* resistance to Wagner is the sign I should like least to see underestimated. It does us honor, it even permits a hope: France would not have that much health any more. The Germans, the *delayers par excellence* in history, are today the most retarded civilized nation in Europe:[1] this has its advantages—by the same token they are relatively the *youngest*.

One pays heavily for being one of Wagner's disciples. Only

---

[1] *Das zurückgebliebenste Kulturvolk Europas.* For the conception of the Germans as "delayers" (*Verzögerer*), cf. *The Antichrist,* section 61, written a few months after *The Case of Wagner* (*Portable Nietzsche,* p. 653ff.) and the chapter on *The Case of Wagner* in *Ecce Homo*.

quite recently have the Germans shed a kind of fear of him—the itch *to be rid of him* they felt at every opportunity.*

It is a curious matter, still remembered, which revealed this old feeling once more at the very end, quite unexpectedly. It happened at Wagner's funeral: the first German Wagner Association, that of Munich, placed a wreath on his grave, with an inscription that immediately became famous. It read: "Redemption for the redeemer!" Everybody admired the lofty inspiration that had dictated this inscription; also the taste that distinguished Wagner's admirers. But many (strangely enough!) made the same small correction: "Redemption *from* the redeemer!"— One heaved a sigh of relief.—

One pays heavily for being one of Wagner's disciples. Let us take the measure of this discipleship by considering its cultural effects. Whom did his movement bring to the fore? What did it breed and multiply?— Above all, the presumption of the layman, the art-idiot. That kind now organizes associations, wants its "taste" to prevail, wants to play the judge even in *rebus musicis et musicantibus.*[2] Secondly: an ever growing indifference against all severe, noble, conscientious training in the service of art; all this is to be replaced by faith in genius or, to speak plainly, by impudent dilettantism (—the formula for this is to be found in the *Meistersinger*). Thirdly and worst of all: *theatrocracy*—the nonsense of a faith in the *precedence* of the theater, in the right of the theater to *lord it* over the arts, over art.—

But one should tell the Wagnerians a hundred times to their faces *what* the theater is: always only *beneath* art, always only something secondary, something made cruder, something twisted

---

* [Nietzsche's] *Note.* Was Wagner a German at all? There are some reasons for this question. It is difficult to find any German trait in him. Being a great learner, he learned to imitate much that was German—that's all. His own nature *contradicts* that which has hitherto been felt to be German— not to speak of a German musician.— His father was an actor by the name of Geyer. A Geyer [vulture] is practically an Adler [eagle].— What has hitherto circulated as "Wagner's Life" is *fable convenue* [a myth that has gained acceptance], if not worse. I confess my mistrust of every point attested to only by Wagner himself. He did not have pride enough for any truth about himself; nobody was less proud. Entirely like Victor Hugo, he remained faithful to himself in biographical questions, too—he remained an actor. [See the letters of August 1888, printed below. W. K.]

[2] Of music and musicians.

tendentiously, mendaciously, for the sake of the masses. Wagner, too, did not change anything in this respect: Bayreuth is large-scale opera—and not even *good* opera.— The theater is a form of demolatry[3] in matters of taste; the theater is a revolt of the masses,[4] a plebiscite *against* good taste.— *This is precisely what is proved by the case of Wagner:* he won the crowd, he corrupted taste, he spoiled even our taste for opera!—[5]

One pays heavily for being one of Wagner's disciples. What does it do to the spirit? *Does Wagner liberate the spirit?*— He is distinguished by every ambiguity, every double sense, everything quite generally that persuades those who are uncertain without making them aware *of what* they have been persuaded. Thus Wagner is a seducer on a large scale. There is nothing weary, nothing decrepit, nothing fatal and hostile to life in matters of the spirit that his art does not secretly safeguard: it is the blackest obscurantism that he conceals in the ideal's shrouds of light. He flatters every nihilistic (Buddhistic) instinct and disguises it in music; he flatters everything Christian, every religious expression of decadence. Open your ears: everything that ever grew on the soil of *impoverished* life, all of the counterfeiting of transcendence and beyond,[6] has found its most sublime advocate in Wagner's art—*not* by means of formulas: Wagner is too shrewd for formulas—but by means of a persuasion of sensuousness which in turn makes the spirit weary and worn-out. Music as Circe.

---

[3] Worship of the people, or of the masses. Cf. Aristotle's disparagement of "spectacle" in his *Poetics* (end of Chapter 6) and, above all, Plato's *Laws*, 700—the passage in which he introduces the term *theatrocracy*, here taken up by Nietzsche.

[4] *Ein Massen-Aufstand:* the phrase is here introduced in the very same sense in which Ortega y Gasset (1883–1955) gave it world-wide currency when he made it the title of his best known book in 1930. Nietzsche's influence on Oretga was very great.

[5] *Er verdarb den Geschmack, er verdarb selbst für die Oper unsren Geschmack!— "Verderben"* can mean "spoil" as well as "corrupt."

If *verdarb* were taken to mean "corrupted" in both places, the meaning of the second part of the sentence would be puzzling: "he corrupted our taste even for opera." Why *"even"* for opera"? One would expect Nietzsche to say that Wagner corrupted not only musical taste, and taste for opera above all, but also taste in general. So Nietzsche presumably means: he corrupted taste and spoiled even our taste for opera.

[6] *Die ganze Falschmünzerei der Transcendenz und des Jenseits.* See section 10, footnote 1, above.

His last work is in this respect his greatest masterpiece. In the art of seduction, *Parsifal* will always retain its rank—as *the stroke of genius* in seduction.— I admire this work; I wish I had written it myself; failing that, *I understand it*.— Wagner never had better inspirations than in the end. Here the cunning in his alliance of beauty and sickness goes so far that, as it were, it casts a shadow over Wagner's earlier art—which now seems too bright, too healthy. Do you understand this? Health, brightness having the effect of a shadow? almost of an *objection?*— To such an extent have we become *pure fools*.— Never was there a greater master in dim, hieratic aromas—never was there a man equally expert in all *small* infinities, all that trembles and is effusive, all the feminisms from the *idioticon*[7] of happiness!— Drink, O my friends, the philters of this art! Nowhere will you find a more agreeable way of enervating your spirit, of forgetting your manhood under a rosebush.— Ah, this old magician! This Klingsor[8] of all Klingsors! How he thus wages war against *us!* us, the free spirits! How he indulges every cowardice of the modern soul with the tones of magic maidens!— Never before has there been such a *deadly hatred* of the search for knowledge!— One has to be a cynic in order not to be seduced here; one has to be able to bite in order not to worship here. Well then, you old seducer, the cynic warns you— *cave canem.*—[9]

One pays heavily for being one of Wagner's disciples. I observe those youths who have been exposed to his infection for a long time. The first, relatively innocent effect is the corruption of taste. Wagner has the same effect as continual consumption of alcohol: blunting, and obstructing the stomach with phlegm. Specific effect: degeneration of the sense of rhythm. In the end the Wagnerian calls rhythmic what I myself call, using a Greek proverb, "moving the swamps." Considerably more dangerous is the corruption of concepts. The youth becomes a moon-calf—an "idealist." He has gone beyond science; in this way he has reached the master's level. And he poses as a philosopher; he writes *Bayreuther Blätter;*[10] he

---

[7] A dictionary confined to a particular dialect.

[8] Magician in *Parsifal.*

[9] Beware of the dog! Greek *kynikos* (cynical) means literally "doglike."

[10] Literally, leaves, leaflets, or papers from Bayreuth: the monthly organ of the Wagner Societies to which Wagner himself contributed copiously.

solves all problems in the name of the father, the son, and the holy master.[11] What is uncanniest, however, is the corruption of the nerves. Let anyone walk through a city: everywhere he will hear how instruments are ravished in a solemn rage—interspersed with a savage howling. What's going on?— The youths are worshiping Wagner.— Bayreuth rhymes on institute for cold-water therapy.[12] — Typical telegram from Bayreuth: *bereits bereut* [already rued].—

Wagner is bad for youths; he is calamitous for women. What is a female Wagnerian, medically speaking?— It seems to me, a doctor can't confront young women too seriously with this alternative for the conscience: one or the other.— But they have already made their choice. One cannot serve two masters when the name of one is Wagner. Wagner has redeemed woman; in return, woman has built Bayreuth for him. All sacrifice, all devotion: one has nothing that one would not give to him. Woman impoverishes herself for the benefit of the master, she becomes touching, she stands naked before him.— The female Wagnerian—the most charming ambiguity that exists today; she *embodies* the cause of Wagner—in her sign his cause triumphs.— Ah, this old robber! He robs our youths, he even robs our women and drags them into his den.— Ah, this old Minotaur! The price we have had to pay for him! Every year trains of the most beautiful maidens and youths are led into his labyrinth, so that he may devour them—every year all of Europe intones the words, "off to Crete! off to Crete!" [13]

Second Postscript

My letter, it seems, is open to a misunderstanding. On certain faces the lines of gratitude appear; I even hear a modest exultation. I

---

[11] *Und des heiligen Meisters* instead of *und des heiligen Geistes.* In English, unlike German, "master" does not sound much like "spirit" or "ghost."

[12] In German this does not rhyme either: *Bayreuth reimt sich auf Kaltwasserheilanstalt.*

[13] See the letter to Gast, August 24, 1888, below.

should prefer to be understood in this matter—as in many others.
— But since a new animal plays havoc in the vineyards of the
German spirit, the *Reich*-worm, the famous *Rhinoxera*,[1] not a
word I write is understood any more. Even the *Kreuzzeitung*[2] testi-
fies to that, not to speak of the *Literarische Zentralblatt*.[3]— I have
given the Germans the most profound books they have—reason
enough for the Germans not to understand a single word.—

When in *this* essay I declare war upon Wagner—and incidentally upon a German "taste"—when I use harsh words against the
cretinism of Bayreuth, the last thing I want to do is start a celebration for any *other* musicians. *Other* musicians don't count compared to Wagner. Things are bad generally. Decay is universal. The
sickness goes deep. If Wagner nevertheless gives his name to the
ruin of music, as Bernini did to the ruin of sculpture, he is certainly
not its cause. He merely accelerated its tempo—to be sure, in such
a manner that one stands horrified before this almost sudden down-
ward motion, abyss-ward. He had the naïveté of decadence: this
was his superiority. He believed in it, he did not stop before any of
the logical implications of decadence. The others *hesitate*—that is
what differentiates them. Nothing else.

---

[1] Nietzsche's coinage. The meaning is unclear, and no previous German or
English edition attempts an explanation. The similarity of the word to
"rhinoceros" probably serves only to make the name sound like that of a
real animal; and the Greek appearance of the name may also be a mere
ruse. Greek *rhinos* can either mean skin or be the genetive of *rhis* (nose);
and *oxēra* means vinegary, while *xēra* means dry, arid. None of this makes
much sense in the context above. It is much more likely that *Rhin* is meant
to refer to the Rhine river, which is central in Wagner's *Ring* and a symbol
of German nationalism; while *ox* may simply mean "ox" (*Ochse* in German)—except that Nietzsche writes *die* . . . *Rhinoxera,* suggesting Teu-
tonic bovinity *feminini generis* (of the feminine gender), to use a phrase he
himself introduces a few pages later. None of this should be taken too seriously, any more than similar coinages in *Zarathustra*. Rather it helps to explain why Christian Morgenstern (1871–1914) placed a motto from Nietzsche at the head of his delightful *Galgenlieder* (Gallow Songs: *Twenty
German Poets,* tr. Walter Kaufmann, New York, The Modern Library,
1963).
[2] A prominent right-wing newspaper; cf. *Ecce Homo,* Chapter III, end of
section 1: "Is it credible that the *Nationalzeitung*—a Prussian newspaper, to
explain this to my foreign readers—I myself read, if I may say so, only the
Journal des Débats—should in all seriousness have understood the book
[*Beyond Good and Evil*] as a 'sign of the times,' as the true and proper
Junker philosophy for which the *Kreuzzeitung* merely lacked the courage?"
[3] A weekly survey of scholarly publications, founded in 1850.

What Wagner has in common with "the others"—I'll enumerate it: the decline of the power to organize; the misuse of traditional means without the capacity to furnish any *justification,* any for-the-sake-of; the counterfeiting[4] in the imitation of big forms for which nobody today is strong, proud, self-assured, *healthy* enough; excessive liveliness in the smallest parts; excitement at any price; cunning as the expression of *impoverished* life; more and more nerves in place of flesh.— I know only one musician who is still capable today of creating an overture that is *of one piece:* and nobody knows him.[5]

Those famous today do not write "better" music than Wagner but merely less decisive music, more indifferent music—more indifferent because what is merely half is dated by *the presence of what is whole.* But Wagner was whole; but Wagner was the whole corruption; but Wagner was courage, the will, *conviction* in corruption—what does Johannes Brahms matter now?— His good fortune was a German misunderstanding: he was taken for Wagner's antagonist—an antagonist was *needed.*— That does not make for *necessary* music, that makes, above all, for too much music.— If one is not rich one should have pride enough for poverty.

The sympathy Brahms inspires undeniably at certain points, quite aside from this party interest, party misunderstanding, long seemed enigmatic to me—until finally I discovered, almost by accident, that he affects a certain type of man. His is the melancholy of incapacity; he does *not* create out of an abundance, he *languishes* for abundance. If we discount what he imitates, what he borrows from great old or exotic-modern styles—he is a master of imitation—what remains as specifically his is *yearning.*— This is felt by all who are full of yearning and dissatisfaction of any kind. He is too little a person, too little a center.— This is understood by those who are "impersonal," those on the periphery—and they love him for that. In particular, he is the musician for a certain type of dissatisfied women. Fifty steps more, and you have got the female Wagnerian—just as fifty steps beyond Brahms you encounter Wagner—the female Wagnerian, a type that is more incisive, more

---

[4] See section 10, note 1.

[5] Nietzsche's young friend and disciple, Heinrich Köselitz, alias Peter Gast. See the letter of August 9, 1888, below.

interesting, and above all *more charming*. Brahms is touching as long as he is secretly enraptured or mourns for himself—in this he is "modern"; he becomes cold and of no further concern to us as soon as he becomes *the heir* of the classical composers.— People like to call Brahms the *heir* of Beethoven: I know no more cautious euphemism.—

Everything in music today that lays claim to a "great style" *either* deceives us *or* deceives itself. This alternative gives enough food for thought; for it includes some casuistry about the value of these two cases. "Deceives *us*": most people's instinct protests against this—they don't want to be deceived—but I myself should still prefer even this type to the other ("deceives *itself*"). This is *my* taste.—

To make this easier to understand, for the benefit of the "poor in spirit": Brahms—*or* Wagner.— Brahms is *no* actor.— A goodly portion of the *other* musicians may be subsumed in the concept of Brahms.—

I waste no words on the clever apes of Wagner, Goldmark, for example: with the *Queen of Sheba*[6] one belongs in a zoo—one can make an exhibit of oneself.— What can be done well today, what can be masterly, is only what is small. Here alone integrity is still possible.—

Nothing, however, can cure music *in* what counts, *from* what counts, from the fatality of being an expression of the physiological contradiction—of being *modern*. The best instruction, the most conscientious training, intimacy on principle, even isolation in the company of the old masters—all this remains merely palliative—to speak more precisely, illusory—for one no longer has the presupposition in one's body, whether this be the strong race of a Handel or whether it be the overflowing animal vitality of a Rossini.— Not everybody has a *right* to every teacher: that applies to whole ages.—

To be sure, the possibility cannot be excluded that somewhere in Europe there are still *rests* of stronger generations, of typically untimely human beings: if so, one could still hope for a *belated*

---

[6] The first and best-known opera (1875) by Karl Goldmark (1830–1915), a Jewish composer who was born in Hungary and died in Vienna.

beauty and perfection in music, too, from that quarter. What we can still experience at best are exceptions. From the *rule* that corruption is on top, that corruption is fatalistic, no god can save music.

Epilogue

Let us recover our breath in the end by getting away for a moment from the narrow world to which every question about the worth of *persons* condemns the spirit. A philosopher feels the need to wash his hands after having dealt so long with "The Case of Wagner."—

I offer my conception of what is *modern*.— In its measure of strength every age also possesses a measure for what virtues are permitted and forbidden to it. Either it has the virtues of *ascending* life: then it will resist from the profoundest depths the virtues of declining life. Or the age itself represents declining life: then it also requires the virtues of decline, then it hates everything that justifies itself solely out of abundance, out of the overflowing riches of strength. Aesthetics is tied indissolubly to these biological presuppositions: there is an aesthetics of *decadence,* and there is a *classical* aesthetics—the "beautiful in itself" [1] is a figment of the imagination, like all of idealism.—

In the narrower sphere of so-called moral values one cannot find a greater contrast than that between a *master morality* [2] and the morality of *Christian* value concepts: the latter developed on soil that was morbid through and through (the Gospels present us with precisely the same physiological types that Dostoevsky's novels describe),[3] master morality ("Roman," "pagan," "classical," "Renaissance") is, conversely, the sign language of what has turned out well, of *ascending* life, of the will to power as the principle of life. Master morality *affirms* as instinctively as Christian morality *negates* ("God," "beyond," "self-denial"—all of them negations). The former gives to things out of its own abundance—it transfigures, it beautifies the world and *makes it more rational*—the latter impoverishes, pales and makes uglier the value of things, it *negates* the world. "World" is a Christian term of abuse.—

---

[1] *"Schönes an sich"* might also be rendered in this context as "inherently beautiful" or "absolutely" or "unconditionally beautiful."

[2] See *Beyond Good and Evil,* section 260.

[3] Cf. *The Antichrist* (in *Portable Nietzsche*), pp. 585, 601, and 603, including the translator's footnotes; also Kaufmann, *Nietzsche,* Chapter 12, section I.

These opposite forms in the optics of value are *both* necessary: they are ways of seeing, immune to reasons and refutations. One cannot refute Christianity; one cannot refute a disease of the eye. That pessimism was fought like a philosophy, was the height of scholarly idiocy. The concepts "true" and "untrue" have, as it seems to me, no meaning in optics.—

What alone should be resisted is that falseness, that deceitfulness of instinct which *refuses* to experience these opposites as opposites—as Wagner, for example, refused, being no mean master of such falsehoods. To make eyes at master morality, at *noble* morality (Icelandic saga is almost its most important document) while mouthing the counterdoctrine, that of the "gospel of the lowly," of the *need* for redemption!—

I admire, incidentally, the modesty of the Christians who go to Bayreuth. I myself wouldn't be able to endure certain words out of the mouth of a Wagner. There are concepts which do *not* belong in Bayreuth.—

What? A version of Christianity adapted for female Wagnerians, perhaps *by* female Wagnerians—for Wagner was in his old days by all means *feminini generis?* To say it once more, the Christians of today are too modest for my taste.—

If Wagner was a Christian, then Liszt was perhaps a church father! [4]— The need for *redemption,* the quintessence of all Christian needs, has nothing to do with such buffoons: it is the most honest expression of decadence, it is the most convinced, most painful affirmation of decadence in the form of sublime symbols and practices. The Christian wants to be *rid* of himself. *Le moi est toujours haïssable.* [5]

Noble morality, master morality, conversely, is rooted in a triumphant Yes said to *oneself*—it is self-affirmation, self-glorification of life; it also requires sublime symbols and practices, but only because "its heart is too full." All of *beautiful,* all of *great*

---

[4] Franz Liszt (1811–86) was the father of Cosima (1837–1930), Wagner's second wife. This is not the first allusion to Cosima in this work; cf. Kaufmann, *Nietzsche* (1950), pp. 28–31; (1956), pp. 38–41; i.e., Chapter 1, section II. Liszt had retired to Rome in 1861, joined the Franciscan order in 1865—and eventually joined the Wagners in Bayreuth, where he died in 1886.

[5] "The ego is always hateful." Cf. *Nietzsche contra Wagner* (in *Portable Nietzsche*), p. 671.

art belongs here: the essence of both is gratitude. On the other hand, one cannot dissociate from it an instinctive aversion *against* decadents, scorn for their symbolism, even horror: such feelings almost prove it. Noble Romans experienced Christianity as *foeda superstitio:*[6] I recall how the last German of noble taste, how Goethe experienced the cross.[7]

One looks in vain for more valuable, more *necessary* opposites.—*

But such falseness as that of Bayreuth is no exception today. We are all familiar with the unaesthetic concept of the Christian *Junker.* Such *innocence* among opposites, such a "good conscience" in a lie is actually *modern par excellence,* it almost defines modernity. Biologically, modern man represents a *contradiction of values;* he sits between two chairs, he says Yes and No in the same breath. Is it any wonder that precisely in our times falsehood itself has become flesh and even genius? that *Wagner* "dwelled among us"? It was not without reason that I called Wagner the Cagliostro of modernity.—

But all of us have, unconsciously, involuntarily in our bodies values, words, formulas, moralities of *opposite* descent—we are, physiologically considered, *false.*— *A diagnosis of the modern soul* —where would it begin? With a resolute incision into this instinctive contradiction, with the isolation of its opposite values, with the vivisection of the *most instructive* case.— The case of Wagner is for the philosopher a *windfall*—this essay is inspired, as you hear, by gratitude.—

---

6 "An abominable superstition."

7 See Goethe's *Venetian Epigrams,* cited in section 3 above; especially:
> Much there is I can stand, and most things not easy to suffer
>   I bear with quiet resolve, just as a god commands it.
> Only a few I find as repugnant as snakes and poison—
>   These four: tobacco smoke, bedbugs, garlic, and †.

For other examples see Kaufmann, *Twenty German Poets,* pp. 28–33; for Nietzsche on Goethe, *Twilight of the Idols* (in *Portable Nietzsche*), pp. 553–55.

* [Nietzsche's] *Note.* The opposition between *"noble* morality" and "Christian morality" was first explained in my *Genealogy of Morals:* perhaps there is no more decisive turning point in the history of our understanding of religion and morality. This book, my touchstone for what belongs to me, has the good fortune of being accessible only to the most high-minded and severe spirits: the *rest* lack ears for it. One must have one's passion in things where nobody else today has it.—

FROM Nietzsche's Correspondence

About *The Case of Wagner*[1]

LETTER TO GAST:
SILS MARIA, *July 17, 1888*

. . . Dear friend, do you recall that in Turin I wrote a little pamphlet? Now we are printing it; and you are requested most urgently to help. Naumann[2] already has your address. The title is:

The Case of Wagner
A Musicians' Problem
By
FRIEDRICH NIETZSCHE.

It is something *amusing* with a *fond* of almost too much seriousness.— Could you get hold of Wagner's coll. writings? I'd like to have a few references, to be able to quote exactly, with the numbers of volumes and pages. (1) In the text of the *Ring* there is a variant of Brünnhilde's last aria that is entirely Buddhistic: I only need the numbers of volume and page, *not* the words. (2) How does this passage in *Tristan* go *literally:*

> *The awful deep mysterious ground,*
> *Who will proclaim it to the world?*

Is this right?

3) In one of his last writings Wagner once said—*in italics* if I remember it right—that "chastity works *miracles*." Here I'd like the exact wording.

For the rest I ask you to offer every kind of objection, of criticism of wording and taste. There are many bold things in this little fabrication.— Procedure with printer's proofs as usual. About appearance, paper, etc., Naumann and I have already reached agreement. The manuscript will be in his hands July 19. . . .

---

[1] For the sources, see the Bibliography below.
[2] The publisher.

FROM GAST'S LETTER
TO NIETZSCHE, *July 31, 1888*

. . . In the *score,* which arrived recently from Venice, Marke's[3] question is:

> *The* unfathomably *deep*
> *mysterious ground, etc.*

The text in the *Collected Edition,* if I am not mistaken, is

> *The unfathomable*
> *awfully deep*
> *mysterious ground.*

It was some such entirely insane piling up of words.—
Instead of Brunhilde Wagner says *Brünnhilde* (pp. 11 and 12). . . .

LETTER TO GAST:
SILS MARIA, *August 9, 1888*

Dear Friend,

In the first lines of the *Preface* I had changed the words "many jokes" to read "a hundred jokes." Looking back, the word "hundred" here seems to me too strong; I suggest that in your revision you restore the original "many."

Today an incredibly beautiful day, colors of the south!

Your friend
NIETZSCHE.

POSTCARD TO GAST:
SILS MARIA, *August 9, 1888*

Dear Friend,

There are still *postscripts* to my "letter" of which proofs must be read; I am sorry. A lot of pepper and salt; in the *second* postscript I take the problem by the horns in amplified form (I shan't easily find another opportunity to speak of these matters *again;* the

---

[3] The name of the King in *Tristan and Isolde.*

form chosen this time allows me many "liberties"). Among other things, a judgment of the dead also for Brahms. At one point I even permitted myself to allude to *you*—in a form that will have your consent, I hope.

Just now I have instructed Naumann to send you the printer's proofs I corrected last, making quite a few changes, for a final *revision*.

With the utmost gratitude,

Your friend

N.

LETTER TO GAST:
SILS MARIA, *August 11, 1888*

. . . The strongest passages are really in the "postscripts"; at one point I even have doubts whether I have not gone too far (*not* in the facts but in speaking of the facts). Perhaps we better *omit* the note[4] (in which something is suggested about Wagner's descent) and instead leave larger spaces between the *major subdivisions* of the "postscript." . . .[5]

FROM GAST'S LETTER
TO NIETZSCHE, *August 11, 1888*

. . . "Redemption for the redeemer" (p. 42, line 8 [6]) are the final words of Wagner's *Parsifal*. Whether the Wagner Association in Munich was the first in Germany I have not been able to confirm, though I have looked in lots of places: but perhaps you don't mean it chronologically?— "Everybody" on p. 42, line 12,[7] you might change to "But many also made."

What you mean by saying "Bayreuth rhymes on institute for cold-water therapy" (p. 46, line 8 from bottom[8]) is not immedi-

---

[4] See the letter of August 18, note 10, below.

[5] To avoid leaving a gap on the printed page.

[6] First Postscript, see p. 182, line 7.

[7] In the sentence with the parenthesis "(strangely enough!)" just a few lines later. Nietzsche accepted this suggestion.

[8] First Postscript, penultimate paragraph.

ately clear to the reader. Neither is "she stands naked before him" (p. 47, line 7 [9]). . . .

LETTER TO GAST:
SILS MARIA, *August 18, 1888*

Dear friend,
delighted with your letter, just received.— Regarding the *note*,[10] I have made up my mind to retain it *in its entirety* (except for a more cautious nuance in the question of descent). For in a kind of epilogue I return with great force to Wagner's falseness: so every hint in this direction becomes valuable. (This epilogue I have *reworked* several times. What you will receive from the printer is *still not* the right version. But send it to me, corrected!)—

I do mean the *Venetian Epigrams* (and *not* the *Roman Elegies*). It is a historical fact (as I have learned from Hehn's book[11]) that *they* gave the greatest offense. . . .

LETTER TO GAST:
SILS MARIA, *August 24, 1888*

Dear friend, I am just mailing the epilogue to Naumann with the request that it be sent to you once more for a *final revision*. It seemed useful to me to say a few things more clearly (it seemed a finesse to shield *Christianity* against Wagner). Also, the very last sentence is stronger now—also more cheerful.

"Off to Crete!" is a famous chorus in *La Belle Hélène*.[12] This I am telling you from malice because you "instructed" me about the final words of *Parsifal*. These "last words" of Wagner had after all been my leitmotif. . . .

---

[9] *Ibid.*, last paragraph. Nietzsche ignored these last two criticisms.

[10] Nietzsche's footnote to the first Postscript, p. 182, in which he insinuates that Wagner's father may have been a Jew, Adler being a Jewish name. The point here depends on Wagner's inveterate and vocal anti-Semitism.

[11] Victor Hehn, *Gedanken über Goethe* (reflections on Goethe), 1887. The reference is to section 3.

[12] By Jacques Offenbach. The words "Off to Crete!" conclude the (first) Postscript.

from GAST'S LETTER TO
NIETZSCHE, *September 11, 1888*

. . . I did not know that "Off to Crete!" comes from *La Belle Hélène*. When I took the liberty of indicating the source of the words "Redemption for the redeemer," I was misled by your expression which leads one to suppose that you accord the honor of invention to the presiding officers of the Wagner Association of Munich. . . .

from NIETZSCHE'S LETTER
TO OVERBECK, *October 18, 1888*

It is surprising how easily one can learn from this essay about the *degree* of my heterodoxy which actually does not leave a single stone standing on another. Against the *Germans* I here advance on all fronts: you'll have no occasion for complaints about "ambiguity." This utterly irresponsible race which has on its conscience all the great disasters of civilization and at all *decisive* moments of history had something "else" on its mind (the Reformation at the time of the Renaissance; Kantian philosophy precisely when a *scientific* way of thinking had just been attained with some trouble in England and France; "Wars of Liberation" when Napoleon appeared, the only man so far who was strong enough to turn Europe into a political and *economic unit*), now has "the *Reich*" on its mind—this recrudescence of petty state politics and cultural atomism—at a moment when the great *question of values* is posed for the first time. There has never been a more important moment in history: but *who might be aware of that?*

BIBLIOGRAPHY

I. THE BIRTH OF TRAGEDY and
THE CASE OF WAGNER

1. *The Birth of Tragedy*

a. First edition: *Die Geburt der Tragödie aus dem Geiste der Musik.*
Leipzig: E. W. Fritzsch, 1872.

b. Second edition with many very slight textual changes (listed at the
end of vol. I of the *Grossoktav* edition of Nietzsche's *Werke;* see
below, II.2), printed in 1874, but not published until 1878 by
E. Schmeitzner, Chemnitz, who had meanwhile become Nietzsche's
publisher.

c. In 1886, after Fritzsch had again become Nietzsche's publisher—
though not for long—the remaining copies of both versions were issued with a new title page and preface: *Die Geburt der Tragödie.
Oder: Griechenthum und Pessimismus. Von Friedrich Nietzsche.
Neue Ausgabe mit dem Versuch einer Selbstkritik.* Leipzig: Verlag
von E. W. Fritzsch.

The only one of these editions to bear any date is the first. The translation in this volume embodies Nietzsche's revisions and includes his "Attempt at a Self-Criticism."

2. *The Case of Wagner*

The first edition of *Der Fall Wagner* was published by C. G. Naumann, Leipzig, in September 1888. All subsequent editions appeared
after Nietzsche's breakdown.

II. NIETZSCHE'S COLLECTED
WORKS IN GERMAN

For Nietzsche scholars 2b, 8 and, within its very narrow limits, 9 are
the only reasonably adequate editions. There is some interesting material in 10 and 11, but these editions cannot take the place of 2b or 8.
Those with a more casual interest in Nietzsche will find 7 most con-

venient, and, except for the editorial postscripts, vols. 70–78 are adequate for most purposes.

The title of 1–6 is Nietzsche's Werke.

1. *Gesamtausgabe,* ed. Peter Gast. Leipzig: Naumann, 1892ff. Discontinued after vol. V.

2. *Grossoktavausgabe,* ed. by various editors under the general supervision of Elisabeth Förster-Nietzsche—the turnover being due in large measure to disagreements about the methods to be followed in publishing the *Nachlass,* i.e., notes, fragments, and other MS material not published by Nietzsche himself. The early volumes were published by Naumann; later the edition was taken over by Kröner, Leipzig, who also published 3–7 below.

   a. First ed.: 15 vols., 1895–1901. Vols. I–VIII contain Nietzsche's books; vols. IX–XV the *Nachlass.*
   b. Second ed.: 19 vols., 1901–13.
   Section I (vols. I–VIII), 1905–10: *Werke* (books).
   Section II (vols. IX–XVI), 1901–11: *Nachlass.*
   Section III (vols. XVII–XIX), 1910–13: *Philologica.*
   The last section, which contains articles, lecture notes, and other materials that reflect Nietzsche's career as a classical philologist, was first added in the second edition, and at the same time section II was revised extensively: only vols. XIII and XIV remained unchanged. Vols. IX and X (1903) and XI and XII (1901) were "completely remodeled," and the former vol. XV (1901), which had contained the first edition of *The Will to Power,* was supplanted by a complete rearrangement in two vols., XV (1910) and XVI (1911). The new vol. XV also contained *Ecce Homo,* which had never before been included in a collected edition.
   In 1926, Richard Oehler's index was added as vol. XX, but this index does not cover section III.

3. *Kleinoktavausgabe,* 16 vols., 1899–1912.
   This edition agrees, page for page, with 2b, but lacks the *Philologica* and is smaller in size.

4. *Taschenausgabe,* 11 vols., 1906 (vol. XI, 1913).
   Selections from the *Nachlass* are included in the volumes which contain the works of the same period.

5. *Klassiker-Ausgabe,* 9 vols., 1919.
   This edition contains only the books and *The Will to Power.*

6. *Dünndruck-Gesamtausgabe,* 6 vols., 1930.
   This thin-paper ed. contains the books, *The Will to Power,* and a

selection of the *Nachlass* of the Basel period. In 1931 two more volumes of *Nachlass* material were added, under the title *Die Unschuld des Werdens* (the innocence of becoming), ed. Alfred Bäumler.

7. *Kröners Taschenausgabe*, vols. 70–78 and 82–83, contains the same material as 6; but these very handy volumes can be bought separately, and vol. 170 (1943) contains Richard Oehler's index for this edition.

8. *Sämtliche Werke in zwölf Bänden*, 12 vols., Kröner, Stuttgart 1964–65, is a reprint of the preceding edition: vols. 70–78, 82–83, and 170 comprise 12 vols. But in this edition *Der Wille zur Macht* (*The Will to Power*) is no longer presented as one of Nietzsche's books: the title page adds *Ausgewählt und geordnet von Peter Gast unter Mitwirkung von Elisabeth Förster-Nietzsche* (selected and arranged by Peter Gast with the aid of Elisabeth Förster-Nietzsche); and in a postscript (pp. 711–15) to his editorial afterword (pp. 699–711) Alfred Bäumler deals with *"Der Nachlass und seine Kritiker"* (The *Nachlass* and its critics—attempting a reply to Karl Schlechta and Erich Podach). It is noteworthy that on the title page of vol. 78 (1930) of edition 7 above no credit was given to Gast and Nietzsche's sister.

9. *Gesammelte Werke, Musarionausgabe*, 23 vols. Munich: Musarion Verlag, 1920–29.
   Books, *Nachlass*, and *Philologica* are arranged in a single chronological sequence; a new volume of *juvenilia* is added as vol. I; and Oehler's index, which covers the *Philologica*, too, comprises half of volume XXI (names) and all of vols. XXII and XXIII (subjects).

10. *Werke und Briefe: Historisch-Kritische Gesamtausgabe*, 9 vols. Munich: Beck, 1933–42. Discontinued after 5 vols. of *Werke* and 4 vols. of *Briefe* had appeared. The arrangement is chronological, and the "works" do not include any of Nietzsche's books but cover only the period from 1854, when Nietzsche was 10, to 1869. But H. J. Mette's discussion of the MSS in *Werke*, I, xxxi–cxxvi, is of interest also regarding the MSS of Nietzsche's later works. For the letters see IV.5 below.

11. *Werke in drei Bänden*, ed. Karl Schlechta, 3 vols. Munich: Carl Hanser, 1954–56.
   Vols. I and II contain all of Nietzsche's books, as well as the so-called *Dionysos-Dithyramben* (some of the late poems); vol. III, a selection from the *Nachlass*, including a wretched rearrangement of *The Will to Power*, as well as 278 letters, a chronology (pp. 1359–1382), and a Philological Postscript (pp. 1383–1432). For some

criticisms of this edition, see my editions of *Beyond Good and Evil* and *The Will to Power*. Moreover, the selections from the *Nachlass* are inadequate for scholarly purposes. In 1965 a fourth volume was added: *Nietzsche-Index*. Like Oehler's earlier indices, this is very helpful but incomplete even as far as proper names are concerned.

12. *Friedrich Nietzsches Werke des Zusammenbruchs* by Erich F. Podach (Heidelberg: Wolfgang Rothe, 1961) seeks to supersede all previous editions of *Nietzsche contra Wagner, Der Antichrist, Ecce Homo,* and *Dionysos-Dithyramben,* and is particularly scornful of Schlechta's edition. For a detailed critique of Podach's editing see my article on "Nietzsche in the Light of his Suppressed Manuscripts" in *Journal of the History of Philosophy,* II.2 (October 1964), pp. 205–25.

III. ADDITIONAL MATERIAL NOT INCLUDED IN THE ABOVE EDITIONS

1. *Vorstufen der Geburt der Tragödie* (stages on the way toward *The Birth of Tragedy*), 3 vols. Leipzig: Hadl, 1926–28.

   a. *Das Griechische Musikdrama* (the Greek music drama, lecture, 1870), 1926.
   b. *Sokrates und die Tragödie* (Socrates and tragedy, lecture, 1870), 1927.
   c. *Die Dionysische Weltanschauung* (The Dionysian world view, essay, 1870), 1928.

2. *Socrates und die Griechische Tragödie: Ursprüngliche Fassung der Geburt der Tragödie aus dem Geiste der Musik,* ed. H. J. Mette. Munich: Beck, 1933 (original version).

3. *Lieder für eine Singstimme mit Klavierbegleitung* (songs for a voice with piano accompaniment): vol. I of *Musikalische Werke von Friedrich Nietzsche,* ed. Georg Göhler. Leipzig: Kistner und Siegel, 1924.

4. *Hymnus an das Leben, für gemischten Chor und Orchester* (hymn to life, for mixed choir and orchestra). Leipzig: Fritzsch, 1887 (text by Lou Salomé).

5. *Friedrich Nietzsches Randglossen zu Bizets Carmen* (Friedrich Nietzsche's marginal glosses to Bizet's *Carmen*), by Hugo Daffner. Regensburg: Bosse, no date (1912).

6. Nietzsche's marginal glosses to Guyau's *Esquisse d'une Morale sans Obligation ni Sanction* (1885: Sketch of an ethic without obligation

or sanction), in a 25-page appendix to the German translation of F. M. Guyau, *Sittlichkeit ohne "Pflicht."* Leipzig: Klinkhardt, 1909.

7. *Der Werdende Nietzsche: Autobiographische Aufzeichnungen* (Nietzsche in the process of becoming: autobiographical sketches), ed. E. Förster-Nietzsche. Munich: Musarion, 1924.

8. *Mein Leben: Autobiographische Skizze des jungen Nietzsche* (My life: an autobiographical sketch of the young Nietzsche, written September 18, 1863). Frankfurt am Main: Moritz Diesterweg, 1936. Facsimile on pp. 5–12; printed transcript on pp. 13–15.

9. *Mein Leben, Mein Lebenslauf: 1861, 1863, 1864* (my life, the course of my life). Berlin: W. Keiper, 1943. Four sketches in facsimile only, pp. 7–31. The second of these is identical with 8 above, but the eight pages of the original are reproduced on seven pages: the first six lines of the third page are printed as if they had been found at the bottom of the second page, etc. Although Nietzsche plainly states that he was born October 15, 1844, both editions state that he was 19 when he wrote *Mein Leben* in September, 1863.

10. *Ein Blick in Notizbücher Nietzsches: Ewige Wiederkunft, Wille zur Macht, Ariadne: Eine schaffensanalytische Studie mit 4 Abbildungen* (a glance into Nietzsche's notebooks: eternal recurrence, will to power, Ariadne: a study in the analysis of creation, with 4 Illustrations—i.e., facsimiles), by Erich F. Podach. Heidelberg: Wolfgang Rothe, 1963. For a brief discussion, see the last section of my article, cited under II.11 above.

IV. NIETZSCHE'S CORRESPONDENCE IN GERMAN

1. *Friedrich Nietzsches Gesammelte Briefe* (Friedrich Nietzsche's collected letters), 5 vols. (the 5th actually consists of 2 vols. with continuous pagination). The first eds. of vols. I–III were published by Schuster & Loeffler, Berlin and Leipzig, 1900ff.; those of vols. IV–V, by the Insel-Verlag, Leipzig, 1908ff., which also published the later editions of I–III.

    Vol. I contains letters to Carl von Gersdorff, Frau Marie Baumgartner, Otto Eiser, Frau Louise Ott, Gustav Krug, Paul Deussen, Carl Fuchs, Reinhart von Seydlitz, Karl Knortz—and in later editions also to Wilhelm Pinder, Theodor Muncker, Theodor Opitz, Heinrich Romundt, Frau Vischer-Heussler, Frau Pinder, and Freifrau von Seydlitz.

Vol. II contains correspondence with Erwin Rohde.

Vol. III contains correspondence with Friedrich Ritschl, Jacob Burckhardt, Hippolyte Taine, Gottfried Keller, Heinrich von Stein, Georg Brandes, Hans von Bülow, Hugo von Senger, and Malwida von Meysenbug.

Vol. IV contains letters to Gast. (Gast's letters to Nietzsche were published separately: *Die Briefe Peter Gasts an Friedrich Nietzsche*, 2 vols., Verlag der Nietzsche-Gesellschaft, Munich 1923–24.)

Vol. V contains letters to Nietzsche's mother and sister—but some of the letters "to the sister" are not authentic: several were really written to the mother, while others are composed of drafts of letters directed to others (see Friedrich Nietzsche, *Werke in drei Bänden*, ed. Karl Schlechta, vol. III, Munich: Carl Hanser Verlag, 1956, pp. 1408ff.; also Schlechta's selection of 278 letters, *ibid.*, pp. 929–1352).

2. *Nietzsches Briefwechsel mit Franz Overbeck*, ed. C. A. Bernoulli and Richard Oehler. Leipzig: Insel, 1916. See also IV.7 below.

3. Elisabeth Förster-Nietzsche, *Wagner und Nietzsche zur Zeit ihrer Freundschaft*. Munich: Müller, 1915; translated by C. V. Kerr, with an introduction by H. L. Mencken, as *The Nietzsche-Wagner Correspondence*. London: Duckworth, 1922.

4. Karl Strecker, *Nietzsche und Strindberg, mit ihrem Briefwechsel*. Munich: Müller, 1921.

5. *Werke und Briefe: Historisch-Kritische Gesamtausgabe* (see II.9 above) offers 4 vols. of letters (Munich: Beck, 1938–42) which span the period from 1850 to 1877. *Briefe*, vol. I, pp. xii–lviii, offer a detailed and valuable survey of the whereabouts of all Nietzsche letters of which the Nietzsche Archive had any knowledge at that time. This survey also lists letters published in periodicals and in biographical works. Many letters are privately owned and as yet unpublished.

6. *Werke in drei Bänden*, ed. Karl Schlechta, vol. III, pp. 929–1352: see II.10 and IV.1, vol. V, above.

7. Podach's *Blick in Notizbücher Nietzsches* (III.10 above), pp. 184–190, contains passages that, when IV.2 was published in 1916, were deleted to avoid embarrassment to persons then still living.

V. NIETZSCHE IN ENGLISH

A. The Oscar Levy Translations

1. *The Complete Works of Friedrich Nietzsche,* 18 vols., ed. Oscar Levy. New York: Macmillan, 1909–11; reissued by Russell & Russell, New York, 1964.

2. *Selected Letters of Friedrich Nietzsche,* ed. Oscar Levy, trans. A. M. Ludovici. New York and Toronto: Doubleday, Page & Co., 1921.

These translations, none of them by Dr. Levy himself, represent an immense labor of love but are thoroughly unreliable. None of the translators were philosophers, few were scholars. Mistakes abound, and it is impossible to form any notion of Nietzsche's style on the basis of these versions. Thomas Common's translation of *Zarathustra,* which replaced Alexander's Tille's earlier attempt, is particularly inadequate but held the field until 1954, while Common's attempt to render *The Case of Wagner* was superseded by A. M. Ludovici's.

B. The Walter Kaufmann Translations

Between 1954 and 1967 all but four of Nietzsche's works appeared in new translations, edited by Walter Kaufmann. The translations of the *Genealogy of Morals* and *The Will to Power* are by Kaufmann and R. J. Hollingdale jointly. All the other translations are by Kaufmann alone, who also contributed introductions and copious notes.

1. *The Portable Nietzsche.* New York: The Viking Press, 1954; paperback ed., with the same pagination, 1958. Contains new translations of four complete books:
   Thus Spoke Zarathustra
   Twilight of the Idols
   The Antichrist
   Nietzsche contra Wagner
and of selections from Nietzsche's other books, his notes, and his letters, as well as 60 pages of editorial material, including a brief commentary on every chapter of *Zarathustra.*

2. *Thus Spoke Zarathustra* has also been issued separately in paperback by The Viking Press, New York, 1966.

3. *Beyond Good and Evil,* with commentary. New York: Vintage Books, Random House, 1966.

4. *The Birth of Tragedy* and *The Case of Wagner,* with commentary. New York: Vintage Books, Random House, 1967.

5. *The Will to Power,* with commentary. New York: Random House, 1967.

6. *On the Genealogy of Morals* and *Ecce Homo,* with commentary. New York: Vintage Books, Random House, 1967.

7. *Twenty German Poets: A Bilingual Collection.* New York: Random House, 1962; reprinted in the Modern Library, New York, 1963. Includes eleven poems by and three about Nietzsche.

C. Other Translations

There are many other versions of single works, but no one else has translated more than two or three, and none of the major works has been rendered into English by another philosopher.

Kaufmann's *Zarathustra* (1954), the third English version in over sixty years and the first to dispense with Victorian archaisms, such as "spake" and "thou" with its attendant verb forms, was followed very closely by two other modern versions; but neither Marianne Cowan (Chicago: Gateway Editions, Henry Regnery, 1957) nor R. J. Hollingdale (Harmondsworth and Baltimore: Penguin Books, 1961) departs from Kaufmann's interpretations.

Francis Golffing's distinctly contemporary versions of *The Birth of Tragedy* and *The Genealogy of Morals* (Garden City: Anchor Books, Doubleday, 1956) depart radically from earlier translations of these works, but often also from the originals. The accent is on freedom, and there are striking omissions.

What is now needed most in this field is obviously not more translations of the same books but new versions of the four early works not included in the Kaufmann translations: *Unzeitgemässe Betrachtungen* (1873–76: Untimely Meditations or, in the Levy edition, *Thoughts out of Season*); *Menschliches, Allzu Menschliches* (1878–80: *Human, All-Too-Human*); *Die Morgenröte* (1881: *The Dawn*); and *Die Fröhliche Wissenschaft* (1882: new edition, with substantial additions, 1887: The Gay Science or, in the Levy edition, *The Joyful Wisdom*). In philosophical importance none of these works, with the exception of the last part of *Die Fröhliche Wissenschaft,* can compare with the later works, but they are all richly rewarding.

The third "meditation" has been attempted by J. W. Hillesheim and Malcolm R. Simpson, *Schopenhauer as Educator* (Chicago: Gateway Editions, Henry Regnery, 1965).

But the three great aphoristic works have not been tackled since before World War I, except for selections in B.1 and B.6; and a set of these books in faithful translations that capture something of Nietzsche's stylistic brilliance would constitute a major contribution and be a delightful asset.

VI. BOOKS ON NIETZSCHE

A. Bibliography

1. *International Nietzsche Bibliography,* ed. Herbert W. Reichert and Karl Schlechta. Chapel Hill: University of North Carolina Press, 1960. Arranged by languages—27 of them, from Bulgarian to Vietnamese—this is by far the most comprehensive bibliography ever attempted, though it is far from complete. Ephemeral articles, encyclopedias, histories, and reference works were excluded deliberately; and some items that should have been included escaped the editors' attention. 3973 items are listed, including translations of items that are listed both under the original language and again under the languages of the translations. In spite of some faults, this bibliography supersedes all earlier efforts. It also obviates any need for a long bibliography below: only a very few titles, available in English, are listed.

B. A Few Books in English

Brandes, Georg. *Friedrich Nietzsche,* trans. from the Danish by A. G. Chater. London: Heinemann, 1914. (Four essays by the critic who "discovered" Nietzsche, dated 1889, 1899, 1900, and 1909.)

Brinton, Crane. *Nietzsche.* Cambridge, Mass.: Harvard University Press, 1941; Torchbook edition with new preface, epilogue, and bibliography, Harper & Row, New York, 1965. In the short preface of 1964 Brinton disowns his chapter on "Nietzsche in Western Thought." The revised bibliography adds some serious new errors, showing that the author, never at home with Nietzsche, has not kept up with his subject. In sum, an undistinguished book by a distinguished historian.

Danto, Arthur C. *Nietzsche as Philosopher.* New York: Macmillan, 1965. A rather hasty study, marred by many old misconceptions, new mistranslations, and unacknowledged omissions in quotations. The context of the snippets cited is systematically ignored, nor is any effort made to take into account all, or most, of what Nietzsche said on a given subject.

Hollingdale, R. J. *Nietzsche: The Man and His Philosophy*. Baton Rouge: Louisiana State University Press, 1965. Sympathetic, informed, and well written, this is the best biography in English. Nietzsche's philosophy is discussed in the context of his life.

Jaspers, Karl. *Nietzsche: An Introduction to the Understanding of His Philosophical Activity*, trans. from the German by Charles F. Wallraff and Frederick J. Schmitz. Tucson: University of Arizona Press, 1965. The original, published in 1936, is one of the most interesting studies of Nietzsche in any language, designed to show the reader at every turn that Nietzsche did not merely say *this;* he also said *that.* "It is the task of the interpreter to be forever dissatisfied until he has *also* found the contradiction." But Jaspers systematically ignores the context—both on the pages from which he quotes and the larger context of Nietzsche's development. Early and late passages, and material from books and ephemeral notes are juxtaposed indiscriminately. In the English version, which is otherwise good, all the references for the abundant quotations are omitted, so that the reader has no clue whatsoever regarding their origins.

————. *Nietzsche and Christianity*, trans. from the German (1938) by E. B. Ashton. Chicago: Gateway Editions, Henry Regnery, 1961. On about 80 small pages we encounter an approach basically similar to that of Jaspers' big volume with its more than 400 large pages.

————. "Kierkegaard and Nietzsche," in *Reason and Existenz*, trans. from the German (1935) by William Earle. New York: Noonday Press, 1955. Also included in Walter Kaufmann, *Existentialism from Dostoyevsky to Sartre*, Meridian Books, New York, 1956, pp. 158–84. This is the pioneering juxtaposition of the two great influences on twentieth-century existentialism, by the man who is generally considered the dean of German existential philosophy.

Kaufmann, Walter. *Nietzsche: Philosopher, Psychologist, Antichrist*. Princeton, N.J.: Princeton University Press, 1950; rev. ed. with different pagination, Meridian Books, New York, 1956. Cited by chapters and sections to facilitate easy reference, regardless of edition. An attempt at a comprehensive reinterpretation.

————. *From Shakespeare to Existentialism*. Boston: Beacon Press, 1959; rev. ed. with different pagination, Anchor Books, Doubleday, Garden City, 1960. All references are to the rev. ed. Five chapters on Nietzsche: one on his ethic, two on his relation to Rilke, one on "Philosophy versus Poetry," and one on "Jaspers' Relation to Nietzsche."

————. "Nietzsche Between Homer and Sartre: Five Treatments of the Orestes Story," in *Revue Internationale de Philosophie*, No. 67 (1964). Demonstrates Nietzsche's tremendous influence on Sartre's *The Flies*.

————. "Nietzsche in the Light of His Suppressed Manuscripts," in *Journal of the History of Philosophy*, II.2 (1964).

————. Exposés of *My Sister and I* as a forgery, falsely attributed to Nietzsche, in *Milwaukee Journal*, February 24, 1952, and *Partisan Review*, May–June 1952; and of the rev. ed., in *The Philosophical Review*, January 1955.

Lea, F. A. *The Tragic Philosopher: A Study of Friedrich Nietzsche*. New York: Philosophical Library, 1957. An attempt to do what Hollingdale did much better, eight years later.

Love, Fredrick R. *Young Nietzsche and the Wagnerian Experience*. Chapel Hill: University of North Carolina Press, 1963. An interesting monograph that takes into account Nietzsche's own compositions.

Löwith, Karl. *From Hegel to Nietzsche*, trans. from the German (1941) by David E. Green. New York: Holt, 1964. By far the best of Löwith's historical studies, this volume is organized by topics, each of which is broken down into sections devoted to different writers, in chronological order. There are eight sections on Nietzsche, including discussions of his views of Goethe and Hegel; his relation to the Hegelians of the forties; his attempt to overcome nihilism; his conception of the herd man and the lead animal; his conception of labor; his critique of education; his conception of the overman; and his critique of Christian morality and culture.

Mann, Thomas. *Nietzsche's Philosophy in the Light of Contemporary Events*. Washington: Library of Congress, 1948. Two essays.

Morgan, George Allen, Jr. *What Nietzsche Means*. Cambridge, Mass.: Harvard University Press, 1941; paperback reprint, Torchbooks, Harper & Row, New York, 1965. Morgan's only book, based on many years of devoted scholarship, first convinced some American scholars that Nietzsche was indeed a philosopher. Morgan deliberately disregards how Nietzsche came to think as he did, but reports his views, topically arranged, and gives copious references to the *Grossoktavausgabe* (II.2.b above). An unusually detailed table of contents and a good index make this book very useful as a reference work.

Royce, Josiah. "Nietzsche," in *The Atlantic Monthly,* March 1917. A sympathetic and perceptive article, "found among the posthumous papers of Professor Royce."

Vaihinger, Hans. "Nietzsche and His Doctrine of Conscious Illusion (The Will to Illusion)," the last chapter of *The Philosophy of 'As if,'* trans. from the German (1911) by C. K. Ogden. New York: Harcourt Brace, 1924, pp. 341–62. This is one of the most interesting studies of Nietzsche's theory of knowledge in any language.

INDEX

for *The Birth of Tragedy*

INDEX

All numbers refer to sections, not to pages. **RW** refers to the Preface to Richard Wagner; **SC,** to the Attempt at a Self-Criticism; **TI,** to the Translator's Introduction; **n** to the Translator's Notes. For references to Nietzsche's works, see Nietzsche.

INDEX

———◆◉◆———

for *The Case of Wagner*

INDEX

Figures refer to sections, not to pages. **TI** refers to the translator's Introduction; **P** to Nietzsche's Preface; **PS1** to Postscript 1; **PS2** to Postscript 2; **E** to the Epilogue; **L** to the letters that follow *The Case of Wagner*; **n** to the translator's notes. For references to Nietzsche's works, see Nietzsche.

FRIEDRICH NIETZSCHE was born in 1844 in Röcken (Saxony) Germany. He studied classical philology at the universities of Bonn and Leipzig, and in 1869 was appointed to the chair of classical philology at the University of Basel, Switzerland. Ill health led him to resign his professorship ten years later. His works include *The Birth of Tragedy* (1872), *Beyond Good and Evil* (1886), *On The Genealogy of Morals* (1887), *The Case of Wagner* (1888), and *Ecce Homo* (1908).

WALTER KAUFMANN was born in Freiburg, Germany, in 1921, came to the United States in 1939, and studied at Williams College and Harvard University. During World War II he served in Europe with Military Intelligence. In 1947 he joined the faculty of Princeton University, where he is now Professor of Philosophy. He has held many visiting professorships, including Fulbright grants at Heidelberg (1955–56) and Jerusalem (1962–63). His books include *Nietzsche* (1950), *Critique of Religion and Philosophy* (1958) *The Faith of a Heretic* (1961), and *Hegel* (1965), as well as a verse translation of Goethe's *Faust* (1961).

VINTAGE WORKS OF SCIENCE
AND PSYCHOLOGY

A free catalogue of VINTAGE BOOKS *will be sent at your request. Write to* Vintage Books, 457 Madison Avenue, New York, New York 10022.

VINTAGE POLITICAL SCIENCE
AND SOCIAL CRITICISM

A free catalogue of VINTAGE BOOKS *will be sent at your request. Write to* Vintage Books, 457 Madison Avenue, New York, New York 10022.